KATAKANA

	a	i	u	e	o
a	ア	イ	ウ	エ	オ
k	カ	キ	ク	ケ	コ
s	サ	シ	ス	セ	ソ
t	タ	チ	ツ	テ	ト
n	ナ	ニ	ヌ	ネ	ノ
h	ハ	ヒ	フ	ヘ	ホ
m	マ	ミ	ム	メ	モ
y	ヤ		ユ		ヨ
r	ラ	リ	ル	レ	ロ
w	ワ				ヲ
n	ン				

	ya	yu	yo
ky	キャ	キュ	キョ
sh	シャ	シュ	ショ
ch	チャ	チュ	チョ
ny	ニャ	ニュ	ニョ
hy	ヒャ	ヒュ	ヒョ
my	ミャ	ミュ	ミョ
ry	リャ	リュ	リョ

	a	i	u	e	o
g	ガ	ギ	グ	ゲ	ゴ
z	ザ	ジ	ズ	ゼ	ゾ
d	ダ	ヂ	ヅ	デ	ド
b	バ	ビ	ブ	ベ	ボ
p	パ	ピ	プ	ペ	ポ

	ya	yu	yo
gy	ギャ	ギュ	ギョ
j	ジャ	ジュ	ジョ
by	ビャ	ビュ	ビョ
py	ピャ	ピュ	ピョ

HIRAGANA

	a	i	u	e	o
a	あ	い	う	え	お
k	か (ka)	き (ki)	く (ku)	け (ke)	こ (ko)
s	さ (sa)	し (shi)	す (su)	せ (se)	そ (so)
t	た (ta)	ち (chi)	つ (tsu)	て (te)	と (to)
n	な (na)	に (ni)	ぬ (nu)	ね (ne)	の (no)
h	は (ha)	ひ (hi)	ふ (fu)	へ (he)	ほ (ho)
m	ま (ma)	み (mi)	む (mu)	め (me)	も (mo)
y	や (ya)		ゆ (yu)		よ (yo)
r	ら (ra)	り (ri)	る (ru)	れ (re)	ろ (ro)
w	わ (wa)				を (o)
n	ん				

	ya	yu	yo
ky	きゃ (kya)	きゅ (kyu)	きょ (kyo)
sh	しゃ (sha)	しゅ (shu)	しょ (sho)
ch	ちゃ (cha)	ちゅ (chu)	ちょ (cho)
ny	にゃ (nya)	にゅ (nyu)	にょ (nyo)
hy	ひゃ (hya)	ひゅ (hyu)	ひょ (hyo)
my	みゃ (mya)	みゅ (myu)	みょ (myo)
ry	りゃ (rya)	りゅ (ryu)	りょ (ryo)

	a	i	u	e	o
g	が (ga)	ぎ (gi)	ぐ (gu)	げ (ge)	ご (go)
z	ざ (za)	じ (ji)	ず (zu)	ぜ (ze)	ぞ (zo)
d	だ (da)	ぢ (ji)	づ (zu)	で (de)	ど (do)
b	ば (ba)	び (bi)	ぶ (bu)	べ (be)	ぼ (bo)
p	ぱ (pa)	ぴ (pi)	ぷ (pu)	ぺ (pe)	ぽ (po)

	ya	yu	yo
gy	ぎゃ (gya)	ぎゅ (gyu)	ぎょ (gyo)
j	じゃ (ja)	じゅ (ju)	じょ (jo)
by	びゃ (bya)	びゅ (byu)	びょ (byo)
py	ぴゃ (pya)	ぴゅ (pyu)	ぴょ (pyo)

* i - adjective

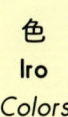
色
Iro
Colors

赤(い)* aka(i)*
red

青(い)* ao(i)*
blue

黄色(い)* kiiro(i)*
yellow

黒(い)* kuro(i)*
black

白(い)* shiro(i)*
white

茶色(い)* / ブラウン
chairo(i)* / buraun
brown

緑 midori
green

オレンジ orenji
orange

ピンク pinku
pink

黄緑 kimidori
yellow-green

紺 kon
dark blue

水色 mizuiro
light blue

紫 murasaki
purple

灰色 / グレー
haiiro / gurē
gray

日本料理
Nihon ryōri
Japanese Food

すき焼き sukiyaki
beef and vegetables cooked in sweet-salty soy sauce

しゃぶしゃぶ shabu shabu
Japanese variant of hot pot

焼肉 yakiniku
grilled meat

天ぷら tempura
deep-fried vegetables or seafood

おでん oden
broth with egg, steamed fish cake etc.

にぎりずし nigiri zushi
sushi

ちらしずし chirashi zushi
sashimi or various toppings on sushi rice

いなりずし inari zushi
sushi rice-stuffed fried tofu

のり巻き norimaki
sushi roll

親子丼 oyako don
chicken and egg rice bowl

牛丼 gyū don
beef rice bowl

かつ丼　katsu don
pork cutlet rice bowl

天丼　ten don
tempura rice bowl

きつねうどん　kitsune udon
thick white wheat noodles with deep-fried tofu

たぬきうどん　tanuki udon
thick white wheat noodles with tempura batter

天ぷらそば　tempura soba
buckwheat noodles with tempura

ざるそば　zaru soba
cold soba with dipping sauce

しょうゆラーメン　shōyu rāmen
soy sauce based ramen

塩ラーメン　shio rāmen
salt based ramen

味噌ラーメン　miso rāmen
miso based ramen

とんこつラーメン　tonkotsu rāmen
pork bone based ramen

焼きそば　yakisoba
fried noodles

お好み焼き　okonomiyaki
Japanese pan-fried pizza with various ingredients

もんじゃ焼き　monjayaki
thin Japanese pan-fried pizza with various ingredients

たこ焼き　takoyaki
octopus dumpling

しょうが焼き　shōgayaki
pork fried with ginger

鶏の照り焼き　tori no teriyaki
chicken teriyaki

肉じゃが　nikujaga
meat and potato stew

さばの塩焼き　saba no shioyaki
grilled mackerel

鮭の塩焼き　sake no shioyaki
salt-grilled salmon

おにぎり　onigiri
rice ball

お茶漬け　ochazuke
rice bowl filled with broth

味噌汁　misoshiru
miso soup

とん汁　tonjiru
pork miso soup with vegetables

洋食
Yōshoku
Japanese Style Western Food

コロッケ　korokke
croquette

えびフライ　ebifurai
fried shrimp

トンカツ　tonkatsu
pork cutlet

ハンバーグ　hambāgu
hamburger meat

カレー（ライス）　karē (raisu)
curry with rice

カツカレー　katsu karē
pork cutlet curry

オムライス　omuraisu
fried omelette stuffed with rice

ハヤシライス　hayashi raisu
rice with hashed meat

ナポリタン　naporitan
pasta with tomato ketchup

グラタン　guratan
gratin

中華料理
Chūka ryōri
Chinese Food

チャーハン　chāhan
fried rice

餃子　gyōza
pot stickers

春巻き　harumaki
spring roll

シュウマイ　shūmai
steamed meat dumpling

デザート
Dezāto
Desserts

ショートケーキ　shōtokēki
strawberry shortcake

シュークリーム　shūkurīmu
cream puff

かき氷　kakigōri
shaved ice

チョコレートパフェ　tyokorēto pafe
chocolate parfait

あんみつ　anmitsu
mitsumame topped with bean jam

漬物
Tsukemono
Pickled Vegetables

梅干　umeboshi
pickled plum

たくあん　takuan
pickled daikon radish

薬味
Yakumi
Condiments

ふくじんづけ　fukujinzuke
pickled vegetables in soy sauce

らっきょう　rakkyō
Japanese leek pickles

キムチ　kimuchi
Korean style pickles

のり　nori
nori seaweed

青のり　aonori
green nori seaweed

かつおぶし　katsuobushi
sliced dried bonito

紅しょうが　beni shōga
pickled ginger

ごま　goma
sesame

ねぎ　negi
green onion

大根おろし　daikon oroshi
grated daikon radish

七味（とうがらし）　shichimi (tōgarashi)
a mixture of red pepper and other spices

その他の食材
Sonota no shokuzai
Other Foods

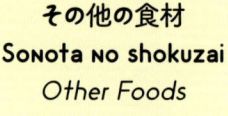

わさび　wasabi
wasabi

からし　karashi
mustard

納豆　nattō
fermented soybeans

豆腐　tōfu
tofu

油揚げ　abura age
deep-fried tofu

かまぼこ　kamaboko
steamed fish cake

こんにゃく　konnyaku
konjac potato gel

わかめ　wakame
wakame seaweed

こんぶ　kombu
kombu seaweed

たらこ　tarako
salted cod roe

明太子　mentaiko
spiced cod roe

飲み物（ノンアルコール）
Nomimono (nonarukōru)
Drink (Non-alcoholic)

コーヒー　kōhī
coffee

アイスコーヒー　aisu-kōhī
iced coffee

オレンジジュース　orenji-jūsu
orange juice

紅茶　kōcha
black tea

アイスティー　aisu-thī
iced tea

ウーロン茶　ūron-cha
oolong tea

緑茶　ryoku-cha
green tea

飲み物（アルコール）
Nomimono (arukōru)
Drink (Alcohol)

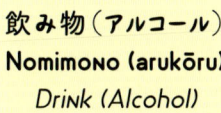
生ビール　nama-bīru
draft beer

ハイボール　haibōru
whisky and soda

レモンサワー　remon sawā
shochu with lemon and soda

梅酒　umeshu
plum wine

焼酎　shōchū
shochu (Japanese liquor similar to vodka)

日本酒　nihon-shu
Japanese sake

熱燗　atsukan
hot sake

冷酒　reishu
cold sake

ストレート　sutorēto
straigh

水割り　mizu-wari
with cold water

ロック　rokku
on the rocks

ソーダ割　sōda-wari
with soda

カクテル　kakuteru
cocktail

（赤／白）ワイン　(aka/shiro) wain
red/white wine

シャンパン　shanpan
champagne

居酒屋メニュー
Izakaya Menyū
Izakaya Menu

枝豆　edamame
boild soybeans

もろきゅう　morokyū
cucumber with miso paste

冷奴　hiyayakko
cold tofu

揚げ出し豆腐　agedashi dōfu
deep-fried tofu with broth

だし巻き卵　dashimaki tamago
Japanese omelette

ポテトサラダ　poteto sarada
potato salad

大根サラダ　daikon sarada
radish salad

シーフードサラダ　sīfūdo sarada
seafood salad

シーザーサラダ　sīzā sarada
caesar salad

コーンバター　kōn batā
corn butter

（フライド）ポテト　(furaido)poteto
french fries

エイヒレ　eihire
ray fin

ほっけ　hokke
atka mackerel

いかの姿焼き　ika no sugatayaki
grilled squid

アサリの酒蒸し　asari no sakamushi
steamed clams with sake

刺身　sashimi
raw fish

カキフライ　kakifurai
fried oysters

串揚げ　kushiage
deep-fried skewers

から揚げ　karaage
fried chicken

焼き鳥　yakitori
grilled chicken skewers

手羽先　tebasaki
chicken wings

サイコロステーキ　saikoro sutēki
diced steak

なべ　nabe
Japanese hot pot

伝統芸能
Dentō geinō
Traditional Performing Art

歌舞伎　kabuki
kabuki

能　nō
noh theatre

茶道　sadō
tea ceremony

華道　kadō
flower arrangement

書道　shodō
calligraphy

俳句　haiku
haiku poetry

落語　rakugo
Japanese comedic storytelling

すもう　sumō
sumo wrestling

剣道　kendō
kendo

合気道　aikidō
aikido

柔道　jūdō
judo

NIHONGO FUN & EASY

Survival Japanese Conversation for Beginners

2nd Edition

緒方 由希子　　角谷 佳奈　　左 弥寿子　　渡部 由紀子
OGATA Yukiko　SUMITANI Kana　HIDARI Yasuko　WATANABE Yukiko

Foreword

This text was planned and published in 2009 in order to create a standard teaching material for practical Japanese language that can be used by beginner level learners, not for grammar, but immediately in daily life before learning "hiragana."

Receiving feedback such as "this text allowed me to enjoy communicating in Japanese in daily life when I had first arrived in Japan and didn't know left from right" made us happy that we were able to create one of the achievements we were aiming for.

This text is characterized by the following four points:
1. Instead of grammar, phrases and their function within a conversation are written out to help students learn natural sounding Japanese.
2. Units are composed of several different elements, with a variety of situations, functions, and topics to allow students to effectively learn genuinely helpful expressions in accordance with their interests.
3. Conversation drills are presented separately from grammatical explanations to help students easily understand both practical exercises and the workings of the Japanese language.
4. Each unit contains a variety of practice exercises to help students naturally acquire target phrases and expressions.

We have tried to make this textbook easy to use for teachers and volunteers who are relatively inexperienced, in order to minimize the burden of class preparation. Students can enjoy various types of exercises just by following along with the text, and especially in the extension exercises, there are various devices that allow students to practice spontaneously and creatively.

When creating this textbook, we envisioned a text that "makes you want to use the phrases you learned immediately," "is practical and intellectually stimulating for adults," and "brings Japan closer to you." At the root of this is our wish that all foreigners who have had the opportunity to come to Japan enjoy Japan.
We will be sincerely happy if this book can make the encounters between Japanese language learners and Japan even more wonderful.

We are pleased to have the opportunity to publish this revised edition more than a decade after its publication in 2009. The vocabulary has been changed to reflect the changing times, and a much-requested Japanese translation has been added.
We would like to thank Yui Hatano, who was responsible for editing, for her great cooperation and support in publishing the revised edition. We would also like to thank our illustrator Noriaki Hiratsuka for his cooperation once again.
We would like to, once again, express our sincere respect and gratitude to the teachers and learners at Coto Japanese Academy, Coto Japanese Club, and Coto Online for their continued use of our materials and the feedback they have given us.

The Authors

はじめに

　本テキストは2009年、ビギナーレベルの方が「ひらがな」を学習する以前に文法ではなく、街ですぐに使える実践的な日本語教材の定番をつくるべく企画出版したものです。

　日本に来たばかりでまだ右も左もわからないなか、このテキストを手に街で日本語でのコミュニケーションを楽しむことができた！ そんなフィードバックを聞いたときにまた一つ自分たちの目指す成果を作ることができたと嬉しく感じました。

　本テキストの特徴は、①文法ではなくフレーズと機能で提示されるため自然な日本語が学べる、②場面、機能、トピックなど様々な要素からユニットを立てているため、本当に役に立つ表現を効果的に学ぶことができる、③文法編を別に作ることで、日本語とはどんな言語なのかという解説と実践練習を行き来しながら学ぶことができる、④各課に様々な形の練習が何度も出てくることで自然に表現が身につく、ということなどです。
　本テキストを使っていただく先生方にとっては、授業準備の負担が少ないように、また、比較的経験の浅い先生やボランティアの方でも使用しやすいものになるよう心がけました。 テキストに沿って進めるだけでいろいろなタイプの練習が楽しめますし、特に拡張練習では、学生が自発的にクリエイティブな練習をできるようにいろいろな仕掛けがしてあります。

　作成にあたって私たちがイメージしたのは、「習ったフレーズをすぐに使ってみたくなる」「実践的かつ知的好奇心をくすぐるような大人向けの」「日本をもっと身近に感じる」テキストです。 そして、その根底にあるのは、「縁あって来日した外国人の皆さんに、日本を楽しんでほしい」という想いです。
　この本を通して日本語学習者の皆さんと日本との出会いがより素敵なものになれば、心から嬉しく思います。

　2009年の出版から十数年の年月を経て、この度改訂版を発行する機会を得ることができました。時代の変化に合わせて語彙を変更し、またリクエストの多かった日本語訳を追加しました。
　改訂版の発行にあたっては編集担当の秦野由衣さんに多大なご協力とご支援をいただきました。また、イラストレーターの平塚徳明さんにも改めてご協力をいただきました。
　日頃から教材をご愛顧くださり、たくさんのフィードバックを下さったCoto Japanese Academy、Coto Japanese Club, Coto Onlineの先生方、並びに学習者の皆様方には改めて心からの敬意と感謝を捧げたいと思います。

著者一同

Contents | 目次

【Pre-text】Pictures | 写真資料 .... i -viii

Foreword | はじめに 2
How to Use This Book | この本の使い方 6
Must-know Words and Phrases | 絶対に覚えておきたい表現 10
Explanatory Notes | 凡例 12

UNIT 1　I am John. 13
Introducing yourself | 自己紹介
Watashi wa Jon desu. / O-shigoto wa? / Ongaku ga suki desu.
I am John. / (What is) your job? / I like music.

UNIT 2　Is there an ATM around here? 25
Asking for directions | 場所を尋ねる
Kono hen ni, ATM arimasu ka. / Toire, doko desu ka. /
Yūbinkyoku ni ikitai n desu ga....... .
Is there an ATM around here? / Where is the restroom? / I'm trying to get to the post office.

UNIT 3　How much is this? 37
Shopping | 買い物
Kasa, arimasu ka. / Kore, ikura desu ka. / Kono T-shatsu, kudasai. /
Mō chotto yasui no, arimasen ka.
Do you have umbrellas? / How much is this? / I'll have this T-shirt. / Do you have one a little cheaper?

UNIT 4　Take out, please. 51
Convenience stores and restaurants | コンビニ・レストラン
Menyū, onegaishimasu. / Kyō no ranchi, nan desu ka. / Mochikaeri de. /
Satō, iranai desu.
Could I have a menu? / What's the lunch of the day? / Take out, please. / No sugar, thank you.

UNIT 5　Can I pay by credit card? 67
Asking permission | 許可を得る
Kādo de ii desu ka. / Kono pen, karite mo ii desu ka.
Can I pay by credit card? / May I borrow this pen?

UNIT 6　Please wait a moment. 79
Making requests | 依頼する
Chotto matte kudasai. / Yukkuri hanashite moraemasen ka.
Please wait a moment. / Could you speak more slowly?

UNIT 7　Does this (train) go to Yokohama? ……… 91
Transportation | 交通
Kore, Yokohama ni ikimasu ka. / Shinjuku made dōyatte ikeba ii desu ka. / Tōkyō kara Kyōto made donogurai kakarimasu ka.
Does this (train) go to Yokohama? / How do I get to Shinjuku? / How long does it take from Tokyo to Kyoto?

UNIT 8　I'm going to an art museum. ……… 105
Talking about plans and activities | 予定や行動について話す
Bijutsukan ni ikimasu. / Kinō wa uchi de Nihon-go o benkyō shimashita. / Sumō o mitai desu.
I'm going to an art museum. / I studied Japanese at home yesterday. / I want to watch sumo wrestling.

UNIT 9　How do you like living in Japan? ……… 119
Talking about impressions | 感想を言う
Nihon no seikatsu wa dō desu ka. / Ryokō wa dō deshita ka.
How do you like living in Japan? / How was your trip?

UNIT 10　What does that taste like? ……… 131
Eating | 食事
Sore, donna aji desu ka. / Oishisō desu ne. / Butaniku wa chotto……… .
What does that taste like? / That looks delicious. / I can't really eat pork.

UNIT 11　It's nice weather today, isn't it? ……… 143
Socializing Ⅰ - Making small talk | 世間話をする
Kyō wa ii tenki desu ne. / Saikin shigoto wa dō desu ka. / Ja, mata.
It's nice weather today, isn't it? / How has your job been lately? / See you later.

UNIT 12　Would you like to have a cup of tea? ……… 155
Socializing Ⅱ - Invitations | 誘う
Ocha o nomimasen ka. / Onsen ni itta koto ga arimasu ka.
Would you like to have a cup of tea? / Have you ever been to an onsen (hot spring)?

Grammar | 文法 ……… 165

Column | コラム ……… 184

Translation of Dialogue | ダイアログ翻訳 ……… 187

Listening Answers and Script | リスニング解答とスクリプト ……… 189

Model Answers for Role playing and "Do you remember?"
| ロールプレイとDo you rememberモデル回答 … 195

【Appendix】Handy Wordbook | 別冊語彙集

How to Use This Book (To Learners)

Introduction

This book is designed to help beginner students, including those with no knowledge of the Japanese language, acquire natural-sounding, essential Japanese that can be used immediately in daily conversation.

Because this book does not develop concepts of grammar as it progresses, students may begin studying from any of the 12 units at their leisure.

Particles, a grammatical device of the Japanese language, are frequently omitted as they are in daily conversation to expose students to natural sounding Japanese as much as possible. Roman letters and kana spellings to approximate the actual pronunciation of certain words are also included.

We recommend that students memorize phrases and expressions as they appear in the included dialogues so as to reproduce them later, and not analyze all elements of each sentence to study grammar.

The Grammar Appendix included at the back of the book is a complement to the main text intended to help students acquire a systematic understanding of the construction of the Japanese language. We recommend that students use the vocabulary list in the Appendix to expand exercises and practice dialogues found in the book, as well as carry around for reference of necessary words for daily conversation. The color pages in the book's pre-text include pictures of foods and traditional performing arts, which should prove useful for conversation practice.

What's in a unit

Unit phrases	**Phrase 1 - 4:** Use note and example sentences to understand how phrases are used.
	Practice A: New words and practice conversation patterns. Use words from Practice A to complete phrases and communicate. Practice until you can say the words you need to know without looking at the book.
	Practice B: Short practice conversations using target phrases. Use words in Practice A to complete brief practice conversations.
General exercises	**Dialogue:** Use the target phrases in each unit to practice longer conversations. **Listening:** Practice listening exercises with Japanese spoken at a natural speed. **Do you remember?:** Use the right word or sentence as indicated by an illustration to see if you have learned target phrases. **Role playing:** Perform role play exercises using the expressions learned in that unit. **Phrases for This Unit:** Review the phrases learned in a unit in addition to other crucial expressions.
Other pages	**Material:** A page of items to help effectively perform practice conversations. **One More Step:** Practice for students wanting to challenge themselves to more difficult expressions. **Remember and Use!:** A page to help students memorize basic Japanese words, including numbers, verbs, and adjectives, for later use. **Good to Know:** Helpful introductions to services and Japanese words and phrases that make life in Japan a breeze.

この本の使い方（先生方へ）

はじめに

　本テキストは、日本語の知識が全くない人から初級前半程度の文法を習得している学習者が、日常生活で必要なすぐに使える自然な日本語を習得できるように作られた教材です。

　本テキストは文法積み上げ式のテキストではありませんので、全部で12あるユニットのうちのどのユニットからでも学習を始めることができます。学習者の希望やレベルに合わせて使用する課をピックアップしたり、ユニットの順番を変えて使用したりしても問題ありません。

　UNIT 1から12まで順に学習を進めていくときには、既習ユニットの文型を取り入れながら学習を拡張していけるような練習も含まれており、効果的な学習をすることができます。

　なるべく自然な日本語に触れてもらえるように、日常的に使われている助詞の省略などはそのまま表記しました。またローマ字表記も、音声と近い表記を採用しました。

　フレーズや談話に出てくる表現については、ひとつずつ分解して文法的な説明を加えるのではなく、そのままフレーズとして覚えることを想定しています。そのため、教師は教えるというよりも、そのフレーズの使用場面を想定した会話練習を一緒にしたり、フレーズや語彙を覚えやすいようにサポートしたりする役割が期待されます。

　動詞や形容詞の活用についても、そのユニット内の会話練習で必要な形だけを練習し、活用形の作り方は教えません。そのような文法的な解説は、文法編にまとめて掲載してあります。ただし、基本練習をしたい人向けに、UNIT 8とUNIT 9のあとのRemember and Use! で、動詞と形容詞の時制・肯定形・否定形の活用練習ができるようになっています。

　文法編は、学習者が日本語の仕組みを体系的に理解できるような読み物としてあり、本文と関連しています。別冊語彙集は、Practice Aの代入練習や談話練習などで学習者がより幅広い語彙から練習をできるように、また、持ち運び可能な単語集としても利用できるよう別冊として付属させました。また、巻頭の料理や伝統芸能のカラー写真もぜひ練習に活用してください。

　本テキストをメイン教材として利用する場合には、授業内でPractice Aの語彙の定着をはかりながら進めていくのが効果的です。また、サブテキストとして使用する場合には、提出されている語彙だけでなく、学習者の使いたい語彙や場面を取り上げて練習を膨らませていくのがよいでしょう。

1ユニットの構成と授業の流れ

① 学習目標の確認・動機づけ

　ユニット扉には、学習するフレーズの使用場面と学習目標（ゴール）が書いてあります。

　まずはここを読んで、これから学習するフレーズがどんな場面で使われるものなのか、また、このユニットを学習することで何ができるようになるのか、という学習目標の確認をし、学習の動機づけを行いましょう。

② フレーズ導入（各ユニットに2～4のフレーズがあります。）
　NOTEとEX.で、フレーズの機能と意味の確認をします。
　クラスではホワイトボードなどを使って本日の学習内容としてのフレーズ提示を行うと流れをうまく作ることができます。

③ フレーズ練習
　Practice Aのパターン練習をします。
　語彙の確認: 教師が指導する場合にはどこまでを覚えさせる語彙とするのかしっかり目標を決めて語彙導入、練習を行うのが効果的です。特に教室ではできるだけカードなどで繰り返し語彙の提示を行って定着を図ってください。
　代入練習: フレーズにPractice Aの語彙を代入した文を言ってもらいます。なるべく文字を追わずにフレーズを言わせるようにしましょう。学習者にあったスピードで、可能な場合は自然なスピードに近づけて言ってみましょう。

④ 談話練習
　Practice Bでフレーズを使った談話練習をします。
　談話の意味確認: 読み合わせ後、下のMEMOや英訳でわからない語彙を確認し、談話の場面をしっかりと理解してもらってください。問題文の指示にしたがって、＜　＞にPratice Aの語彙などを入れ替えながら、談話練習をしてください。ここでも、なるべく文字を見ずに談話ができるよう繰り返し練習を行ってください。PracticeBで＜　＞が空欄になっている箇所については、音声で回答例を確認できます。
　本テキストでは、UNIT 1～UNIT 7をサバイバルパート、UNIT 8～UNIT 12をコミュニケーションパートと位置づけています。サバイバルパートでは日本人役と外国人役がはっきりしている談話が多いので、教師と行う際には教師が店員や駅員などの日本人役を担当するようにしましょう。

⑤ 総合談話練習
　Dialogueでユニット内の複数のフレーズを使った談話練習をします。
　ユニット内で出てきた複数のフレーズをひとつの場面の中で使ってみる総合的な談話練習です。本文内に英訳がないので、読み合わせをして学習者の理解度を確認してから練習に入ってください。談話の理解や入れ替えを助けるために、右ページにMaterialがつけられていることもあります。これもできるだけ文字を追わずに談話ができるよう繰り返し練習を行ってください。また、可能な場合は学習者のオリジナルパターンを作ってみるよう促してみてください。

⑥ リスニング練習
　Listeningで、ユニットで学習したフレーズを使った会話の聞き取り練習をします。
　各ユニットに4問出題されます。自然に近いスピードで話されているので、全てを聞き取るのではなく必要な情報をスキャンする能力を高めることを目指しています。p.189にリスニングの答えとスクリプトがあります。

⑦ ロールプレイ練習
　Role playingで、学習したフレーズを使って自分で会話を組み立てる練習をします。
　必ず決まった答えがあるわけではないので、ロールカードを見て、ここまでの学習内容を応用し、自分なりの会話を組み立てるように促しましょう。既にいくつかのユニットを学習済みであれば、既習のフレーズや語彙も会話に盛り込めるように教師が学習者をリードできると、より効果的です。p.195 にロールプレイのローマ字表記での回答例があります。

⑧ 場面練習
　Do you remember? では、日常場面で起こりがちな場面のイラストを見て、学習したフレーズがぱっと出てくるかを確認する練習をします。
　フレーズの確認だけでなく、そこから会話を発展させたり、その場面で考えられる他の会話を考えたりするなど、応用練習の素材としても活用してください。p.197にDo you remember? のローマ字表記での回答例があります。

⑨ フレーズ復習・到達度チェック
　Phrases for This Unit では、ユニットに出てきたターゲットフレーズと、談話練習で出てきた便利な表現をまとめてあるので、1ユニットの内容を簡単に振り返ることができます。
　また、ユニットの最後の項目では、ユニット扉で設定した学習目標が達成できたかどうかをチェックすることができます。

⑩ その他
　Remember and Use!：最低限覚えておきたい動詞や形容詞、数字を定着させるための練習ページです。場面会話だけでなく文章作成の力もつけたい人にお勧めです。また、このコーナーをユニット学習に入る前に学習しておくのも効果的です。
　One More Step: メインの学習項目に加えて、更に高度な語彙や表現に挑戦できるよう作られたページです。
　Good to Know：日本の生活の中で知っておくと便利なサービス、日本語の仕組みや運用に関する情報を紹介するコーナーです。
　コラム：初級の学生からよく出る質問（文脈によって複数の意味を持つ表現など）についてまとめてあります。
　下記の付属資料をダウンロードにてご利用いただけます。
　　ダウンロード用URL：https://www.ask-books.com/jp/fun&easy
　　・音声ファイル：各ユニットのPhrase、Practice A、B、
　　　　　　　　　　Dialogue、Listening
　　・日本語訳：Good to Know、Role playing、Grammar、コラム
　　・イラスト：フレーズ導入用イラスト、Do you remember?

参考カリキュラム例
・**30時間コース**
　メインユニット練習 … 約24時間：UNIT 1～12（1ユニット2時間×12ユニット）
　定着・応用練習 ……… 約6時間：Remember & Use!、One More Step

Must-know Words and Phrases | 絶対に覚えておきたい表現

● **Survival Phrases**

1. すみません。*
   Sumimasen. *
   Sorry. / Excuse me. / Thank you.

   *An all-purpose phrase that can be used when calling out to a person, apologizing, or thanking someone.

2. a) はい。 b) いいえ。
   a) Hai. b) Iie.
   a) Yes. b) No.

3. a) そうです。 b) ちがいます。
   a) Sō desu. b) Chigaimasu.
   a) That's right. b) That's wrong. / No.

4. 英語は話せますか。
   Eigo wa hanasemasu ka.
   Do you speak English?

5. 英語が話せる人はいますか。
   Eigo ga hanaseru hito wa imasu ka.
   Is there anyone (here) who speaks English?

6. Q: わかりますか。
   Q: Wakarimasu ka.
   Q: Do you understand?

   A: a) わかります。 b) わかりません。
   A: a) Wakarimasu. b) Wakarimasen.
   A: a) I understand. b) I don't understand.

7. Q: わかりましたか。
   Q: Wakarimashita ka.
   Q: Did you get that? / Did that make sense?

   A: a) わかりました。 b) わかりません。
   A: a) Wakarimashita. b) Wakarimasen.
   A: a) I got it. b) I don't get it.

8. 日本語はわかりません。
   Nihon-go wa wakarimasen.
   I don't understand Japanese.

9. Q: 大丈夫ですか。
   Q: Daijōbu desu ka.
   Q: Are you alright?

   A: 大丈夫です。
   A: Daijōbu desu.
   A: I'm alright.

10. Q: いいですか。
    Q: Ii desu ka.
    Q: Can I ...? / Is it okay?

    A: a) どうぞ。 b) すみません、ちょっと……。
    A: a) Dōzo. b) Sumimasen, chotto….
    A: a) Please./Okay./Go ahead. b) Sorry, but... .

11. もう一度いいですか。
    Mō ichido ii desu ka.
    Would you say that one more time?

● Greetings

1. おはよう（ございます）。
   Ohayō (gozaimasu).
   Good morning.

2. こんにちは。
   Konnichiwa.
   Hello. / Good afternoon.

3. こんばんは。
   Kombanwa.
   Good evening.

4. じゃ、また。
   Ja, mata.
   See you (later).

5. ありがとう（ございます）。
   Arigatō (gozaimasu).
   Thank you (very much).

6. いただきます。
   Itadakimasu.
   I humbly receive this food.
   [said before a meal]

7. ごちそうさま（でした）。
   Gochisōsama (deshita).
   Thank you.
   [a set phrase said at the end of a meal]

● Helpful Words and Phrases

1. （お）元気ですか。*
   (O)genki desu ka. *
   How are you?
   *Typically not asked to people seen on a daily basis.

2. 元気です。
   Genki desu.
   I'm fine.

3. がんばって（ください）。
   Gambatte (kudasai).
   Do your best. / Good luck. / Break a leg.

4. どうぞ。
   Dōzo.
   Go ahead. / Please.

5. どうも。
   Dōmo.
   Thanks. [casual]

6. すごい
   sugoi
   awesome/amazing/great/a lot

7. 本当
   hontō
   really/true

8. もちろん
   mochiron
   of course

● Numbers

1	2	3	4	5	6	7	8	9	10
いち	に	さん	よん／し	ご	ろく	なな／しち	はち	きゅう／く	じゅう
ichi	ni	san	yon / shi	go	roku	nana / shichi	hachi	kyū / ku	jū

Explanatory Notes | 凡例

A note about *kana* / *kanji* and the Romanization

Because this book is designed to help learners acquire conversational skills regardless of their ability to read Japanese, text is displayed in both a mixture of *kana* and *kanji* as well as Roman letters. However, some areas of the book only feature Roman letters due to space constraints.

Kanji are printed wherever they would normally be used in written Japanese, along with their readings in *hiragana*.

This book mainly incorporates the Hepburn system of Romanization.

Long vowels are indicated with a horizontal line (eg. Tōkyō = Tookyoo).

However, the long [i] found at the end i-adjectives, such as in "tanoshii" are spelled out to more easily demonstrate conjugations. Long [e] sounds are written as "ee" or "ei" depending on the original spelling of the word in question, although many times words with an [ei] sound are pronounced more like [ee].

Compound words include hyphens to indicate boundaries between individual words to aid pronunciation, such as "100-en" and "hon-ya."

Characters in this book

ジョン／John
American, Engineer
アメリカ人　エンジニア

カレン／Karen
British, John's wife/English teacher
イギリス人　ジョンの妻　英語教師

クマール／Kumar
Indian, John's co-worker/Engineer
インド人　ジョンの同僚　エンジニア

田中／Tanaka
Japanese, John's co-worker in the general affairs division
日本人　ジョンの同僚　総務

佐藤／Sato
Japanese, John and Karen's friend/Student
ジョンとカレンの友達　学生

鈴木／Suzuki
Japanese, John and Karen's friend/Consultant
日本人　ジョンとカレンの友達
コンサルタント

UNIT 1

I am John.

私はジョン です。
<small>わたし</small>
Watashi wa Jon desu.

Introducing yourself
自己紹介

GOALS FOR UNIT 1

- Provide a simple self-introduction
  簡単な自己紹介をする

- Ask a person you just met for their name and occupation
  初対面の人に名前と職業を聞く

- Have a conversation about hobbies and interests
  趣味や興味のあることについて会話する

Phrase 1   Introducing oneself.

🔊 Track 1

私 **は**ジョン**です**。
わたし

Watashi wa Jon **desu.**   *I am John.*

> **NOTE** "A wa B desu" means "A = B." "wa" marks the topic/subject of the sentence, while "desu" means something similar to **"to be"** in English, and comes after a noun or adjective in polite sentences. Japanese speakers often omit the topic, or **"____ wa"** portion of a sentence, when the identity of the topic is obvious from context.
>
> 「AはBです」はA＝Bという意味です。「は」は、文の主題あるいは主語を表し、「です」には英語での "to be" と似た機能があります。丁寧文では「です」の前に、名詞や形容詞がきます。日本語では文脈からそれが明らかな場合、主題や「〜は」の部分が省略されることがあります。

Ex.

ジョン ：私**は**ジョン**です**。
　　　　わたし

　　　　(私は)アメリカ人**です**。どうぞよろしく。
　　　　 わたし　　　　じん

Jon ： Watashi **wa** Jon **desu.**

　　　(Watashi wa) Amerika-**jin desu.** Dōzo yoroshiku.

> John ： I am John.
> 　　　　(I'm) American.
> 　　　　It's nice to meet you.

Practice A   私は＿＿＿です。
　　　　　　　　わたし

Let's use the following words with the phrase **"Watashi wa ＿＿＿ desu."**
下記の言葉を使って「私は＿＿＿です」のフレーズを練習してください。

🔊 Track 2

ジョン	アメリカ人[*1]	エンジニア
Jon	Amerika-jin	enjinia
John	*American*	*engineer*
→ "Your name"	→ See Appendix, Countries	→ See Appendix, Jobs

Jobs

学生	先生／教師	会社員	コンサルタント
gakusei	sensei / kyōshi[*2]	kaishain	konsarutanto
student	*teacher*	*company worker*	*consultant*

Countries

日本	インド	イギリス	オーストラリア
Nihon	Indo	Igirisu	Ōsutoraria
Japan	*India*	*United Kingdom*	*Australia*

＊1 "[country]+ jin" = people / person from that country / area.
＊2 Use "kyōshi" for yourself and the respectful "sensei" for another person.
＊1 「国名＋人」は国籍や出身を表します。
＊2 「教師」は自分について言う時に使います。「先生」はその他の人について言及する時の敬意表現です。

Practice B-1

Provide a self-introduction with the words found in Practice A.
Practice Aの言葉で自己紹介してください。 🔊 Track 3

ジョン ：はじめまして。私は〈ジョン〉です。
　　　　〈エンジニア〉です。〈アメリカ〉人です。どうぞよろしく。

クマール：〈クマール〉です。〈インド〉から来ました。
　　　　こちらこそ、どうぞよろしく。

Jon : Hajimemashite. Watashi wa <Jon> desu.
　　　 <Enjinia> desu. <Amerika>-jin desu.
　　　 Dōzo yoroshiku.
Kumāru : <Kumāru> desu. <Indo> kara kimashita.
　　　 Kochira koso, dōzo yoroshiku.

> Jon : How do you do? I'm John.
> 　　　I'm an engineer. I'm American.
> 　　　It's nice to meet you.
> Kumar : I'm Kumar. I'm from India.
> 　　　The pleasure is mine.

Practice B-2

Ask for the listener's job and nationality using the words in Practice A.
Practice Aの言葉を使って仕事と国籍を尋ねてください。 🔊 Track 4

佐藤 ：ジョンさんは〈学生〉ですか。
ジョン：いいえ、〈学生〉じゃありません。*〈エンジニア〉です。

Satō : Jon-san wa <gakusei> desu ka.
Jon　: Iie, <gakusei> ja arimasen.*
　　　 <Enjinia> desu.

> Sato : Are you a student, John-san?
> John : No, I'm not a student.
> 　　　 I'm an engineer.

＊ To answer affirmatively, say "Hai, gakusei desu."
＊ 肯定する時は「はい、学生です」と答えます。

MEMO

はじめまして。／Hajimemashite.／*How do you do?*

どうぞよろしく。／Dōzo yoroshiku.／*It's nice to meet you.*

〜から来ました。／… kara kimashita.／*(I'm) from … .*

こちらこそ／kochira koso／*an emphatic way to say "I'm the one" that can be translated as "me too"*
　　　強調表現で、英語では「私も (me too)」と訳されます。

〜か。／… ka.／Add "ka" to the end of a declarative sentence to make it question. Ex. Jon-san desu ka. = *Are you John?*
　　　文末に「か」を付けることで、疑問文になります。

はい／いいえ／hai / iie／*yes / no*

(Aは) Bじゃありません。／(A wa) B ja arimasen.／*A is not B.*

Phrase 2 — Ask the listener for information about him/herself.

🔊 Track 5

お仕事は？
しごと

O-shigoto wa? *(What is) your job?*

> **NOTE** "＿＿wa?" is an abbreviated version of a question. Japanese speakers often omit the question words of a sentence and only state the topic when it is obvious they are asking a question from context. Rising intonation signifies that the "＿＿wa?" statement is an abbreviated question. Ex. **O-shigoto wa?** (↗)
>
> 「～は？」は疑問文の後半を省略したものです。日本語では文脈からそれが明らかな場合、疑問詞を省略したり、主題だけを述べたりします。語尾が上がることで「～は？」が疑問文の働きをします。例：「お仕事は？」

Ex.

① 田中：お仕事は（なんですか）？　　ジョン：エンジニアです。

② 田中：お住まいは（どこですか）？　　ジョン：千葉です。

① Tanaka : O-shigoto wa (nan desu ka) ?
　Jon　　 : Enjinia desu.
② Tanaka : O-sumai wa (doko desu ka) ?
　Jon　　 : Chiba desu.

① Tanaka : (What is) your job?
　John　　: (I'm) an engineer.
② Tanaka : (Where do) you live?
　John　　: (I live) in Chiba.

Practice A

＿＿＿は？

Use the following words with the phrase "＿＿＿ wa?"

下記の言葉を使って「＿＿は？」のフレーズを練習してください。

🔊 Track 6

（お*)仕事 しごと (O*)shigoto *job* → See Appendix, Jobs	（お)国 くに (O)kuni *country* → See Appendix, Countries	（ご*)出身 しゅっしん (Go*)shusshin *birth place/hometown*
（お)名前 なまえ (O)namae *name*	（お)住まい／うち す (O)sumai / uchi *place of residence / home*	（お)勤め／会社 つとめ　かいしゃ (O)tsutome / kaisha *company*

＊ Attaching the prefix お (o) or ご (go) to a noun makes that noun polite. Use these prefixes when talking about another person, and never for yourself. → See p.183, Grammar

＊ 名詞に「お」や「ご」などの接頭辞をつけると丁寧な表現になります。ただし、接頭辞は自分以外の他の人に関して言う時だけつけます。p.183 文法ページ参照。

B-1 Place your own name and information in < > to complete the following sentences. 🔊 Track 7

自分自身の情報を〈　〉に入れて下記の文を完成させてください。

鈴木　：〈ジョン〉さん、お国は？
ジョン：〈アメリカ〉です。
鈴木　：お住まいは？
ジョン：〈千葉〉です。〈鈴木〉さんは？
鈴木　：私も〈千葉〉です。／私は〈東京〉です。
ジョン：お仕事は？
鈴木　：〈コンサルタント〉です。

Suzuki : < Jon >-san, o-kuni wa?
Jon　　: < Amerika > desu.
Suzuki : O-sumai wa?
Jon　　: < Chiba > desu. < Suzuki >-san wa?
Suzuki : Watashi mo <Chiba > desu. /
　　　　 Watashi wa < Tōkyō> desu.
Jon　　: O-shigoto wa?
Suzuki : < Konsarutanto > desu.

Suzuki : Where are you from, John-san?
John　 : I'm from the United States.
Suzuki : Where do you live?
John　 : I live in Chiba. How about you, Suzuki-san?
Suzuki : I live in Chiba, too. /
*　　　　 I live in Tokyo.*
John　 : What is your job?
Suzuki : I'm a consultant.

 B-2 Make your own conversation using the words in Practice A.

Practice Aの言葉を使って自分自身について話してください。

MEMO

私も〜です。／Watashi mo … desu.／*I'm also … .*

Phrase 3 — Talk about your interests.

🔊 Track 8

音楽が好きです。
おんがく　す

Ongaku **ga suki desu.**　　　　　*I like music.*

NOTE "[Noun] ga suki desu" means "I like [noun]." → See p.169, Grammar
In sentences like the examples below, the **"watashi wa___"** portion of the sentence that denotes the subject is often omitted in spoken conversation.

「[名詞] が 好きです」は "I like [Noun]" という意味です。p.169文法ページ参照。
以下の例文にあるように、会話文では「私は」という部分が省略されることがあります。

Ex.

ジョン：(私は)音楽が好きです。
　　　　わたし　おんがく　す
　　　でも、カラオケは好きじゃありません。
　　　　　　　　　　　　す

Jon : (Watashi wa) ongaku **ga suki desu.**
　　　 Demo, karaoke wa suki ja arimasen.

John : *I like music.*
　　　　 But, I don't like karaoke.

Practice A

___が好きです。
　　　　す

Use the following words with the phrase "___ ga suki desu."
下記の言葉を使って「___が好きです」のフレーズを練習してください。

🔊 Track 9

音楽 おんがく ongaku *music* 	映画 えいが eiga *movie* 	カラオケ karaoke *karaoke* 
アウトドア autodoa *the outdoors* 	旅行 りょこう ryokō *travel* → See Appendix, Hobbies	サッカー sakkā *soccer/football* → See Appendix, Sports 
(お)すし (O)sushi *sushi* → See Appendix, Food	ビール bīru *beer* → See Appendix, Drinks	イタリア料理 りょうり Itaria ryōri *Italian food* → See Appendix, Countries

Practice B

Use words from Practice A in < > to practice having a conversation.
Practice Aの言葉を〈　〉に入れて会話練習をしてください。

🔊 Track 10

UNIT 1

①

鈴木(すずき)：私(わたし)は〈ビール〉が好(す)きです。カレンさんは？
カレン：私(わたし)も好(す)きです。／私(わたし)はあまり好(す)きじゃありません。

Suzuki : Watashi wa < bīru > ga suki desu.
　　　　 Karen-san wa?
Karen　 : Watashi mo suki desu.
　　　　 / Watashi wa amari suki ja arimasen.

> *Suzuki : I like beer. How about you, Karen-san?*
> *Karen　: I like beer, too. / I don't really like beer.*

②

田中(たなか)：〈カラオケ〉は*好(す)きですか。
ジョン：はい、好(す)きです。
　　　　／いいえ、〈カラオケ〉はあまり……。でも〈音楽(おんがく)〉は好(す)きです。
田中(たなか)：そうですか。

Tanaka : < Karaoke > wa* suki desu ka.
Jon 　　: Hai, suki desu.
　　　　　/ Iie, < karaoke > wa amari... .
　　　　　Demo, < ongaku > wa suki desu.
Tanaka : Sō desu ka.

> *Tanaka : Do you like karaoke?*
> *John　 : Yes, I do.*
> *　　　　 / No, not really. But, I like music.*
> *Tanaka : I see.*

＊は **(wa)** can be used to denote a topic or subject, it can also be used to imply a comparison or contrast. Because of this nuance, は **(wa)** often appears instead of が **(ga)** in statements that contain a nuance of comparison, such as negative or interrogative sentences, like in the example sentence above.

＊「は」は主題や主語以外に、比較や対称の意味も持ちます。このため上記の例文にあるように、否定文や疑問文においては、「が」より比較のニュアンスを持つ「は」が使われることが多いです。

MEMO

あまり／amari／*not very much, not really*

でも／demo／*but*

そうですか。／Sō desu ka. ／*I see.*

Dialogue

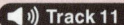 Track 11

Practice having a conversation by replacing the words in (1)–(3) with the words below. Put your own name and information in < >.
〈　〉には自分自身の情報を、(1)〜(3)はピンクの枠内の言葉に置き換えて、会話練習をしてください。

ジョン　：はじめまして。〈ジョン〉です。
　　　　　どうぞよろしく。

田中　　：はじめまして。〈田中〉です。
　　　　　こちらこそ、どうぞよろしく
　　　　　お願いします。
　　　　　ジョンさん、(1)お国は？

ジョン　：〈アメリカ〉です。

田中　　：そうですか。(2)お住まいは？

ジョン　：〈千葉〉です。〈田中さん〉は？

田中　　：私は〈中野〉です。
　　　　　ジョンさん、(3)日本料理は好き
　　　　　ですか。

ジョン　：はい、〈天ぷら〉が好きです。
　　　　　／いいえ、あまり……。

田中　　：そうですか。

Jon　　　: Hajimemashite. < Jon > desu.
　　　　　 Dōzo yoroshiku.

Tanaka　: Hajimemashite. < Tanaka > desu.
　　　　　 Kochira koso, dōzo yoroshiku
　　　　　 onegaishimasu.
　　　　　 Jon-san, (1) o-kuni wa?

Jon　　　: < Amerika > desu.

Tanaka　: Sō desu ka. (2) O-sumai wa?

Jon　　　: < Chiba > desu. < Tanaka >-san wa?

Tanaka　: Watashi wa < Nakano > desu.
　　　　　 Jon-san, (3) Nihon ryōri wa suki desu
　　　　　 ka.

Jon　　　: Hai, < tempura > ga suki desu.
　　　　　 / Iie, amari.......

Tanaka　: Sō desu ka.

---

①
(1) ご出身　　　　　　　　　go-shusshin
(2) お仕事　　　　　　　　　o-shigoto
(3) スポーツ　　　　　　　　supōtsu

②
(1) お国　　　　　　　　　　o-kuni
(2) お勤め　　　　　　　　　o-tsutome
(3) お酒　　　　　　　　　　o-sake

Listening

Two people who just met are having a conversation. Listen to what they say and select the correct answer.
会ったばかりの2人が話しています。何を話しているか聞いて正しい答えを選んでください。

Q1

1. The man is English.
2. The man is Australian.
3. The man is Indian.

Q2

1. The woman asked the man for his name and hometown.
2. The woman asked the man where he works and lives.
3. The woman asked the man about his hometown and job.

Q3

1. The woman doesn't like karaoke.
2. The man likes karaoke.
3. The man doesn't like karaoke.

Q4

1. The woman likes wine.
2. The woman doesn't like alcohol.
3. The man likes beer.

Role playing

Role play using the cards below.
下記のカードを使ってロールプレイしてください。

At a party　パーティーで

A: You meet B-san, a Japanese person, for the first time at a friend's party. Say hello to B-san and introduce yourself. (Please use your own answers.)

B: You are a Japanese person. Ask where A-san is from, where he/she works and lives in Japan, what he/she likes, and what his/her interests are.

Do you remember?

Use the phrases you have learned in this unit in situations ①–③ below.
このユニットで学習したフレーズを下記の①〜③の状況に合わせて使ってください。

Phrases for This Unit

Unit Phrases

- 私(わたし)はジョンです。 — Watashi wa Jon desu. — *I am John.*
- お仕事(しごと)は？ — O-shigoto wa? — *(What is) your job?*
- 音楽(おんがく)が好(す)きです。 — Ongaku ga suki desu. — *I like music.*

Useful expressions

- ～から来(き)ました。 — ... kara kimashita. — *I'm from ... .*
- どうぞよろしく。 — Dōzo yoroshiku. — *It's nice to meet you.*

UNIT 1

Check!

Now I can...

☐ Provide a simple self-introduction
簡単な自己紹介ができる

☐ Ask a person I just met for their name and occupation
初対面の人に名前と職業が聞ける

☐ Have a conversation about hobbies and interests
趣味や興味のあることについて会話できる

One More Step

● **Talking about family**　家族について話す

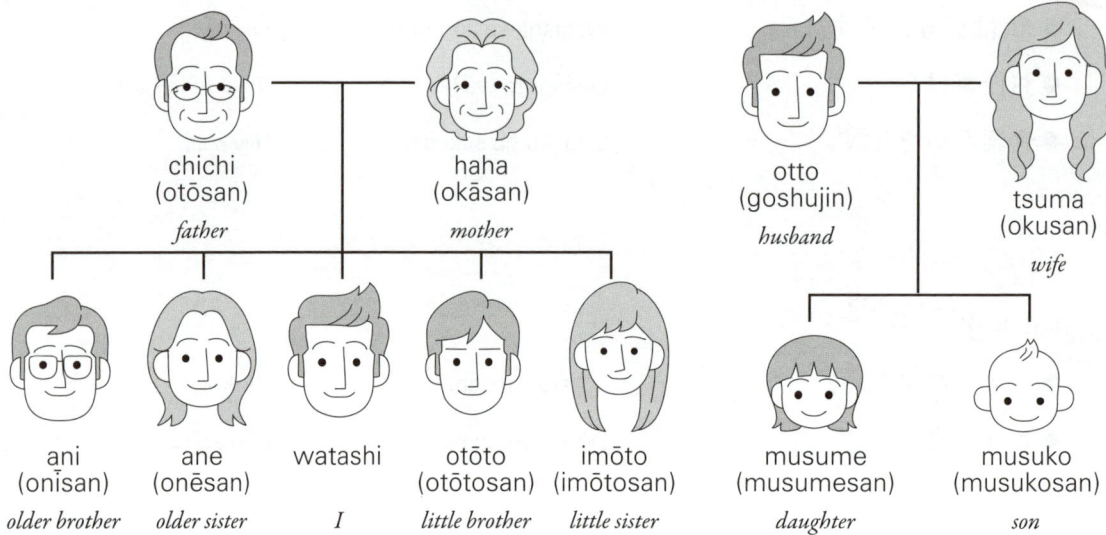

chichi (otōsan)	haha (okāsan)	otto (goshujin)	tsuma (okusan)
father	mother	husband	wife

ani (onīsan)	ane (onēsan)	watashi	otōto (otōtosan)	imōto (imōtosan)	musume (musumesan)	musuko (musukosan)
older brother	older sister	I	little brother	little sister	daughter	son

＊ Words in (　) are used to respectfully address another person's family members
＊ (　) の中は他の人の家族に対する丁寧な呼び方

Let's practice

(1) Use the examples below to describe where your family members are from (a), what they do (b), and where they live (c).
下記の例のように自分の家族について、出身地、何をしているか、どこに住んでいるかなどを説明してみましょう。

　a. Watashi no*¹ tsuma wa Igirisu-jin desu.

　b. Watashi no haha wa kyōshi desu.

　c. Watashi no musuko wa Ōsutoraria ni sunde imasu.*²

(2) Fill in the blanks below to have a conversation about someone's siblings and children.
下記に言葉を入れて、兄弟やこどもについての会話を作ってみましょう。

　Q. Go-kyōdai*³ / okosan*⁴ ga imasu ka.*⁵

　A. a. Hai, ＿＿ to*⁶ ＿＿ ga imasu.

　　 b. Hai, ＿＿ ga [number] imasu.

　　 c. Iie, imasen.

Counting people

one person	hitori
two people	futari
three people	san-nin
four people	yo-nin

Say the number word + **nin** when counting three or more people

*1 watashi no = *my*　*2 ...wa [place] ni sunde imasu = ... *live in [place]*　*3 go-kyōdai = *(Your) brothers and sisters* ("kyōdai" refers to one's own siblings)　*4 okosan = *(Your) children* ("kodomo" refers to one's own children)　*5 ... ga imasu ka. = *Do you have ... ?* (for animate objects)
→ See p.170, Grammar　*6 A to B = *A and B*

Is there an ATM around here?

このへんに、ATMありますか。
Kono hen ni , ATM arimasu ka.

Asking for directions
場所を尋ねる

GOALS FOR UNIT 2

- Ask if a store or place you want to go to is in the nearby area
  行きたい店や場所が近くにあるかどうか尋ねる

- Ask for the location of a store or place you want to go to
  行きたい店や場所を尋ねる

- Ask and understand simple directions
  道を尋ねたり、簡単な道案内を理解したりする

Phrase 1
Ask if a store or place you want to go to is in the nearby area.

このへんに、ATMありますか。

Kono hen ni, ATM arimasu ka. *Is there an ATM around here?*

🔊 Track 16

> **NOTE** "___ (wa) arimasu ka." = "Is there ___?", "Kono hen ni" means "around here." "Arimasu" is used only for inanimate objects. → *See p.170, Grammar*
>
> 「～（は）ありますか」は "Is there …?" という意味です。「このへんに」は "around here" という意味です。「あります」が使われるのは無生物に対してのみです。p.170文法ページ参照。

Ex.

ジョン ：すみません。**このへんに、ATM（は）ありますか。**

女の人 ：ええ、あそこにありますよ。

Jon : Sumimasen. **Kono hen ni, ATM (wa) arimasu ka.**
Onna no hito : Ee, asoko ni arimasu yo.

> John : Excuse me. Is there an ATM around here?
> Woman : Yes, over there.

Practice A

このへんに、_____ ありますか。
Use the following words with the phrase **"Kono hen ni, _____ arimasu ka."**
下記の言葉を使って「このへんに、_____ ありますか」のフレーズを練習してください。

🔊 Track 17

ATM ATM *ATM*	地下鉄の駅 ちかてつ えき chikatetsu no eki *subway station*	バス停  てい basu-tei *bus stop*
交番 こう ばん kōban *police box*	駐車場 ちゅうしゃ じょう chūshajō *parking lot*	コンビニ kombini *convenience store* → *See Appendix, Shops*
電気屋  でん き や denkiya *electronics store*	スーパー sūpā *super market*	100円ショップ えん hyaku-en shoppu *100-yen store*	ドラッグストア  doraggusutoa *drugstore*

Practice B

Put the words from Practice A into < > to complete the exercise.
Practice Aの言葉を〈　〉に入れ下記の文を完成させてください。

🔊 Track 18

①

-On a street- 道で

ジョン　：すみません。このへんに、〈コンビニ〉ありますか。

女の人　：ええ、あそこにありますよ。

ジョン　：ありがとうございます。

女の人　：どういたしまして。

Jon : Sumimasen. Kono hen ni < kombini > arimasu ka.	John : Excuse me, is there a convenience store around here?
Onna no hito : Ee, asoko ni arimasu yo.	Woman : Yes, it's over there.
Jon : Arigatō gozaimasu.	John : Thank you.
Onna no hito : Dō itashimashite.	Woman : You're welcome.

②

-On a street- 道で

ジョン　：すみません。このへんに、〈ドラッグストア〉ありますか。

男の人　：さあ、ちょっとわかりません。

ジョン　：じゃ、いいです。ありがとうございます。

Jon : Sumimasen. Kono hen ni <doraggusutoa> arimasu ka.	John : Excuse me, is there a drug store around here?
Otoko no hito : Sā, chotto wakarimasen.	Man : Hmm, I'm not sure [if there is].
Jon : Ja, ii desu. Arigatō gozaimasu.	John : That's alright. Thank you.

MEMO

ええ／ee／yes

あそこにありますよ。／Asoko ni arimasu yo.／It's over there.
[The particle "yo" is used to emphasize new information to a person.
助詞の「よ」は、聞き手にとって、それが新しい情報であることを強調したい場合に使います。]

どういたしまして。／Dō itashimashite.／You're welcome.

さあ／sā／I don't know. [said to indicate a lack of sureness　確信が持てない時に使います。]

ちょっとわかりません。／Chotto wakarimasen.／I'm not sure.

じゃ、いいです。／Ja, ii desu.／That's alright.

Phrase 2 — Ask where something is.

🔊 Track 19

トイレ、**どこですか。**

Toire, **doko desu ka.** *Where is the restroom?*

NOTE "Doko" means "where.", "_____ (wa) doko desu ka." is used to ask for the location of something.

「どこ」は "where" の意味で、「〜（は）どこですか」は、ものの場所を尋ねる時に使います。

Ex.

ジョン ：すみません。トイレ（は）どこですか。

店員(てんいん) ：こちらです。

Jon   : Sumimasen. <u>Toire</u> **(wa) doko desu ka.**
Ten'in : Kochira desu.

John : Excuse me. Where is the restroom?
Clerk : This way.

Practice A-1

_____、どこですか。
Use the following words with the phrase "_____, doko desu ka."
下記の言葉を使って「_____、どこですか」のフレーズを練習してください。

🔊 Track 20

トイレ toire *restroom* 	レジ reji *cash register* 	エレベーター erebētā *elevator*
コインロッカー koin rokkā *coin locker* 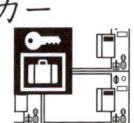	入り口(いりぐち) iriguchi *entrance*	本屋(ほんや) hon-ya *bookstore*  → **See Appendix, Shops**

Practice A-2

_____です。
Answer the questions from above using the following words with the phrase "_____ desu."
上記(A-1)の質問に下記の言葉と「_____です」を使って答えてください。

🔊 Track 21

ここ／こちら* koko / kochira* *here*	そこ／そちら* soko / sochira* *there*	あそこ／あちら* asoko / achira* *over there*

＊ Kochira, sochira, and achira are polite versions of these expressions.
＊「こちら」「そちら」「あちら」は、それぞれ「ここ」「そこ」「あそこ」の丁寧な言い方です。

1階 いっかい ikkai *first floor / ground floor*	2階 に かい ni-kai *second floor*	3階 さん かい san-kai* *third floor*	4階 よん かい yon-kai *fourth floor*

* **"San-gai"** (third floor) and **"san-kai"** (third floor) are also being used.
  Please see Counters on p.178 of Grammar for counting floors higher than 4.
*「3階（さんがい）」「3階（さんかい）」ともに使われます。
  5階以上の数字については p.178 の助数詞のページを参照。

Have a practice conversation using the words from practice A-1 and A-2 in 〈 〉
(A-1), (A-2) の言葉を〈　　〉に入れ会話練習をしてください。 🔊 Track 22

ジョン ：すみません、^{A-1}〈トイレ〉、どこですか。
店員　：^{A-2}〈あちら〉です。
てんいん
ジョン ：ありがとうございます。

Jon　　：Sumimasen, ^{A-1}< toire >, doko desu ka.
Ten'in　：^{A-2}< Achira > desu.
Jon　　：Arigatō gozaimasu.

John　：Excuse me, where is the restroom?
Clerk ：It's over that way.
John　：Thank you.

Ask what floor the following shops are on with the conversation pattern below.
以下(1.2.3)の店が何階にあるか下記の会話例を使って尋ねてください。 🔊 Track 23

1. Bookstore　　2. 100-yen store　　3. Restaurants
1. 本屋　　　　2. 100円ショップ　　3. レストラン

-At the reception desk-　受付で
　　　　　　　　　　　うけつけ

ジョン ：すみません、〈　　〉は何階ですか。
　　　　　　　　　　　　　　　　なんかい
受付　：〈　　〉でございます。
うけつけ
ジョン ：え？　もう一度いいですか。
　　　　　　　　　いちど
受付　：〈　　〉です。
うけつけ

Jon　　　　：Sumimasen, <　> wa nan-kai desu ka.
Uketsuke　：<　> de gozaimasu.
Jon　　　　：E? Mō ichido ii desu ka.
Uketsuke　：<　> desu.

4F	Restaurants
3F	Bookstore
2F	100-yen store
1F	Reception / Front desk

John　：Excuse me, what floor is the <　> on?
Clerk ：It's on the <　>.
John　：Pardon? Would you say that one more time?
Clerk ：It's <　>.

MEMO

もう一度いいですか。／Mō ichido ii desu ka.／*Would you say that one more time?*
　いち ど

〜は何階ですか。／... wa nan-kai desu ka.／*What floor is the ... on?*
　なん かい

Phrase 3 — Gather information about a place you are trying to go.

郵便局に行きたいんですが……。
ゆうびんきょく　い

Yūbinkyoku ni ikitai n desu ga...... . *I'm trying to get to the post office.*

🔊 Track 24

> **NOTE** "__ ni ikitai" means "I would like to go to __" or "I am trying to get to __."
> "__ n desu ga" frequently precedes a sentence requesting information, but because this nuance is so obvious from context, the rest of the sentence following "__ n desu ga" is often left out.
>
> 「〜に行きたい」は "I would like to go (行きたい)" あるいは "I am trying to get to (行こうとしている)" という意味です。「〜んですが」のあとには、その情報を求める文（教えてもらえませんか、など）が続きますが、文脈からニュアンスが明らかな場合には省略されることが多いです。

Ex.

ジョン　：すみません。郵便局に行きたいんですが……。
　　　　　　　　　ゆうびんきょく　い
警察官　：あの公園の左ですよ。
けいさつかん　　こうえん　ひだり

Jon　　　　　: Sumimasen. Yūbinkyoku ni ikitai n desu ga...... .
Keisatsu-kan : Ano kōen no hidari desu yo.

John　　　　　: Excuse me, I'm trying to get to the post office, but....
Police officer : It's to the left of that park.

Practice A-1

_____に行きたいんですが……。
Use the following words with the phrase "_____ ni ikitai n desu ga...... ."
下記の言葉を使って「_____に行きたいんですが…」のフレーズを練習してください。

🔊 Track 25

郵便局 ゆうびんきょく yūbinkyoku *post office* 	映画館 えいがかん eigakan *movie theater* 	銀行 ぎんこう ginkō *bank* 
タクシーのりば takusī-noriba *taxi stand*	公園 こうえん kōen *park*	病院 びょういん byōin *hospital*	美術館 びじゅつかん bijutsukan *art museum*

Practice A-2

_____ですよ。
Answer the questions from above using the following words with the phrase "_____ desu yo."
上記(A1)の質問に下記の言葉と「_____ですよ」を使って答えてください。

🔊 Track 26

ここまっすぐ koko massugu *straight up / down here* 	あっち acchi *over that way / over there* 

～の左(ひだり) 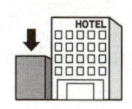 -no hidari *to the left of*	～の右(みぎ)  -no migi *to the right of*	～の前(まえ)  -no mae *in front of*
～のうしろ 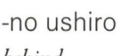 -no ushiro *behind*	～のとなり  -no tonari *next to*	～の近(ちか)く  -no chikaku *near*

 Practice B Look at the map on p. 33 and ask for items 1-4 with the conversation template below. 🔊 Track 27
下記の会話例を使い、p.33の地図を見ながら1-4の場所を尋ねてください。

Ex. ふじ病院(びょういん) Fuji byōin
1. 本屋(ほんや) hon-ya 2. 映画館(えいがかん) eigakan 3. さくらホテル Sakura hoteru 4. 郵便局(ゆうびんきょく) yūbinkyoku

ジョン：すみません、〈ふじ病院(びょういん)〉に行(い)きたいんですが……。
警察官(けいさつかん)：〈ここまっすぐ〉ですよ。／〈美術館(びじゅつかん)の前(まえ)〉ですよ。
ジョン：近(ちか)いですか。
警察官(けいさつかん)：はい、近(ちか)いですよ。／いいえ、ちょっと遠(とお)いですよ。

Jon	: Sumimasen, <Fuji byōin> ni ikitai n desu ga... .
Keisatsu-kan	: <Koko massugu> desu yo. / <Bijutsukan no mae> desu yo.
Jon	: Chikai desu ka.
Keisatsu-kan	: Hai, chikai desu yo. / Iie, chotto tōi desu yo.

John	: Excuse me, I'm trying to get to Fuji Hospital.
Police officer	: It's straight down here. / It's in front of the museum.
John	: Is it near here?
Police officer	: Yes. / No, it's a little far.

MEMO
近(ちか)いですか。／Chikai desu ka. ／*Is it near here?*
ちょっと遠(とお)いですよ。／Chotto tōi desu yo. ／*It's a little far.*

Dialogue 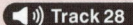 Track 28

Look at the picture on the right page and have a practice conversation replacing the words in (1) - (4).
右のページを見ながら、(1)〜(4)の言葉をピンクの枠内の言葉に置き換えて会話練習をしてください。

-In front of a station- 駅の前で

クマール	：すみません。	Kumāru	: Sumimasen.
女の人	：はい。	Onna no hito	: Hai.
クマール	：(1)<u>さくら公園</u>に行きたいんですが……。	Kumāru	: (1) <u>Sakura kōen</u> ni ikitai n desu ga....... .
女の人	：えっと……、ここまっすぐですよ。	Onna no hito	: Etto......, koko massugu desu yo.
クマール	：そうですか。あ、それから、このへんに、(2)<u>ATM</u>ありますか。	Kumāru	: Sō desu ka. A, sorekara, kono hen ni (2) <u>ATM</u> arimasu ka.
女の人	：そうですね……。あ、(3)<u>コンビニ</u>にありますよ。	Onna no hito	: Sō desu ne....... . A, (3) <u>kombini</u> ni arimasu yo.
クマール	：(3)<u>コンビニ</u>はどこですか。	Kumāru	: (3) <u>Kombini</u> wa doko desu ka.
女の人	：(4)<u>さくら公園の前</u>です。	Onna no hito	: (4) <u>Sakura kōen no mae</u> desu.
クマール	：ありがとうございます。	Kumāru	: Arigatō gozaimasu.

---

① (1) ふじ病院   Fuji byōin
    (2) 花屋   hana-ya (= *flower shop*)
    (3) スーパー   sūpā
    (4) 病院の近く   byōin no chikaku

② (1) 現代美術館   Gendai bijutsukan (= *Modern art museum*)
    (2) コインロッカー   koin rokkā
    (3) 地下鉄の駅   chikatetsu no eki
    (4) ホテルのとなり   hoteru no tonari

MEMO

それから / sorekara / *and*
[Used when uttering an additional statement or question. 平叙文・疑問文を追加する時に使います。]

そうですね / sō desune / *Let me see.*

Material

Look at the map while doing the practice conversation on the left page.
下記の地図を見ながら、左ページの会話練習をしてください。

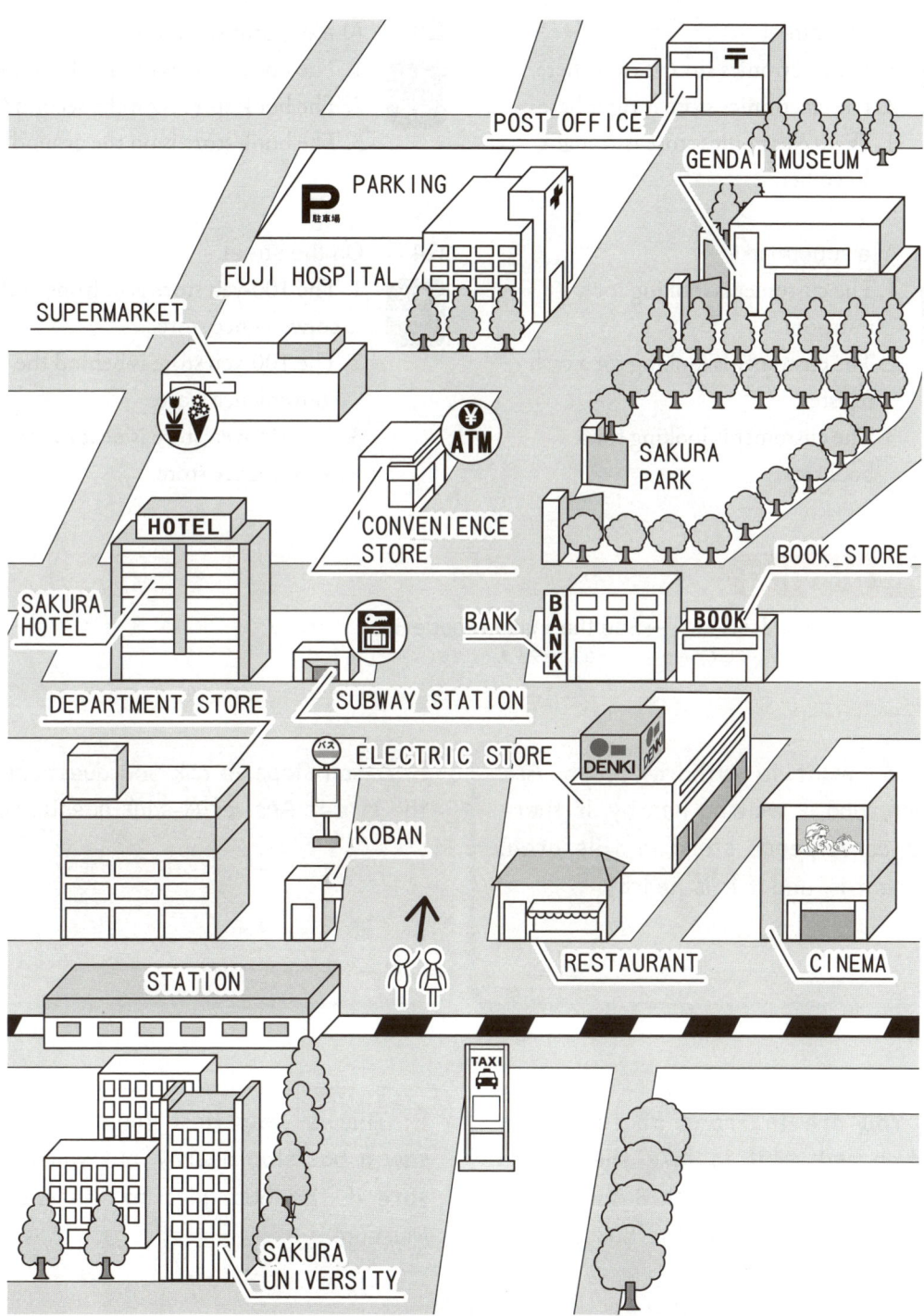

Listening

Listen to the conversation between the man and woman and choose the correct answer.
男の人と女の人の会話を聞いて正しい答えを選んでください。

Q1 On the street

1. The electronics store is over there.
2. The electronics store is right here.
3. There electronics store is straight down here.

Q3 At a department store

1. The book store is on the third floor.
2. The book store is on the second floor.
3. The book store is on the ground floor.

Q2 At a supermarket

1. The customer is looking for a restroom.
2. The customer is looking for a cash register.
3. The customer is looking for a bookstore.

Q4 On the street

1. The 100-yen store is in front of the convenience store.
2. The 100-yen store is behind the convenience store.
3. The 100-yen store is next to the convenience store.

Role playing

Role play using the cards below.   →See the map on page 33.
下記のカードを使ってロールプレイしてください。 →p.33の地図を見てください。

1.

A: You want to withdraw cash. Ask B-san, who is walking nearby, if there is a convenience store in this area, where it is, and if it is nearby.

B: A-san stops to ask you questions in the street. Answer A-san's questions.

2.

A: You are in front of the train station and want to take the bus to the Gendai Museum. Ask B-san where the bus stop is and if the bus goes to the museum.

B: This is your first time here. You saw a bus stop nearby, but you're not sure if the bus goes to the Gendai Museum.

Do you remember?

Use the phrases you have studied in this unit in situations ①–③ below.
このユニットで学習したフレーズを下記の①〜③の状況に合わせて使ってください。

Phrases for This Unit

Unit Phrases

- このへんに、ATM ありますか。 — Kono hen ni, ATM arimasuka. — *Is there an ATM around here?*
- トイレ、どこですか。 — Toire, doko desu ka. — *Where is the restroom?*
- 郵便局に行きたいんですが……。 — Yūbinkyoku ni ikitai n desu ga....... . — *I'm trying to go to the post office.*

Useful expressions

- じゃ、いいです。 — Ja, ii desu. — *That's alright.*
- もう一度いいですか。 — Mō ichido ii desu ka. — *Would you say that one more time?*
- 〜は何階ですか。 — ...wa nan-kai desu ka. — *What floor is the ... on?*
- 近いですか。 — Chikai desu ka. — *Is it near here?*
- それから、〜 — sorekara, ... — *and* [Used when uttering an additional statement or question.]

Check!

✓ Now I can...

- ☐ Ask if the store or place I want to go to is in the nearby area
  行きたい店や場所が近くにあるかどうか尋ねられる
- ☐ Ask for the location of the store or place I want to go to
  行きたい店や場所が尋ねられる
- ☐ Ask and understand simple directions
  道を尋ねたり、簡単な道案内を理解したりできる

How much is this?

これ、いくらですか。
Kore, ikura desu ka.

Shopping
買い物

- Ask if a store has what you are looking for
  探しているものが店にあるかどうか尋ねる

- Ask for the price of something you want to buy
  買いたいものの値段を尋ねる

- Request what you would like from a store
  店の人に、その他のリクエストをする

Phrase 1
Ask if a store has what you want to buy.

🔊 Track 33

かさ、**ありますか**。

Kasa, **arimasu ka**.

Do you have umbrellas?

NOTE "___ (wa) arimasu ka." was introduced as a way to ask if something exists in Unit 2. It can also mean "**Do you have___?**" → See p.170, Grammar

「〜（は）ありますか」には、ユニット2で取り上げたように、存在の有無について尋ねる用法の他、"Do you have...?" のように所有の意味があります。p.170文法ページ参照。

Ex.

ジョン　：すみません。<u>かさ</u>（は）ありますか。

店員（てんいん）：はい、あります。こちらです。

Jon　　：Sumimasen. <u>Kasa</u> **(wa) arimasu ka.**
Ten'in ：Hai, arimasu. Kochira desu.

John　：Excuse me, do you have umbrellas?
Clerk ：Yes, we do. They're right here.

Practice A

_____、ありますか。

Use the following words with the phrase "_____ , arimasu ka."

🔊 Track 34

下記の言葉を使って「_____、ありますか」のフレーズを練習してください。

かさ kasa *umbrella*	充電器（じゅうでんき） jūdenki *battery charger*	ボールペン bōru-pen *ball point pen* → **See Appendix, Stationery**
ティッシュ thisshu *tissue*	（お*）水（みず） (o*)mizu *water*	（お）酒（さけ） (o)sake *alcoholic drink/Japanese sake*
牛乳（ぎゅうにゅう） gyūnyū *milk*	塩（しお） shio *salt* → **See Appendix, Seasoning**	薬（くすり） kusuri *medicine* → **See Appendix, Medicine**

＊ The prefix "o-" makes nouns more polite. → See p.183, Grammar
＊ 名詞の前の接頭辞「お」は丁寧表現です。p.183文法ページ参照。

Put the words from A in < > to complete the conversation exercise.
Practice Aの言葉を〈　〉に入れて会話練習をしてください。

🔊 Track 35

①

ジョン：すみません。〈かさ〉、ありますか。
店員（てんいん）：はい、こちらです。
ジョン：ありがとうございます。

Jon : Sumimasen. <Kasa>, arimasu ka.	John : Excuse me. Do you have umbrellas?
Ten'in : Hai, kochira desu.	Clerk : Yes. They're right here.
Jon : Arigatō gozaimasu.	John : Thank you.

②

ジョン：すみません。〈充電器（じゅうでんき）〉、ありますか。
店員（てんいん）：申し訳（もうしわけ）ありません。〈充電器（じゅうでんき）〉は、ないんです。
ジョン：わかりました。

Jon : Sumimasen. < Jūdenki >, arimasu ka.	John : Excuse me. Do you have a battery charger?
Ten'in : Mōshiwake arimasen. 　< Jūdenki > wa, naindesu.	Clerk : I'm sorry, but we don't [have any battery chargers].
Jon : Wakarimashita.	John : Okay.

MEMO

申し訳（もうしわけ）ありません。／Mōshiwake arimasen.／*I'm sorry.*
　　　　　　　　　　　　　["I have no excuse"; extremely polite　非常に丁寧な表現です。]

ないんです。／Naindesu.／"…n desu" can be used to make a negative answer softer.
　　　　　　　　　　　「〜んです」を使うことで否定的な回答を柔らかい印象にできます。

"Naindesu" = "We don't have it."

Phrase 2

Ask how much something costs.

これ、いくらですか。

Kore, ikura desu ka.   *How much is this?*

🔊 Track 36

NOTE "Ikura" means "how much." "___ (wa) ikura desu ka." means "How much is ___?" and is used to ask how much something costs.

「いくら」は、"How much is...?" の意味で、ものの値段について聞く表現です。

Ex.

ジョン ：これ(は)いくらですか。

店員(てんいん) ：500円です。
　　　　　　　ごひゃくえん

Jon   : Kore (wa) ikura desu ka.
Ten'in : 500 [gohyaku]-en desu.

John : How much is this?
Clerk : It's 500 yen.

_____、いくらですか。

Let's use the following words with the phrase "_____ , ikura desu ka."

下記の言葉を使って「_____、いくらですか」のフレーズを練習しましょう。

🔊 Track 37

これ	それ	あれ
kore	sore	are
this	*that*[*1]	*that*[*2]

Speaker　Listener   Speaker　Listener   Speaker Listener

*1 *'That' which is close to the listener* / 聞き手に近い that
*2 *'That' which is far from both the speaker and listener* / 聞き手、話し手両者から遠い that

Practice A-2 Study the numbers from 10 to 10,000 (→see p. 47) and say the following prices in (1) – (7) with the phrase "_____-en desu."
🔊 Track 38

10から10,000までの数字を学習しましょう。(p.47参照)　また「_____円です」を使って(1) – (7)の値段を言ってください。

(1) ¥55　(2) ¥99　(3) ¥270　(4) ¥360　(5) ¥890　(6) ¥1,500　(7) ¥2,700

Practice B Practice talking about prices with the pictures below.
🔊 Track 39

下記のイラストを見て値段を言う練習をしてください。

ジョン　：すみません。〈紙袋〉、いくらですか。
　　　　　　　　　　かみぶくろ

店員　　：〈10円〉です。
てんいん　　じゅうえん

Jon　　　: Sumimasen. < Kami-bukuro >, ikura desu ka.
Ten'in　 : < 10 [jū]-en > desu.

John　　: Excuse me. How much is this paper bag?
Clerk　　: It's 10 yen.

Ex. 紙袋
かみ ぶくろ
kami-bukuro
paper bag

¥10

① ペン
pen
pen
¥220

② お弁当
べん とう
o-bentō
bento-box
¥850

③ タオル
taoru
towel

¥980

④ 時計
と けい
tokei
clock

¥1,980

⑤ バッグ／かばん
baggu/kaban
bag

¥4,600

⑥ マフラー
mafurā
scarf

¥5,300

⑦ くつ
kutsu
shoes

¥8,800

Phrase 3 — Make a purchase.

🔊 Track 40

このTシャツ、ください。

Kono T-shatsu, kudasai. *I'll have this T-shirt.*

NOTE "___(o) kudasai." means "Please give me ___." and is used when making a purchase. "kono" is always used before a noun. "kore" means "this" and is also used before "kudasai."

「〜（を）ください」は、"Please give me" の意味で、買い物をする時に使われる表現です。「この」はいつも名詞の前につきます。「これ」は "this" の意味で、これも「ください」の前にきます。

Ex.

① すみません。このTシャツ（を）ください。

② すみません。これ（を）ふたつください。

① Sumimasen. Kono T-shatsu (o) kudasai.
② Sumimasen. Kore (o) futatsu kudasai.

① : *Excuse me. I'll have this T-shirt.*
② : *Excuse me. I'll have two of these.*

Practice A-1

_____ 、ください。

Use the following words with the phrase "_____ , kudasai."

下記の言葉を使って「_____ ください」のフレーズを練習してください。

🔊 Track 41

このTシャツ	そのTシャツ	あのTシャツ
kono T-shatsu	sono T-shatsu	ano T-shatsu
this T-shirt	*that T-shirt*	*that T-shirt*
これ	それ	あれ
kore	sore	are
this	*that/it*	*that*

Practice A-2 これ、＿＿＿＿ください。
Say how many of each item you want with the phrase **"Kore, ＿＿＿＿ kudasai."**
「これ、＿＿＿＿ください」のフレーズを使っていくつほしいか言ってみましょう。

🔊 Track 42

ひとつ	ふたつ	みっつ	よっつ
hitotsu	futatsu	mittsu	yottsu
one	two	three	four

* 5 = itsutsu, 6 = muttsu, 7 = nanatsu, 8 = yattsu, 9 = kokonotsu, 10 = tō
　Saying the number word with "ko" can also be used to count objects. → *See p.178, Grammar*

* これ以外に、数字に「個」をつける言い方もあります。p.178 文法ページ参照。

Practice B Put the words from Practice A-1 and A-2 into <　> to complete the conversation below.
(A-1)と(A-2)の言葉を〈　　〉に入れて会話練習をしてください。

🔊 Track 43

ジョン：すみません。 A-1＜このTシャツ＞、A-2＜ふたつ＞ください。

店員（てんいん）：はい。ありがとうございます。

ジョン：あ、それから、A-1＜これ＞もください。

店員（てんいん）：かしこまりました。お支払（しはら）いは？

ジョン：カードでお願（ねが）いします。

店員（てんいん）：一回（いっかい）でよろしいですか。

ジョン：はい。一回（いっかい）で。

Jon　　： Sumimasen. A-1< Kono T-shatsu >, A-2< futatsu > kudasai.	John　　： Excuse me, I'll have two of these T-shirts.
Ten'in ： Hai. Arigatō gozaimasu.	Clerk　： Okay. Thank you.
Jon　　： A, sorekara, A-1< kore > mo kudasai.	John　　： And I'll take this, too.
Ten'in ： Kashikomari mashita. Oshiharaiwa?	Clerk　： Alright. What is your payment method?
Jon　　： Kādo de onegai shimasu.	John　　： I'd like to pay by credit card.
Ten'in ： Ikkai de yoroshiidesuka.	Clerk　： Is one instalment OK?
Jon　　： Hai. Ikkai de.	John　　： Yes. One, please.

それから、～もください。／Sorekara, … mo kudasai. ／ *And I'll have … , too.*

かしこまりました。／Kashikomarimashita. ／ *Certainly/Yes/Right away.*

カードでお願（ねが）いします。／Kādo de onegaishimasu. ／ *I'd like to pay by credit card.*

一回（いっかい）でよろしいですか。／Ikkai de yoroshiidesuka. ／ *Is one instalment OK?*

UNIT 3

Phrase 4 — Making requests at a store.

🔊 Track 44

もうちょっと安(やす)いの、ありませんか。

Mō chotto yasui no, arimasen ka. *Do you have one a little cheaper?*

> **NOTE** "Mō chotto" means "a little more" and can be used with adjectives. "Mō chotto ____ no arimasen ka." is often used to make a request while shopping. Although "arimasen ka" can also be used in the affirmative, is considered more polite to ask with a negative form.
>
> 「もうちょっと」は、"a little more" の意味で形容詞とともに使われます。「もうちょっと____のありませんか」は買い物の場面で、依頼の機能（____のください）としても使われます。もちろん「ありますか」と肯定疑問文でも使いますが、否定疑問文のほうがより丁寧です。

Ex.

ジョン　：もうちょっと安(やす)いの（は）ありませんか。

店員(てんいん)：こちらはいかがですか。

Jon　　：**Mō chotto <u>yasui</u> no (wa) arimasen ka.**
Ten'in　：Kochira wa ikaga desu ka.

> John　：Do you have one a little cheaper?
> Clerk　：How about this one?

 Practice A

もうちょっと_____の、ありませんか。 🔊 Track 45

Let's use the following words with the phrase "**Mō chotto _____ no, arimasen ka.**"

下記の言葉を「もうちょっと_____の、ありませんか」を使って練習してください。

安(やす)い yasui *cheap*	大(おお)きい ōkii *big*	小(ちい)さい chiisai *small*	軽(かる)い karui *light/light weight*
長(なが)い nagai *long*	短(みじか)い mijikai *short*	他(ほか)の*メーカー hoka no* mēkā *another makers*	他(ほか)の*色(いろ) hoka no* iro *another colors* → **See Appendix, Colors**

* You don't use "mō chotto" with "hoka no" (another, the other).
*「他の」の前には「もうちょっと」という表現はつけません。

Practice B-1 Put the words from Practice A in < > and practice the conversation below. 🔊 Track 46
Practice Aの言葉を〈　〉に入れて会話練習をしてください。

-Looking at something in a shop- 店で品物を見ている

ジョン：すみません。これ、もうちょっと〈安い〉の、ありませんか。

店員：すみません。これだけなんです。

ジョン：そうですか。じゃあ、ちょっと考えます。

Jon	: Sumimasen. Kore, mō chotto < yasui > no arimasen ka.
Ten'in	: Sumimasen. Kore dake nan desu.
Jon	: Sō desu ka. Jā, chotto kangaemasu.

> John : Excuse me. Do you have a cheaper one of these?
> Clerk : I'm sorry, this is all we have.
> John : Okay, I'll think about it then.

 **Practice B-2** Study the numbers from 10 to 100,000 (p. 47) and practice the conversation with the words below. 🔊 Track 47
10から100,000までの数字を学習しましょう。(p.47参照)　下記のイラストを使って練習してください。

ジョン：すみません。この〈自転車〉、いくらですか。

店員：〈23,980〉円です。

| Jon | : Sumimasen. Kono <jitensha>, ikura desu ka. |
| Ten'in | : <23,980> -en desu. |

> John : Excuse me. How much is this bicycle?
> Clerk : It's 23,980 yen.

Ex. 自転車　① スマホ　② ワイヤレスイヤホン　③ パソコン
jitensha　　sumaho　　waiyaresu iyahon　　pasokon
bicycle　　*smart phone*　　*wireless earphone*　　*personal computer*

 ¥23,980
 ¥76,000
  ¥10,500
 ¥98,000

MEMO

こちらはいかがですか。／Kochira wa ikaga desu ka.／*How about this one?*

これだけなんです。／Kore dake nan desu.／*This is all we have.*

じゃあ、ちょっと考えます。／Jā, chotto kangaemasu.／*I'll think about it then.*

Dialogue

Track 48

Look at the picture on the right page and have a practice conversation replacing the words in (1) – (5).
右のページを見ながら、(1)～(5)の言葉をピンクの枠内の言葉に置き換えて会話練習をしてください。

ジョン	：すみません。	Jon	: Sumimasen.
	(1)Tシャツ、ありますか。		(1) T-shatsu, arimasu ka.
店員	：はい、ございます。こちらです。	Ten'in	: Hai, gozaimasu. Kochira desu.
ジョン	：それはいくらですか。	Jon	: Sore wa ikura desu ka.
店員	：(2)3,900円です。	Ten'in	: (2) 3,900-en desu.
ジョン	：(3)もうちょっと安いの、ありませんか。	Jon	: (3) Mō chotto yasui no, arimasen ka.
店員	：(4)こちらは1,980円です。	Ten'in	: (4) Kochira wa 1,980-en desu.
ジョン	：じゃあ、(5)それ、みっつください。	Jon	: Jā, (5) sore, mittsu kudasai.
店員	：ありがとうございます。	Ten'in	: Arigatō gozaimasu.

❶
(1) 水　　　　　　　　　　　　　　　　mizu
(2) 150円　　　　　　　　　　　　　　150-en
(3) もうちょっと小さい　　　　　　　Mō chotto chiisai
(4) こちらは100円です　　　　　　　Kochira wa 100-en desu
(5) それ、ひとつ　　　　　　　　　　sore, hitotsu

❷
(1) 充電器　　　　　　　　　　　　　　jūdenki
(2) 4,990円　　　　　　　　　　　　　4,990-en
(3) 他の色　　　　　　　　　　　　　Hoka no iro
(4) 青いのと黒いのがあります　　　Aoi no to kuroi no ga arimasu
(5) 黒いの　　　　　　　　　　　　　kuroi no

MEMO

ございます。／Gozaimasu.／[A politer way to say "arimasu (=have)"「あります(所有)」の丁寧な表現です。]

Material

1 Look at the pictures below and complete the practice conversation on the left page.
下記の絵を見ながら左ページの会話練習を完成させましょう。

2 Counting 1 – 100,000
1から100,000までの数の言い方

1-10	11-20	10-100	100-1,000	1,000-10,000	10,000-100,000
1 ichi	11 jū-ichi	10 jū	100 hyaku	1,000 sen	10,000 ichi-man
2 ni	12 jū-ni	20 ni-jū	200 ni-hyaku	2,000 ni-sen	20,000 ni-man
3 san	13 jū-san	30 san-jū	300 sambyaku	3,000 san-zen	30,000 sam-man
4 yon/shi	14 jū-yon	40 yon-jū	400 yon-hyaku	4,000 yon-sen	40,000 yon-man
5 go	15 jū-go	50 go-jū	500 go-hyaku	5,000 go-sen	50,000 go-man
6 roku	16 jū-roku	60 roku-jū	600 roppyaku	6,000 roku-sen	60,000 roku-man
7 nana/shichi	17 jū-nana	70 nana-jū	700 nana-hyaku	7,000 nana-sen	70,000 nana-man
8 hachi	18 jū-hachi	80 hachi-jū	800 happyaku	8,000 hassen	80,000 hachi-man
9 kyū/ku	19 jū-kyū	90 kyū-jū	900 kyū-hyaku	9,000 kyū-sen	90,000 kyū-man
10 jū	20 ni-jū	100 hyaku	1,000 sen	10,000 ichi-man	100,000 jū-man

The pink numbers are those whose pronunciation varies by a euphonic change.
ピンク色の数字は音便によって発音が変化するものです。記憶に残るように抜き出して練習をすると効果的です。

UNIT 3

Listening

Listen to the conversation between the man and woman and choose the correct answer.
男の人と女の人の会話を聞いて正しい答えを選んでください。

Q1 At a convenience store

1. They don't have newspapers.
2. They have cigarettes.
3. They don't have cigarettes (Tabako).

Q2 At a kiosk

1. The umbrella is 400 yen.
2. The umbrella is 600 yen.
3. The umbrella is 800 yen.

Q3 Inside a *shinkansen*

1. The man wants a bento box.
2. The man wants 2 bento boxes.
3. The man wants 3 bento boxes.

Q4 At a department store

1. The woman wants a bigger one.
2. The woman wants a cheaper one.
3. The woman wants a smaller one.

Role playing

Role play using the cards below.
下記のカードを使ってロールプレイしてください。

1. At a kiosk　キオスクで

A: You are at a kiosk. Ask if they have a battery charger (mobairu batterī) for your cellular phone, how much it costs, and if they have one that costs less.

B: You are a clerk at a kiosk. The store has chargers for 1,000 and 1,500 yen. If asked about prices, first recommend the more expensive model.

2. At a shop　店で

A: You are at a shop and want to buy an umbrella. Ask the clerk for it, how much it is, and if they have any smaller ones.

B: You work at a shop. The shop has a small umbrella for 1,500 yen and big umbrella for 2,800 yen. If asked, first recommend the bigger umbrella.

Do you remember?

Use the phrases you have studied in this unit in situations ①–④ below.
このユニットで学習したフレーズを下記の①〜④の状況に合わせて使ってください。

Phrases for This Unit

Unit Phrases

- かさ、ありますか。　　Kasa, arimasu ka.　　*Do you have umbrellas?*
- これ、いくらですか。　　Kore, ikura desu ka.　　*How much is this?*
- このTシャツ、ください。　　Kono T-shatsu, kudasai.　　*I'll have this T-shirt.*
- もうちょっと安いの、ありませんか。　　Mō chotto yasui no, arimasen ka.　　*Do you have one a little cheaper?*

Useful expressions

- ちょっと考えます。　　Chotto kangaemasu.　　*I will think about it.*
- お支払いは？　　O-shiharai wa?　　*What is your payment method?*
  ―カードでお願いします。　　― Kādo de onegaishimasu.　　*― I'd like to pay by credit card.*
- それから、これもください。　　Sorekara, kore mo kudasai.　　*I'll take this, too.*

Check!

✓ Now I can...

- ☐ Ask if a store has what I am looking for
  探しているものが店にあるかどうか尋ねられる

- ☐ Ask for the price of something I want to buy
  買いたいものの値段が尋ねられる

- ☐ Request what I would like from a store
  店の人に、その他のリクエストができる

Take out, please.

持ち帰りで。
Mochikaeri de.

Convenience stores and restaurants
コンビニ・レストラン

GOALS FOR UNIT 4

- Make orders at restaurants
  レストランで注文する

- Request and ask about items on the menu
  メニューの内容についてリクエストしたり、尋ねたりする

- Communicate with people at convenience stores and restaurants
  コンビニやレストランの店員とコミュニケーションをとる

Phrase 1 — Make a request at a restaurant.

メニュー、お願いします。
Menyū, **onegaishimasu.**

Could I have a menu?

🔊 Track 53

> **NOTE** "**[Noun] (o) onegaishimasu**" is used when ordering food and making a request to receive something or have something done. A counter word can optionally come after the noun. → *See p.43 and p.178, Counters*
>
> 「[名詞]（を）お願いします」は、食事のオーダーや何かがほしい、あるいはしてほしい時の依頼の表現として使われます。必要に応じ、助数詞も名詞のあとにきます。p.43, p.178の助数詞のページを参照。

Ex.

① すみません。<u>メニュー（を）</u>お願いします。

② <u>カレー（を）</u><u>ひとつ</u>、お願いします。

① Sumimasen. <u>Menyū **(o)**</u> **onegaishimasu.**
② <u>Karē **(o)**</u> <u>hitotsu</u>, **onegaishimasu.**

① *Excuse me. Could I have a menu?*
② *One curry, please.*

Practice A-1

＿＿＿＿、お願いします。
Use the following words with the phrase "＿＿＿＿ , **onegaishimasu.**"
下記の言葉を使って「＿＿＿＿、お願いします」のフレーズを練習してください。

🔊 Track 54

メニュー menyū *menu*	注文（ちゅうもん） chūmon *order*	おしぼり oshibori *rolled wet towel [used to wash one's hands]*
取り皿（とざら） torizara *small plate*	これと同じの（おな） kore to onaji no *the same as this*	グラス gurasu *glass*
お会計（かいけい） okaikei *bill / check*	カレー karē *curry with rice* → *See Appendix, Food*	生ビール（なま） nama bīru *draft beer* → *See Appendix, Drinks*

Practice A-2

[A-1] _____、お願いします。

Ask for words in Practice A-1 in the quantities below using **" [A-1] _____ , onegaishimasu."**

Practice A-1の言葉に以下の助数詞を使って「[A-1] _____、お願いします」のように尋ねてください。

🔊 Track 55

ひとつ	ふたつ	みっつ	よっつ
hitotsu	futatsu	mittsu	yottsu
one	two	three	four

* 5 = itsutsu, 6 = muttsu, 7 = nanatsu, 8 = yattsu, 9 = kokonotsu, 10 = tō → *See p.178, Grammar*
* p.178 文法ページ参照

UNIT 4

Practice B

Put the words from Practice A-1 and A-2 into < > to complete the conversation below.
Practice A-1とA-2の言葉を〈　〉に入れて会話練習をしてください。

🔊 Track 56

店員　：ご注文、お決まりですか。
ジョン：はい。^A-1〈カレー〉^A-2〈ひとつ〉と^A-1〈生ビール〉^A-2〈ひとつ〉、お願いします。
店員　：以上でよろしいですか。
ジョン：はい、以上で。あ、あとお水もらえますか。
店員　：かしこまりました。

Ten'in : Go-chūmon, o-kimari desu ka.
Jon : Hai. ^A-1<Karē> ^A-2<hitotsu> to
　　　　^A-1<nama bīru> ^A-2<hitotsu>, onegaishimasu.
Ten'in : Ijō de yoroshii desu ka.
Jon : Hai, ijō de. A, ato o-mizu moraemasu ka.
Ten'in : Kashikomarimashita.

> Waiter : *Are you ready to order?*
> John : *Yes. I'll have one curry and one draft beer, please.*
> Waiter : *Will that be all for you?*
> John : *Yes, that's all. Oh, could I also have some water?*
> Waiter : *Right away.*

MEMO

（ご注文、）お決まりですか。／(Go-chūmon,) o-kimari desu ka. ／*Are you ready to order?*

以上でよろしいですか。／Ijō de yoroshii desu ka. ／*Will that be all for you?*

以上で。／Ijō de. ／*That's all.*

あと〜／ato... ／*also...*

〜もらえますか。／... moraemasu ka. ／*Could I have ... ?*

かしこまりました。／Kashikomarimashita. ／*Certainly/Yes/Right away.*

Phrase 2
Ask about things you don't understand or don't know about.

🔊 Track 57

今日(きょう)のランチ、**なんですか**。

Kyō no ranchi, **nan desu ka.**   *What's the lunch of the day?*

NOTE "Nan" means "what." "___(wa) nan desu ka" means "What is___?"
「なん」は、"what" の意味で、「___(は)なんですか」は、"What is ___?" という意味です。

Ex.

ジョン ：すみません。今日(きょう)のランチ(は)なんですか。

店員(てんいん)：カレーです。

Jon ： Sumimasen. <u>Kyō no ranchi</u> **(wa) nan desu ka.**

Ten-in ： Karē desu.

> John ： Excuse me, what's the lunch of the day?
> Waiter ： Curry.

Practice A

_____、なんですか。
Use the following words with the phrase "_____ , **nan desu ka.**"
下記の言葉を使って「_____、なんですか」のフレーズを練習しましょう。

🔊 Track 58

今日(きょう)のランチ	日替(ひが)わり*定食(ていしょく)	おすすめ
kyō no ranchi	higawari* teishoku	osusume
lunch of the day	*today's set meal*	*recommendation*
これ 	あれ 	デザート 
kore	are	dezāto
this	*that*	*dessert*
セットのドリンク 	この〈白(しろ)い・黒(くろ)い・赤(あか)い〉の	
setto no dorinku	kono <shiroi / kuroi / akai> no	
included drink	*this <white / black / red > one* → See p.i Colors	

* **Higawari** ["day change"] originally comes from the practice of restaurants offering a different meal each day. Restaurants now offer special menus each day, such as daily set meals and lunches, which are referred to as **higawari**.
*「日替わり」という言葉は、もともと飲食店がその日その日で異なるメニューを出していたことに由来しています。今でもレストランでは「日替わり」という名で、定食やランチメニューなど、その日だけの特別なメニューを提供しています。

 Using the menu on page 61, put the words from Practice A into < > and complete the conversation.　🔊 Track 59
p.61のメニューを見ながらPractice Aの言葉を〈　〉に入れて会話練習をしてください。

ジョン　：〈今日のランチ〉、なんですか。
　　　　　　　きょう
店員　　：〈カレー〉です。
てんいん

John　　: < Kyō no ranchi >, nan desu ka.
Ten'in　 :< Karē > desu.

> John　　: What's the lunch of the day?
> Waiter　: Curry and rice.

 Look at the Pre-text and ask questions about items on the menu using the template below.　🔊 Track 60
巻頭の写真を見ながら、以下の会話例をもとにメニューにある料理について尋ねてください。

ジョン　：すみません。これ、なんですか。
店員　　：〈牛丼〉です。
てんいん　　ぎゅうどん
ジョン　：この〈赤い〉の、なんですか。
　　　　　　　　あか
店員　　：〈しょうが〉ですよ。
てんいん
ジョン　：〈しょうが〉？　〈しょうが〉って、なんですか。
店員　　：〈Ginger〉です。
てんいん

Jon　　 : Sumimasen. Kore, nan desu ka.
Ten'in　: < Gyūdon > desu.
Jon　　 : Kono < akai > no, nan desu ka.
Ten'in　: < Shōga > desu yo.
Jon　　 : < Shōga > ? < Shōga > tte, nan desu ka.
Ten'in　: < Ginger > desu.

> John　　: Excuse me. What is this?
> Waiter　: It's gyu-don.
> John　　: What is this red stuff?
> Waiter　: That's shoga.
> John　　: Shoga? What is shoga?
> Waiter　: It's ginger.

MEMO
〜って、なんですか。／ ...tte nan desu ka.／ What is ...?
[Used to ask about the meaning of a word or something you do not understand.
わからないことや、言葉の意味を尋ねる時に使います。]

Phrase 3
Choose an option and then explain it in a natural-sounding way.

🔊 Track 61

持ち帰りで。
も　かえ

Mochikaeri **de**.

Take out, please.

NOTE Use **"de"** when choosing from a series of options. Saying "____**de onegai shimasu**" is more polite.

「で」は、選択肢の中から何かを選ぶ時に使います。「_____で、お願いします」と言えば、より丁寧な表現になります。

Ex.

店員　：こちらでお召し上がりですか。
てんいん　　　　　　　　　め　あ
ジョン：いいえ、持ち帰りで。
　　　　　　　　も　かえ

Ten'in : Kochira de omeshiagari desu ka.
Jon   : Iie, mochikaeri **de**.

Staff : Would you like to eat in?
John : No, take out, please.

Practice A

_____で。

Use the following words with the phrase "_____ **de**.", when asked the question below.
以下の質問を下記の言葉と「_____で」を使って練習してください。

🔊 Track 62

Q. Would you like to eat in?
店内ご利用ですか。

ここ／店内	持ち帰り
てんない	も　かえ
koko / tennai	mochikaeri
here / eat in	*take out*

Q. That comes hot or cold.
ホットとアイスがございますが。

ホット	アイス
hotto	aisu
hot (drink)	*iced (drink)*

Q. What size would you like?
どちらのサイズをご希望ですか。

エス／エム／エル
esu / emu / eru
small / medium / large

Q. Would you like a bag?/Would you like these in separate bags?
袋をご利用ですか。／別々にしますか。

そのまま	一緒*	別々*
	いっ しょ	べつ べつ
sonomama	issho	betsu betsu
The way it is	*together*	*separate*

* **"issho"** (together), **"betsu betsu"** (separate) [also used when determining how many bills are necessary]
* 「一緒」と「別々」はお支払いの時にも使える表現です。

Practice B-1

Practice ordering with the menu below.
下記のメニューを見ながら注文する練習をしてください。

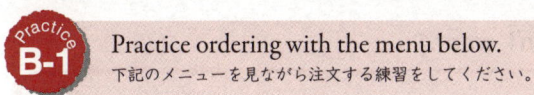 Track 63

店員 ：いらっしゃいませ。こちらでお召し上がりですか。
ジョン：はい、ここで。／いいえ、持ち帰りで。
店員 ：ご注文をどうぞ。
ジョン：〈チーズバーガー〉と〈コーラ〉、お願いします。
店員 ：〈コーラ〉のサイズは？
ジョン：〈エム〉で。

Ten'in : Irasshaimase. Kochira de omeshiagari desu ka.	Staff : Welcome. Would you like to eat in?
Jon : Hai, koko de. / Iie, mochikaeri de.	John : Yes. / No, take out, please.
Ten'in : Go-chūmon o dōzo.	Staff : May I take your order?
Jon : < Chīzu bāgā> to < kōra >, onegai shimasu.	John : I'll have a cheeseburger and a cola, please.
Ten'in : < Kōra > no saizu wa?	Staff : What size cola would you like?
Jon : < Emu > de.	John : Medium, please.

~MENU~

Burger

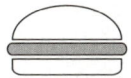
Hamburger

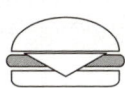
Cheese burger

Teriyaki Burger

Drink
Cola
Iced coffee
Iced tea

Side Menu

French fries

Salad

Practice B-2

Make your own conversation using the words in Practice A.
Practice Aの言葉を使って自分で会話文を作ってください。

 いらっしゃいませ。／Irasshaimase.／Welcome.／May I help you?

こちらでお召し上がりですか。／Kochira de omeshiagari desu ka.／Would you like to eat in?

ご注文をどうぞ。／Go-chūmon o dōzo.／May I take your order?

Phrase 4 Refuse something you don't want.

砂糖、いらないです。
Satō, iranai desu.   *No sugar, thank you.*

🔊 Track 64

NOTE "Iranai desu." can be used to say "No thank you." and is a way to refuse things you don't need.

「いらないです」は、必要がないという意味です。

Ex.

ジョン ：砂糖(は)いらないです。
店員　 ：かしこまりました。

Jon　　：Satō (wa) iranai desu.
Ten'in　：Kashikomarimashita.

John　：No sugar, thank you.
Clerk　：Okay.

Practice A

＿＿＿、いらないです。
Let's use the following words with the phrase "＿＿＿, iranai desu."
下記の言葉を使って「＿＿＿、いらないです」のフレーズを練習してください。

🔊 Track 65

砂糖 (さとう) satō *sugar* 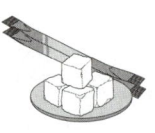	ミルク miruku *cream*	ガムシロップ gamu shiroppu *liquid sugar* 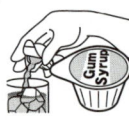
(お)はし (o)hashi *chopsticks* 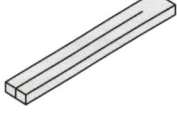	スプーン／フォーク supūn / fōku *spoon / fork*	ストロー sutorō *straw* 
袋 (ふくろ) fukuro *bag / plastic bag* 	紙袋 (かみぶくろ) kami-bukuro *paper bag* 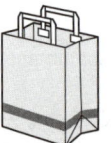	レシート reshīto *receipt* 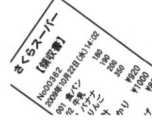

Put the words from Practice A in < > and practice the conversation below.
Practice Aの言葉を〈　〉に入れて会話練習をしてください。

🔊 Track 66

店員　：〈砂糖〉、ご利用ですか。
ジョン：いいえ、いらないです。／はい、お願いします。

Ten'in　: < Satō > go-riyō desu ka.
Jon　　: Iie, iranai desu. / Hai, onegaishimasu.

> Clerk : Would you like sugar?
> John : No, thank you. / Yes, please.

 Look at the picture below and tell the shop staff what you don't need.
下記のイラストを見ながら、いらないものを店員に伝えてください。

🔊 Track 67

ジョン：あ、〈　　　〉、いらないです。
店員　：かしこまりました。

Jon　　: A, <　> iranai desu.
Ten'in　: Kashikomarimashita.

> John : Oh, I don't need a _____.
> Clerk : Okay.

① 　② 　③ 　④

MEMO

～、ご利用ですか。／..., go-riyō desu ka. ／ *Would you like to use...?* [polite expression　丁寧な表現です。]

Dialogue

🔊 Track 68

Look at the menu on page 61 and have a practice conversation replacing the words in (1)-(4), then make your own conversation.
p.61のメニューを見ながら、(1)〜(4)の言葉をピンクの枠内の言葉に置き換えて会話練習をしてください。さらに自分で会話を作ってみましょう。

店員	：ご注文、お決まりですか。	Ten'in	: Go-chūmon, okimari desu ka.
ジョン	：おすすめはなんですか。	Jon	: Osusume wa nan desu ka.
店員	：(1)今日のランチです。	Ten'in	: (1) Kyō no ranchi desu.
ジョン	：じゃあ、それ(2)ひとつ、お願いします。	Jon	: Jā, sore (2) hitotsu, onegaishimasu.
店員	：お飲み物は？	Ten'in	: O-nomimono wa?
ジョン	：(3)コーラで。	Jon	: (3) Kōra de.
店員	：ご一緒にデザートはいかがですか。	Ten'in	: Go-issho ni dezāto wa ikaga desu ka.
ジョン	：いらないです。	Jon	: Iranai desu.
-During a meal- 食事中		~During a meal~	
ジョン	：すみません。(4)お水もらえますか。	Jon	: Sumimasen. (4) O-mizu moraemasu ka.

①
- (1) パスタランチ — pasuta ranchi
- (2) ふたつ — futatsu
- (3) 生ビール — nama-bīru
- (4) おしぼり — oshibori

②
- (1) 日替わり定食 — higawari-tēshoku
- (2) みっつ — mittsu
- (3) アイスコーヒー — aisu-kōhī
- (4) ストロー — sutorō

③ Make your own conversation
自分で会話を作ってみましょう

MEMO

ご注文お決まりですか。／Go-chūmon, o-kimari desu ka. ／*Are you ready to order?*

(お)飲み物／(o)nomimono／*beverage*

ご一緒に〜はいかがですか。／Go-issho ni...wa ikaga desu ka. ／*Would you like ...with that?*

Material

Look at the picture below and practice the conversation on the left page.
下記の絵を見ながら左ページの会話を練習しましょう。

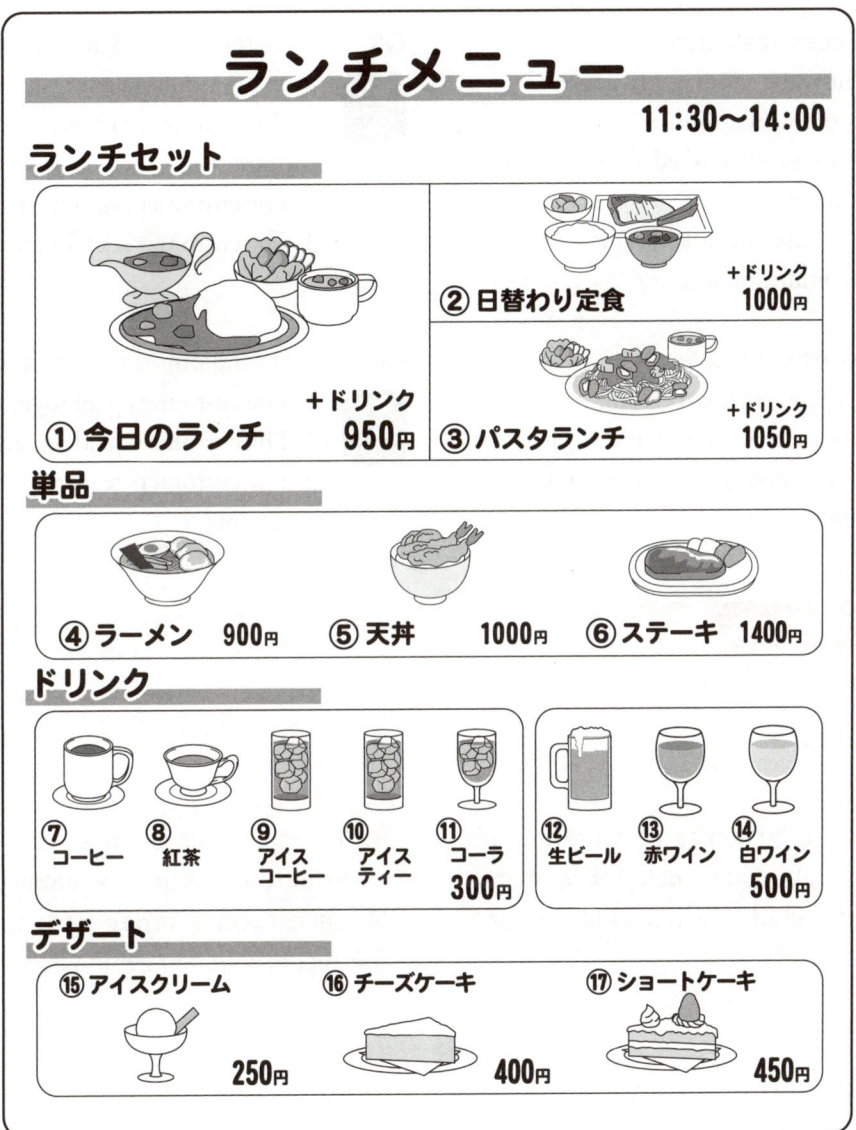

① 今日のランチ／kyō no ranchi／*lunch of the day*　② 日替わり定食／higawari-tēshoku／*today's set meal*
③ パスタランチ／pasuta ranchi／*pasta lunch*　④ ラーメン／rāmen／*ramen*
⑤ 天丼／ten-don／*tendon*　⑥ ステーキ／sutēki／*steak*　⑦ コーヒー／kōhī／*coffee*
⑧ 紅茶／kōcha／*black tea*　⑨ アイスコーヒー／aisu-kōhī／*iced coffee*
⑩ アイスティー／aisu-thī／*iced tea*　⑪ コーラ／kōra／*cola*　⑫ 生ビール／nama-bīru／*draft beer*
⑬ 赤ワイン／aka-wain／*red wine*　⑭ 白ワイン／shiro-wain／*white wine*
⑮ アイスクリーム／aisu-kurīmu／*ice cream*　⑯ チーズケーキ／chīzu-kēki／*cheesecake*
⑰ ショートケーキ／shōto-kēki／*strawberry shortcake*

Listening

Listen to the conversation between the man and woman and choose the correct answer.
男の人と女の人の会話を聞いて正しい答えを選んでください。

Q1 At a sushi restaurant

1. The waiter does not have any recommendations.
2. The customer asked about the lunch of the day.
3. The customer asked for a recommendation.

Q2 At a fast food restaurant

1. The customer got cream.
2. The customer got liquid sugar.
3. The customer got both cream and liquid sugar.

Q3 A waiter at an izakaya comes to take away an empty glass

1. The customer orders another glass of draft beer.
2. The customer asks for a glass of water.
3. The customer asks for another plate.

Q4 Checking out at a restaurant

1. The customers paid together.
2. The customers paid separately.
3. The customers received separate receipts.

Role playing

Role play using the cards below.
下記のカードを使ってロールプレイしてください。

1.

A: You are a customer at a restaurant. Call the waiter and ask for a menu, then order what you would like to eat.

B: You are part of the wait staff at a restaurant. Using the menu on page 61, take A-san's order and ask if he/she would like something to drink.

2.

A: You are talking to the cashier at a fast food restaurant. Make a take-out order for one hamburger and one iced coffee. Please say that you do not want a bag.

B: You are the cashier at a fast food restaurant. Take A-san's order, ask if he/she would like liquid sugar and milk with the iced coffee, and if A-san wants them in a bag.

Do you remember?

Use the phrases you have studied in this unit in situations ①–④ below.
このユニットで学習したフレーズを下記の①〜④の状況に合わせて使ってください

Phrases For This Unit

Unit Phrases

- メニュー、お願いします。 — Menyū, onegaishimasu. — *Could I have a menu?*
- 今日のランチ、なんですか。 — Kyō no ranchi, nan desu ka. — *What's the lunch of the day?*
- 持ち帰りで。 — Mochikaeri de. — *Take out, please.*
- 砂糖、いらないです。 — Satō, iranai desu. — *No sugar, thank you.*

Useful expressions

- 〜ってなんですか。 — ...tte nan desu ka. — *What is ...?* [Used to ask about the meaning of a word or something you do not understand.]
- 〜、ご利用ですか。 — ... go-riyō desu ka. — *Will you be using ...?* [Polite expression]
- 以上で。 — Ijō de. — *That's all.*
- 〜はいかがですか。 — ... wa ikaga desu ka. — *Would you like ...?*

Check! Now I can...

- ☐ Make orders at restaurants
  レストランで注文できる
- ☐ Request and ask about items on the menu
  メニューの内容についてリクエストしたり尋ねたりできる
- ☐ Communicate with people at convenience stores and restaurants
  コンビニやレストランの店員とコミュニケーションがとれる

One More Step

● Useful expressions at restaurants レストランで使える便利な表現

1. Entering a restaurant
入店時

(1) 店員　：何名様ですか。
　　客　　：ひとりです。(ふたり、さんにん、よにん…)

　　Ten'in　：Nan-mei sama desu ka.
　　Kyaku　：Hitori desu. [futari, san-nin, yo-nin …]

　　Waiter　　：How many people?
　　Customer　：One. (Two, three, four, etc.)

(2) 店員　：テーブル席とカウンター席がございますが。
　　客　　：① テーブル席、お願いします。
　　　　　　② カウンター席、お願いします。

　　Ten'in　：Tēburu seki to kauntā seki ga gozaimasuga.
　　Kyaku　：① Tēburu seki, onegaishimasu.
　　　　　　② Kauntā seki, onegaishimasu.

　　Waiter　　：We have both table and counter seating.
　　Customer　：① Table seating, please.
　　　　　　　② A counter seat please.

(3) 店員　：すみません。ただいま満席です。
　　客　　：どのぐらい待ちますか。
　　店員　：15分ぐらいです。

　　Ten'in　：Sumimasen, tadaima man-seki desu.
　　Kyaku　：Donogurai machimasu ka.
　　Ten'in　：Jūgo-fun gurai desu.

　　Waiter　　：I'm sorry, but we're full right now.
　　Customer　：How long is the wait?
　　Waiter　　：About 15 minutes.

2. Asking about food
メニューについての質問やリクエスト

(1) 客　　：これ、肉入ってますか。
　　店員　：はい、入ってます。／いいえ、入ってません。

　　Kyaku　：Kore, niku haittemasu ka.
　　Ten'in　：Hai, haittemasu. / Iie, haittemasen.

　　Customer　：Is there meat in this?
　　Waiter　　：Yes, there is. / No, there's not.

(2) 客　　：たまねぎ抜きで、お願いします。

　　Kyaku　：Tamanegi nuki de, onegaishimasu.

　　Customer　：Without onions, please.

UNIT 4

3. Leaving a restaurant
退店時

(1) 客　　：すみません。お会計、お願いします。
　　 店員　：お会計はご一緒でよろしいですか。
　　 客　　：はい、一緒で。／いいえ、別々で。

Kyaku　：Sumimasen. O-kaikei, onegaishimasu.
Ten'in　：O-kaikei wa go-issho de yoroshii desu ka.
Kyaku　：Hai, issho de. / Iie, betsu betsu de.

> Customer　：Excuse me, could I have the bill, please?
> Waiter　　：Will you pay together?
> Customer　：Yes, together. / No, separately.

(2) 客　　：ごちそうさまでした。おいしかったです。

Kyaku　：Gochisōsama deshita. Oishikatta desu.

> Customer　：Thank you. It was delicious.

Good to Know

Japanese fast food - Keywords -

● 食券 shokken

Several restaurants in Japan, like tachi-gui (stand and eat) soba bars and gyūdon (beef rice bowl) counters, use a shokken, or food ticket, system. Upon entering a restaurant, customers purchase a shokken ticket for what they want to eat from an automated vending machine and hand it to a server, who exchanges it for food. After inserting money into a shokken machine, buttons featuring food you can buy for that amount of money light up. After pushing the lit up button for the food you want, be sure to hit the otsuri (change) button to receive your change.

● セルフサービス serufu-sābisu

Several Japanese fast food restaurants are "self-service," meaning customers are responsible for retrieving their own water, seasonings, and condiments that are placed on most counters and tables. After customers finish eating, they dispose of their own garbage, and if a tray has been used, they return it to the tray collection counter.

● 並 nami・大盛 ōmori / 大 dai・中 chū・小 shō

Sometimes customers must specify the size of the dish they would like when ordering food, especially at gyūdon restaurants. Whereas the words nami (regular) and ōmori (large) are used to describe donburi dishes, restaurants like noodle houses use the terms dai (large), chū (regular), and shō (small). A typical order can be made by saying "Gyūdon, nami de onegaishimasu." (I'll have a regular beef rice bowl, please.) or "Udon no dai, onegaishimasu." (I'll have a large bowl of udon, please.)

Can I pay by credit card?

カードでいいですか。

Kādo de ii desu ka.

Asking permission
許可を得る

GOALS FOR UNIT 5

- Use simple sentences to ask for permission
  簡単な文を使って許可を得る

- Confirm about a process
  手続きについて確認する

Phrase 1
Use nouns to ask for permission.

カードでいいですか。

Kādo de ii desu ka.

Can I pay by credit card?

🔊 Track 73

> **NOTE** "[Noun] de ii desu ka." is used to ask for permission, and means **"Can I do something with/by [noun]?"** or **"Is [noun] okay?"**
>
> 「[名詞]でいいですか」は、許可を求める表現です。"Can I do something with/by [noun]?" "Is [noun] okay?" の意味です。

Ex.

ジョン：すみません。カードでいいですか。

店員（てんいん）：はい、だいじょうぶですよ。

Jon　　： Sumimasen, kādo de ii desu ka.
Ten'in ： Hai, daijōbu desu yo.

> John　　： Excuse me, can I pay by credit card?
> Cashier ： Yes, that's okay.

Practice A

_____ でいいですか。

Use the following words with the phrase "_____ de ii desu ka."

下記の言葉を使って「_____でいいですか」のフレーズを練習してください。

🔊 Track 74

カード kādo *(credit) card*	これ kore *this*	一万円（札） いち まん えん さつ ichiman-en (satsu) *ten-thousand yen (note)*
英語 えいご Eigo *English*	ローマ字 じ Rōma-ji *Roman letters*	今度 こんど kondo *next time*
あと ato *later*	予約なし よやく yoyaku nashi *without a reservation*	くつ kutsu *shoes*

Practice B Use words from Practice A in < > to practice having a conversation.
* Choose words suitable for the situations in ②.
Practice Aの言葉を〈 〉に入れて会話練習をしてください。
* ②は状況に合う言葉を選んでください。

🔊 Track 75

①

ジョン：すみません、〈カード〉でいいですか。
店員（てんいん）：ええ、だいじょうぶですよ。／申（もう）し訳（わけ）ありませんが、ちょっと……。

Jon : Sumimasen, < kādo > de ii desu ka.
Ten'in : Ee, daijōbu desu yo.
／Mōshiwake arimasen ga, chotto…… .

> John : Excuse me, can I pay by credit card?
> Cashier : Yes, that's okay.
> ／I'm terribly sorry, but [we don't accept credit cards].

②

1. Checking out at a store 店でお会計をしている

店員：980円です。
ジョン：すみません、〈　　〉でいいですか。

Ten'in : 980-en desu.
Jon : Sumimasen, <　> de ii desu ka.

> Cashier : That comes to 980 yen.
> John : Excuse me, could I use a _____ ?

2. Filling out an application 申込書を書いている

店員：こちらにご記入（きにゅう）ください。
ジョン：〈　　〉でいいですか。

Ten'in : Kochira ni go-kinyū kudasai.
Jon : <　> de ii desu ka.

> Clerk : Please fill out [the form] here.
> John : Can I use a _____ ? / Is _____ okay?

3. Entering a restaurant レストランに入る

店員：いらっしゃいませ。
ジョン：すみません、〈　　〉でいいですか。

Ten'in : Irasshaimase.
Jon : Sumimasen, <　> de ii desu ka.

> Clerk : Welcome.
> John : Excuse me, is _____ alright?

MEMO
だいじょうぶですよ。／Daijōbu desu yo. ／That's okay.
こちらにご記入（きにゅう）ください。／Kochira ni go-kinyū kudasai. ／Please fill out (the form) here.
いらっしゃいませ。／Irasshaimase. ／Welcome. ／May I help you?
申（もう）し訳（わけ）ありませんが、ちょっと……。／Mōshiwake arimasen ga, chotto …… . ／
I'm terribly sorry, but [we don't accept credit cards].

UNIT 5

Phrase 2 — Use verbs to ask for permission.

🔊 Track 76

このペン、借(か)りてもいいですか。

Kono pen, kari**te mo ii desu ka**.   *May I borrow this pen?*

> **NOTE** "[Verb-te] mo ii desu ka." is also used to ask for permission, and means "May/Can I [verb]?" → See Grammar p.173, Verb te-form
>
> 「て形」もいいですか」もまた、許可を求める表現です。"May/Can I [Verb]?" の意味です。p.173の動詞て形を参照。

Ex.

ジョン　　　：すみません。このペン、借(か)りてもいいですか。

受付(うけつけ)の人(ひと)：どうぞ。

Jon　　　　　　　: Sumimasen. Kono pen, kari**te mo ii desu ka**.
Uketsuke no hito : Dōzo.

John　　　　　: Excuse me. May I borrow this pen?
Receptionist : Yes.

Practice A

[Verb-te]もいいですか。
Use the following words with the phrase " [Verb-te] mo ii desu ka."
下記の言葉を使って「「て形」もいいですか」のフレーズを練習してください。

🔊 Track 77

借(か)りて karite *borrow*	見(み)て mite *see/look/watch*	使(つか)って tsukatte *use*
入(はい)って haitte *come in*	座(すわ)って suwatte *sit here*	もらって  moratte *receive/have*
電話(でんわ)して denwa shite *call*	写真(しゃしん)を撮(と)って  shashin o totte *take a picture*	着(き)て／履(は)いて  kite / haite *put on (upper body)/put on (lower body)*

Practice B: Put the right word in < > and practice having a conversation. Several words may fit in the blanks.
正しい言葉を〈　　〉に入れて会話練習をしてください。複数の言葉が入れられます。

🔊 Track 78

1
- At a temple -　おてらで

ジョン　：すみません。ここ、〈　　　　〉もいいですか。
係員　　：はい、どうぞ。
ジョン　：あと、これ、〈　　　　〉もいいですか。
係員　　：ええ、いいですよ。
　　　　／すみません。それはちょっと……。

Jon　　　: Sumimasen. Koko, <　　> mo ii desu ka.
Kakari-in : Hai, dōzo.
Jon　　　: Ato, kore, <　　>mo ii desu ka.
Kakari-in : Ee, ii desu yo.
　　　　　/ Sumimasen. Sore wa chotto…… .

John　: Excuse me, can I _____ here?
Staff　: Yes.
John　: Also, could I _____ this?
Staff　: Yes, that's fine.
　　　　/ I'm sorry, but that's not allowed.

2
- At the office -　オフィスで

ジョン　：このパソコン、〈　　　　〉もいいですか。
田中　　：今はちょっと……。
ジョン　：じゃ、あとで〈　　　　〉もいいですか。
田中　　：はい、いいですよ。

Jon　　　: Kono pasokon, <　　>mo ii desu ka.
Tanaka　: Ima wa chotto…… .
Jon　　　: Ja, atode <　　>mo ii desu ka.
Tanaka　: Hai, ii desu yo.

John　　: Can I _____ this computer?
Tanaka : Now's not a good time.
John　　: Okay, then could I _____ it later?
Tanaka : Yes, that's fine.

MEMO

どうぞ。／Dōzo.／Please / Feel free.
あと、〜／Ato, ...／Also, ...
それはちょっと……。／Sore wa chotto…… ./ I'm sorry but that's not allowed.
今はちょっと……。／Ima wa chotto…… ./ Now's not a good time.

UNIT 5

Dialogue

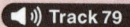 Track 79

Do tasks on the right page using the following conversation template and changing words (1) - (5).
(1)～(5)の言葉をピンクの枠内の言葉に置き換えて会話練習をしてください。下記の会話例を使って右ページのタスクをしましょう。

ジョン：	すみません、 (1)会員になりたいんですが……。	Jon：	Sumimasen, (1)<u>Kai-in ni naritai</u> n desu ga....... .
店員：	本日、身分証明書はお持ちですか。	Ten'in：	Honjitsu, mibun shōmei sho wa o-mochi desu ka.
ジョン：	(2)在留カードでいいですか。	Jon：	(2)<u>Zairyū kādo</u> de ii desu ka.
店員：	はい、けっこうです。 それから、(3)写真はお持ちですか。	Ten'in：	Hai, kekkō desu. Sorekara, (3)<u>shashin</u> wa o-mochi desu ka.
ジョン：	えっと、(4)今度でいいですか。	Jon：	Etto, (4)<u>kondo</u> de ii desu ka.
店員：	はい、だいじょうぶです。 では、こちらにご記入ください。	Ten'in：	Hai, daijōbu desu. Dewa, kochira ni go-kinyū kudasai.
ジョン：	(5)このペン、借りてもいいですか。	Jon：	(5)<u>Kono pen, karite</u> mo ii desu ka.
店員：	ええ、いいですよ。	Ten'in：	Ee, ii desu yo.

---

①
- (1) 口座を開きたい　　　　kōza o hirakitai
- (2) パスポート　　　　　　pasupōto
- (3) 印鑑　　　　　　　　　inkan
- (4) サイン　　　　　　　　sain
- (5) 英語で　　　　　　　　Eigo de

②
- (1) プールを利用したい　　pūru o riyō shitai (riyō = *use*)
- (2) 学生証　　　　　　　　gakusei-shō
- (3) 水着とぼうし　　　　　mizugi to bōshi (= *swimsuit and cap*)
- (4) これ　　　　　　　　　kore
- (5) ここに座って　　　　　koko ni suwatte

MEMO

～はお持ちですか。／ ... wa o-mochi desu ka. ／ *Do you have ... ?* [polite expression　丁寧な表現です。]

それから／sorekara／*also, and*

けっこうです。／Kekkō desu.／*That's alright.* → See p.185 "Kekkō desu."

Material

Check the words and situations of the three tasks below, then practice having a conversation using the left page.
下記の3つのタスクの言葉や状況を確認してから左ページを使って会話練習をしましょう。

Ex. Registering with a gym or a store
ジムやお店で会員登録する

会員になりたいんですが……。
Kai-in ni naritai n desu ga……. / I'd like to become a member.

① Opening a bank account
銀行口座を開設する

口座を開きたいんですが……。
Kōza o hirakitai n desu ga……. / I'd like to open a bank account.

② Using a pool, gym, or other public facility
プール、ジムなど公共の施設を利用する

プールを利用したいんですが……。
Pūru o riyō shitai n desu ga……. / I'd like to use the swimming pool.

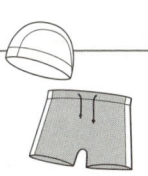

You are often asked for:
よく聞かれるもの

1) 身分証明書 / mibun shōmei sho / *ID*

- 在留カード / zairyū kādo / *residence card*
- パスポート / pasupōto / *passport*
- 運転免許証 / unten menkyo shō / *driver license*
- 学生証 / gakusei shō / *student ID*
- 健康保険証 / kenkō hokenshō / *health insurance card*

2) 住所がわかるもの / jūsho ga wakaru mono / *Proof of address*

- 公共料金の請求書 / kōkyō-ryōkin no seikyū sho / *utility bills*

3) その他 / sonota / *Others*

- 写真 / shashin / *photo*
- 印鑑 / inkan / *signature seal*

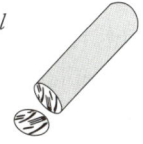

Listening

Listen to the conversation between the man and woman and choose the correct answer.
男の人と女の人の会話を聞いて正しい答えを選んでください。

Q1 At a restaurant

1. The customer is not allowed to smoke because it is non-smoking area.
2. The customer wants to buy cigarettes.
3. The customer is not allowed to smoke because the waitress does not like cigarettes.   *sutte = smoke

Q2 At a drugstore

1. The man receives only a pamphlet.
2. The man can take either a pamphlet or a free sample.
3. The man receives both a pamphlet and a free sample.

Q3 At a front desk

1. The woman said you cannot write in Roman letters.
2. The woman said you can write in Roman letters.
3. The woman would not let the man fill out an application.

Q4 In a taxi

1. The passenger paid with a 1,000-yen note.
2. The passenger paid with a 10,000-yen note.
3. The passenger paid with a credit card.

Role playing

Role play using the cards below.
下記のカードを使ってロールプレイしてください。

1.

A: You go to a restaurant with good reviews, but it seems crowded. Ask if you can get a table without a reservation. If you are refused, ask whether you can receive the store's customer card.

B: You work at a restaurant. Right now there are no empty tables, so no one without a reservations may enter. Deny entry to anyone who does not have a reservation.

2.

A: You want to become a member at a gym. Tell this to the person behind the counter. Explain that you have no time to fill out forms today, and ask if you can take them home to fill out, bring back later, and if you may fill them out in English.

B: You work at a gym. A-san wants to become a member, so ask him/her to fill out the necessary paperwork. It is fine for A-san to take the forms home and bring them back later, and it is also okay if the forms are filled out in English.

Do you remember?

Use the phrases you have studied in this unit in situations ①–④ below.
このユニットで学習したフレーズを下記の①〜④の状況に合わせて使ってください。

Phrases for This Unit

Unit Phrases

- カードでいいですか。 　　Kādo de ii desu ka. 　　*Can I pay by credit card?*
- このペン、借(か)りてもいいですか。 　　Kono pen, karite mo ii desu ka. 　　*May I borrow this pen?*

Useful expressions

- 〜たいんですが……。 　　… tai n desu ga……. 　　*I would like to…. / I want to….*
- 〜お持(も)ちですか。 　　…o-mochi desu ka. 　　*Do you have …? [polite expression]*

Check!

✓ **Now I can…**

☐ Use simple sentences to ask for permission
簡単な文を使って許可が得られる

☐ Confirm about a process
手続きについて確認できる

Remember and Use!

● 8 Basic Verbs ● 基本動詞

to eat たべる／taberu (→ たべて／tabete)	*to drink* のむ／nomu (→ のんで／nonde)
to sit すわる／suwaru (→ すわって／suwatte)	*to enter* はいる／hairu (→ はいって／haitte)
to write かく／kaku (→ かいて／kaite)	*to use* つかう／tsukau (→ つかって／tsukatte)
to see, look, watch みる／miru (→ みて／mite)	*to copy* コピーする／kopī suru (→ コピーして／kopī shite)

Learn the eight basic verbs above and use them with the phrase **"[verb-te] mo ii desu ka."**
上記8つの基本動詞を学び、これを「～(て)もいいですか」のフレーズの中で使ってみましょう。

～(て)もいいですか。／ [Verb-te] mo ii desu ka. ／ *May/can I ...?*

→ **See p.78 for more verbs.**
その他の動詞についてはp.78を参照。

Japanese Verbs (dictionary form, masu-form and te-form)

Although Japanese verbs assume a variety of conjugations depending on tense and their function within a sentence, the three most basic verb forms are the **dictionary form, masu-form,** and **te-form**.

The **dictionary form** is the basic **verb form** which all verbs are conjugated from. It frequently appears in casual conversation and is also used in different grammatical expressions. The **masu-form** appears in more polite conversation.

The **te-form**, which appears in Units 5 and 6, does not express tense, but can be conveniently used to create a wide array of grammatical expressions.

Verbs are divided into one of three groups depending on how they conjugate: **ru-verbs**, which have a simplistic conjugation, or **u-verbs**, ,which are the largest in number and the two **irregular verbs**.

See p.171, Grammar for more detailed explanations on verb conjugations and other issues.

● Verb Conjugation List ●

Ru-verbs	Dictionary form		Masu-form		Te-form	
eat	たべる	taberu	たべます	tabemasu	たべて	tabete
see, look	みる	miru	みます	mimasu	みて	mite
open	あける	akeru	あけます	akemasu	あけて	akete
put on (upper body)	きる	kiru	きます	kimasu	きて	kite

U-verbs	Dictionary form		Masu-form		Te-form	
use	つかう	tsukau	つかいます	tsukaimasu	つかって	tsukatte
meet	あう	au	あいます	aimasu	あって	atte
buy	かう	kau	かいます	kaimasu	かって	katte
enter	はいる	hairu	はいります	hairimasu	はいって	haitte
sit	すわる	suwaru	すわります	suwarimasu	すわって	suwatte
go home	かえる	kaeru	かえります	kaerimasu	かえって	kaette
drink	のむ	nomu	のみます	nomimasu	のんで	nonde
read	よむ	yomu	よみます	yomimasu	よんで	yonde
play, have fun	あそぶ	asobu	あそびます	asobimasu	あそんで	asonde
write	かく	kaku	かきます	kakimasu	かいて	kaite
put on (lower body)	はく	haku	はきます	hakimasu	はいて	haite

Irregular verbs	Dictionary form		Masu-form		Te-form	
do	する	suru	します	shimasu	して	shite
copy	コピーする	kopī suru	コピーします	kopī shimasu	コピーして	kopī shite
work	しごとする	shigoto suru	しごとします	shigoto shimasu	しごとして	shigoto shite
shop	かいものする	kaimono suru	かいものします	kaimono shimasu	かいものして	kaimono shite
come	くる	kuru	きます	kimasu	きて	kite

Please wait a moment.

ちょっと待ってください。
Chotto matte kudasai.

Making requests
依頼する

GOALS FOR UNIT 6

- Use simple sentences to make requests
  簡単な文を使って依頼する

- Invite someone to have something
  人に何かを勧める

- Give simple directions to a destination in a taxi
  タクシーで目的地までの行き方を伝える

Phrase 1 — Making simple requests.

🔊 Track 84

ちょっと待(ま)って**ください**。

Chotto ma**tte kudasai**.   *Please wait a moment.*

> **NOTE** "**[Verb-te] kudasai**" is used to ask someone to please do something, and can be used to make a request or invite someone to do something.
>
> 「[て形]ください」は、相手に何かをしてほしい時に使われる表現です。依頼と提案(勧め)の意味があります。

Ex.
① ちょっと待(ま)って**ください**。
② どうぞ食(た)べて**ください**。

① Chotto ma**tte** kudasai.
② Dōzo tabe**te** kudasai.

① *Please wait a moment.*
② *Please help yourself.*

Practice A-1

[Verb-te]ください。
Make requests using the following words with the phrase "[Verb-te] kudasai."
下記の言葉を使って「「て形」ください」のフレーズを練習してください。

🔊 Track 85

| ちょっと待(ま)って
chotto matte
wait a moment | ちょっと来(き)て
chotto kite
come [here for a second] | それを見(み)せて
sore o misete
show me that | 手伝(てつだ)って
tetsudatte
help |

Practice A-2

どうぞ[Verb-te]ください。
Invite someone to do something using the phrase "Dōzo [Verb-te] kudasai."
下記の言葉を「どうぞ「て形」ください」を使って勧めてください。

🔊 Track 86

| 食(た)べて
tabete
eat | 飲(の)んで
nonde
drink | 座(すわ)って
suwatte
sit |
| 入(はい)って
haitte
enter | 使(つか)って
tsukatte
use | 見(み)て
mite
see, look, watch |

 **Practice B-1** What you can say with the phrase **"[Verb-te] kudasai."** in the following situations? 🔊 Track 87
There may be more than one correct answer.
下記の状況で「「て形」ください」を使ってどんな文が言えますか。正しい答えは一つとは限りません。

1. You are at a restaurant. You are not ready to order but the waiter has already come to your table.
   レストランにいます。あなたがまだ注文を決めていないのにウェイターが注文を取りに来ました。

2. The photocopy machine that you are using at a convenience store has a paper jam. Call one of the store clerks over.
   コンビニのコピー機が紙詰まりを起こしました。店員を呼んでください。

3. You see a watch in a display case that you would like to take a closer look at. Ask the store clerk for help.
   ディスプレイケースの中にある時計をもっと近くで見たいです。店員に頼んでください。

 Practice B-2 Put the words from Practice A-2 in < > and practice the conversation below. 🔊 Track 88
Practice A-2の言葉を〈 〉に入れて会話練習をしてください。

UNIT 6

 ①

田中：ジョンさん、これ〈食べて〉もいいですか。
ジョン：はい、どうぞ〈食べて〉ください。

Tanaka : Jon-san, kore <tabete> mo ii desu ka.
Jon   : Hai, dōzo <tabete> kudasai.

> *Tanaka : John-san, can I eat this?*
> *John   : Yes, please do.*

②

ジョン：田中さん、ここ〈座って〉もいいですか。
田中：ええ、どうぞ〈座って〉ください。

Jon   : Tanaka-san, koko <suwatte> mo ii desu ka.
Tanaka : Ee, dōzo <suwatte> kudasai.

> *John   : Tanaka-san, can I sit here?*
> *Tanaka : Yes, by all means.*

MEMO

〜てもいいですか。／[verb-te] mo ii desu ka.／*Can I / May I ... ?* →See p.70, Unit 5

Practice A-3

[Verb-te]ください。
Use the following words with the phrase " **[Verb-te] kudasai.**"
下記の言葉を使って「「て形」ください」のフレーズを練習してください。

🔊 Track 89

- In a taxi -   タクシーで

角を左に曲がって かど ひだり ま kado o hidari ni magatte *turn left at the corner*	信号を右に曲がって しんごう みぎ ま shingō o migi ni magatte *turn right at the traffic light*	(もうちょっと) まっすぐ行って い (mōchotto) massugu itte *go straight (a little further)*
そこで止めて と soko de tomete *stop there*	(明治)通りを行って めいじ どお い (Meiji)-dōri o itte *go down Meiji street*	その道をわたって みち sono michi o watatte *cross the street*

Practice B-3

Give directions to the taxi driver for where you want to go using the map on the right page.
右ページの地図を使いながらタクシー運転手に行きたい場所への指示を出してください。

🔊 Track 90

Take a taxi to places (1) – (3) on the right page. Think about the example sentences and first ask the driver to take you to a nearby landmark. Once you arrive at the landmark, give directions to your final destination.
右ページの(1)～(3)の場所へ行くためにタクシーに乗りましょう。例文を参考に、まずは近くの目印になるところに行ってもらうよう頼んでください。目印の場所に着いたら目的地への行き方を伝えてください。

運転手　：どちらまでですか。
うんてんしゅ

ジョン　：〈ニューホテル〉の近くまでお願いします。
ちか　　　　　　　ねが

運転手　：かしこまりました。
うんてんしゅ

– Near your destination –   行きたい場所の近く

運転手　：このへんですか。
うんてんしゅ

ジョン　：〈もうちょっとまっすぐ行って〉ください。
い

　　　　　あ、その〈ゲストハウス〉です。

　　　　　そこで止めてください。
と

Taxi driver	: Where to?
John	: Take me to around the New Hotel, please.
Taxi driver	: Right away.
- Near your destination -	
Taxi driver	: Is this the area?
John	: Please <go straight a little>. Ah, that <guest house> is. Please stop there.

Untenshu　：Dochira made desu ka.
Jon　　　　：<Nyū hoteru> no chikaku made onegaishimasu.
Untenshu　：Kashikomarimashita.
– Near your destination –
Untenshu　：Kono hen desu ka.
Jon　　　　：<Mō chotto massugu itte> kudasai.
　　　　　　A, sono <gesuto-hausu> desu.
　　　　　　Soko de tomete kudasai.

Map

Look at the map below and practice the conversation on the left page.
下記の地図を見て左ページの会話練習をしてください。

Ex. Destination: **Gesuto-hausu** / *Guesthouse*　　Landmark: **Nyū hoteru** / *The New Hotel*
　　　　行き先：ゲストハウス　　　　　　　　　　　　　　　目印：ニューホテル

(1) Destination: **(COTO) biru** / *The COTO Building*　Landmark: **Fuji byōin** / *Fuji Hospital*

(2) Destination: **Apāto** / *Your apartment*　　　　　Landmark: **Sakura kōen** / *Sakura Park*

(3) Destination: **Sushi-ya** / *A sushi restaurant*　　Landmark: **Sakura daigaku** / *Sakura University*

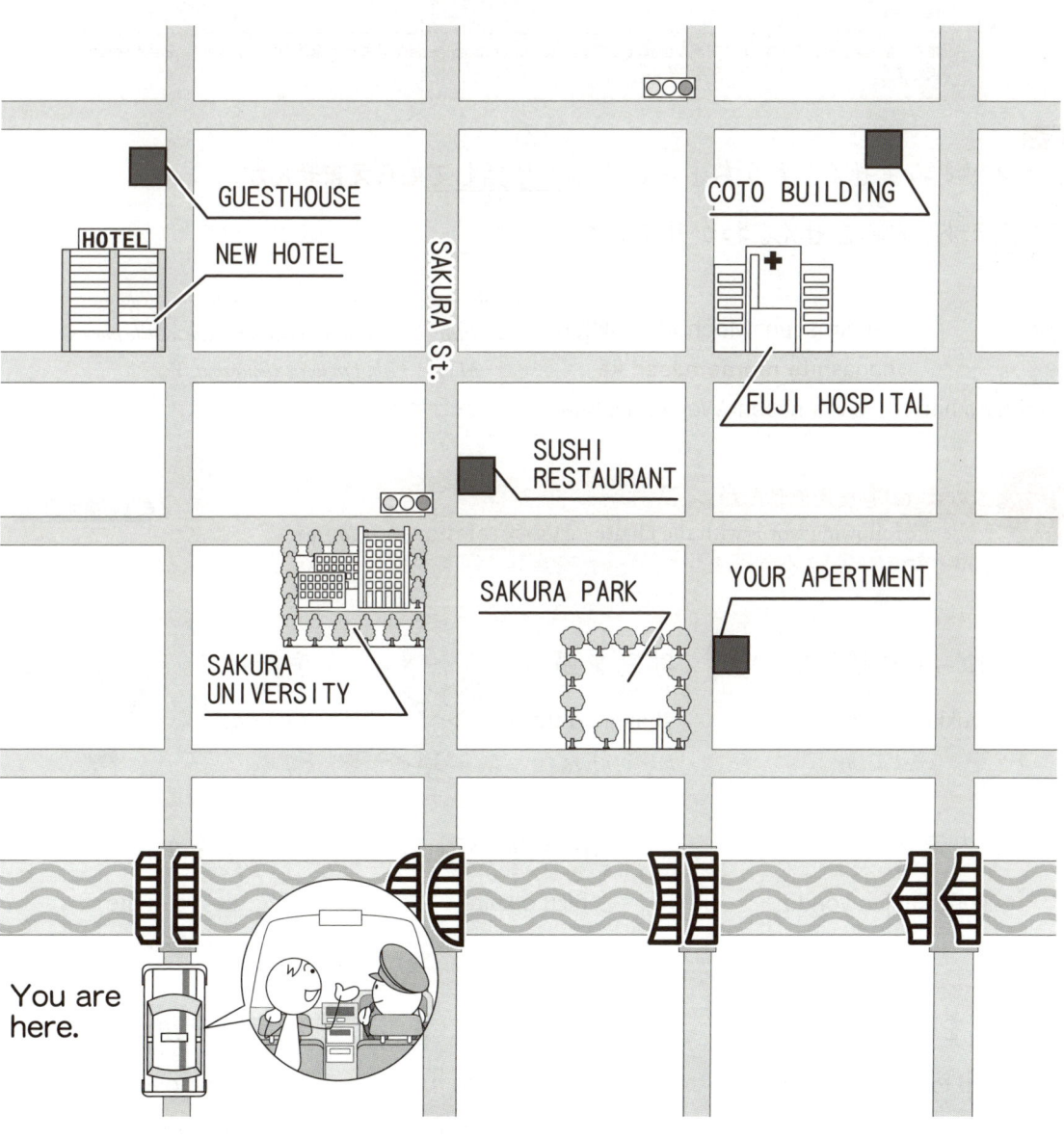

Phrase 2 — Use negative questions to make requests more polite.

🔊 Track 91

ゆっくり話してもらえませんか。
はな

Yukkuri hanashi**te moraemasen ka**. *Could you speak more slowly?*

NOTE "**[Verb-te] moraemasen ka**" is a polite way to make a request. (= "Could I have you ...?") It uses the negative form of "**moraemasu**," which means "**to be able to receive**."

「[て形] もらえませんか」は、より丁寧な依頼表現です。"to be able to receive" という意味の「もらえます」を否定疑問文にして使います。

Ex.

ジョン　：すみません。もうちょっとゆっくり話してもらえませんか。
　　　　　　　　　　　　　　　　　　　　はな

男の人　：あ、すみません。わかりました。
おとこ ひと

Jon　　　　　　： Sumimasen. Mōchotto yukkuri hanashi**te moraemasen ka**.
Otoko no hito : A, sumimasen. Wakarimashita.

> John : I'm sorry, could you speak a little more slowly?
> Man　 : Ah, I'm sorry about that. Yes.

Practice A — [Verb-te]もらえませんか。
Use the following words with the phrase "**[Verb-te] moraemasen ka**."
下記の言葉を使って「「て形」もらえませんか」のフレーズを練習してください。

🔊 Track 92

ゆっくり話して はな yukkuri hanashite *speak slowly*	写真を撮って しゃ しん と shashin o totte *take a picture*	手伝って て つだ tetsudatte *help me*
この漢字を読んで かんじ よ kono kanji o yonde *read this Kanji*	地図を描いて ち ず か chizu o kaite *draw a map*	席をかえて せき seki o kaete *change seats*
それを取って と sore o totte *pass that to me* 	これを貸して か kore o kashite *lend me this/let me use*	荷物を預かって に もつ あず nimotsu o azukatte *keep one's belongings*

Practice B

Ask for help from someone around you in the following situations.
下記の状況に合わせて自分の近くにいる人に頼んでください。

🔊 Track 93

1. You are in a movie theater. The reserved seat is hard to see.
   あなたは映画館にいます。予約した席が見にくいです。

2. You have a map with only Japanese written on it, and can't read the kanji for some of the place names, but want to know what they say.
   あなたは地図を持っていますが、いくつかの場所の漢字が読めません。何と書いてあるか知りたいです。

3. After you check out of a hotel, you want to go to a few tourist attractions. Ask the hotel staff if they will look after your bags.
   あなたはホテルをチェックアウトしたあと、観光名所にいくつか行きたいです。ホテルスタッフに荷物を預かってほしいと頼んでください。

4. You are at a temple by yourself and want someone to take your picture.
   あなたは1人でお寺にいます。誰かにあなたの写真を撮ってほしいです。

5. You are at a convenience store and need to use the restroom.
   あなたはコンビニにいます。トイレを使いたいです。

UNIT 6

Column

There are different levels of politeness when making requests in Japanese. After the most simplistic phrase, **[verb-te] + kudasai,** there are the affirmative and negative forms of **moraeru, [verb-te] moraemasu/moraemasen ka,** which are used in questions. These are followed by **itadakeru,** the *keigo*-form of **moraeru,** in expressions like **[verb-te] itadakemasu/itadakemasen ka,** which frequently appear in conversation. The politeness of a request can be modified simply by changing the words that come after the **te-form** of a verb. Use different request words depending on the situation and difficulty of a request.

Verb te-form +
- **itadakemasen ka**
- **itadakemasu ka**
- **moraemasen ka**
- **moraemasu ka**
- **kudasai**

↑ Expressions with increasing politeness

85

Dialogue

🔊 Track 94

Practice having a conversation by replacing the words in (1) – (3) with the words below.
(1)～(3)の言葉をピンクの枠内の言葉に置き換えて会話練習をしてください。

-Tanaka-san is late to a party at an izakaya-　田中さんは飲み会に遅れました

ジョン	：あ、田中さん。	Jon	: A, Tanaka-san.
	どうぞ (1)座ってください。		Dōzo (1) <u>suwatte</u> kudasai.
田中	：ありがとうございます。	Tanaka	: Arigatō gozaimasu.
ジョン	：どうぞ (2)飲んでください	Jon	: Dōzo (2) <u>nonde</u> kudasai.
田中	：あ、どうも。	Tanaka	: A, dōmo.
ジョン	：おはし、取りましょうか。	Jon	: O-hashi, torimashōka.
田中	：あります。だいじょうぶです。	Tanaka	: Arimasu. Daijōbu desu.

- Later -

ジョン	：すみません、田中さん。	Jon	: Sumimasen, Tanaka-san.
	(3)塩、取ってもらえませんか。		(3) <u>Shio</u>, totte moraemasen ka.
田中	：はい、どうぞ。	Tanaka	: Hai, dōzo.

---

①
(1) 入って　　　　　　　haitte
(2) 食べて　　　　　　　tabete
(3) しょうゆ　　　　　　shōyu

②
(1) こっちに来て　　　　kocchi ni kite
(2) この(お)皿、使って　　kono (o)sara, tsukatte
(3) さしみ　　　　　　　sashimi

MEMO

どうも。／Dōmo.／*Thanks.*

(お)はし、取りましょうか。／(O)hashi, torimashō ka.／*Should I get you chopsticks?*

塩／shio／*salt*

しょうゆ／shōyu／*soy sauce*

Listening

Listen to the conversation between the man and woman and choose the correct answer.
男の人と女の人の会話を聞いて正しい答えを選んでください。

Q1 At the front desk of a hotel

1. The woman borrows an umbrella.
2. The woman lends an umbrella.
3. The woman buys an umbrella.

Q2 At an izakaya

1. The customer has already ordered some food.
2. The customer is not ready to leave the restaurant.
3. The customer is not ready to order.

Q3 In a taxi

1. The passenger asked the driver to turn left at a traffic light.
2. The passenger asked the driver to turn right.
3. The passenger asked the driver to go straight.

Q4 At a friend's house party

1. The man wants food.
2. The man wants an empty glass.
3. The man wants a clean plate.

Role playing

Role play using the cards below.
下記のカードを使ってロールプレイしてください。

1.

A: A Japanese friend has stopped by your house. After inviting your friend to come inside and sit down, offer him/her a cup of tea.

B: You have come to A-san's house to give him/her a box of chocolate. Present the chocolate and suggest A-san eat it. If A-san offers you something, say thank you and accept it.

2.

A: You are at an information center. Ask a staff member to show you a bus time table (=jikoku-hyō), and also ask them to make a copy of any pages you need.

B: You work at an information center. Provide assistance with A-san's requests.

Do you remember?

Use the phrases you have studied in this unit in situations ①–③ below.
このユニットで学習したフレーズを下記の①〜③の状況に合わせて使ってください。

Phrases for This Unit

Unit Phrases

- ちょっと待ってください。   Chotto matte kudasai.   *Please wait a moment.*
- ゆっくり話してもらえませんか。   Yukkuri hanashite moraemasen ka.   *Could you speak more slowly?*

Useful expressions

- どうぞ、食べてください。   Dōzo tabete kudasai.   *Please help yourself.*
- どうも。   Dōmo.   *Thanks.*
- 〜までお願いします。   … made onegaishimasu.   *Please take me to … .* [used when giving directions to a taxi driver]

UNIT 6

Check!

Now I can...

- ☐ Use simple sentences to make a request
  簡単な文を使って依頼できる
- ☐ Invite someone to have something
  人に何かを勧められる
- ☐ Give simple directions to a destination in a taxi
  タクシーで目的地までの行き方が伝えられる

Good to Know

Taxi

In large cities, such as Tokyo, people are often asked about the route to their destinations. In that case, if you say, "Omakase shimasu," they should take you there in the fastest way possible. However, if you want to avoid expressways that incur an additional fee, add, "demo, kōsoku wa tsukawanaide kudasai." If speed is a priority even if it's expensive, say, "kōsoku demo daijōubu desu."

Untenshu : Dochira made?

Kyaku   : xx kōen no chikaku made, onegaishimasu.

Untenshu : Gokibou no rūto ga gozaimasuka.

Kyaku   : Iie, omakase shimasu. (Demo, kōsoku wa tsukawanaide kudasai.)

~ near xxx park ~

Untenshu : kono hen desuka.

Kyaku   : xx taishikan no mae de, tomete kudasai.

Taxi driver : Where would you like to go?

Customer   : Near XXX Park, please.

Taxi driver : Do you have a preferred route?

Customer   : No, I'll leave it to you (but please don't take the highway).

(near xxx park)

Taxi driver : Around here?

Customer   : Please stop in front of the XX Embassy.

Does this (train) go to Yokohama?

これ、横浜に行きますか。
Kore, Yokohama ni ikimasu ka.

Transportation
交通

GOALS FOR UNIT 7

- Confirm how to get to a place with public transportation
  公共交通機関で行く方法を確認する

- Ask for the best route somewhere with public transportation
  公共交通機関を使った一番いい行き方を尋ねる

- Ask about the time and cost required to reach a destination
  目的地までの時間や料金を尋ねる

Phrase 1

Ask if a train goes where you want to go.

🔊 Track 99

これ、横浜に行きますか。
(よこはま) (い)

Kore, Yokohama ni ikimasu ka.   *Does this (train) go to Yokohama?*

> **NOTE** "Ikimasu" means "to go." The phrase "Kore, [place] ni ikimasu ka?" is used to ask if a nearby mode of transportation goes to a specific destination.
>
> 「行きます」は、"to go" の意味で、「これ、[場所] に行きますか」という表現を使うことで、その交通機関が、ある特定の場所に行くかどうかを尋ねることができます。

Ex.

ジョン　：すみません。**これ、横浜に行きますか。**

駅員　　：ええ、行きますよ。
(えきいん)

Jon   : Sumimasen. **Kore, Yokohama ni ikimasu ka.**
Eki-in : Ee, ikimasuyo.

John   : Excuse me. Does this (train) go to Yokohama?
Station staff : Yes, it does.

Practice A-1

これ、＿＿＿に行きますか。

Use the following words with the phrase **"Kore, ＿＿＿ ni ikimasu ka."**

下記の言葉を使って「これ、＿＿＿に行きますか」のフレーズを練習してください。

🔊 Track 100

横浜 (よこはま) Yokohama	東京 (とうきょう) Tōkyō	新大阪 (しんおおさか) Shin-Ōsaka	成田空港 (なりたくうこう) Narita kūkō
Yokohama	*Tokyo*	*Shin-Osaka*	*Narita Airport*

Practice A-2 [Place]は、_____ですよ。
Answer the questions from Practice A-1 using the phrase **"[Place] wa, _____ desu yo."**
Practice A-1の質問に「場所は、_____ですよ」を使って答えてください。 🔊 Track 101

2番線 に ばん せん ni-ban sen *Platform 2*	ちがうホーム chigau hōmu *a different platform*	ちがう線 せん chigau sen *a different train line*
次の電車 つぎ でん しゃ tsugi no densha *the next train*	あっち acchi *over there*	反対 はん たい hantai *the opposite side*

Practice B Put the words from Practice A-1 or A-2 in < > and practice the conversation below.
Practice A-1やA-2の言葉を〈 〉に入れて会話練習をしてください。 🔊 Track 102

- A train is stopped at the platform - 電車がホームに止まっています

ジョン ：すみません、これ、^A-1〈横浜〉に行きますか。
　　　　　　　　　　　　　　よこはま　　　い

駅員 ：はい、行きますよ。／いいえ、^A-1〈横浜〉は ^A-2〈2番線〉ですよ。
えきいん　　　　い　　　　　　　　　　　　　　　よこはま　　　　に ばん せん

ジョン ：ありがとうございます。

Jon	: Sumimasen, kore, ^A-1<Yokohama> ni ikimasu ka.
Eki-in	: Hai, ikimasu yo. / Iie, ^A-1<Yokohama> wa ^A-2< ni-ban sen > desu yo.
Jon	: Arigatō gozaimasu.

John	: Excuse me, does this (train) go to Yokohama?
Station staff	: Yes, it does. / No, the train for Yokohama stops at Platform 2.
John	: Thank you.

UNIT 7

Phrase 2 — Confirm how to get to a destination.

🔊 Track 103

新宿までどうやって行けばいいですか。
しんじゅく　　　　　　　　　　い

Shinjuku made dōyatte ikeba ii desu ka.

How do I get to Shinjuku?

> **NOTE** "Made" and "dōyatte" mean "to" and "how", respectively. The phrase "Dōyatte ikeba ii desu ka." is used when asking directions to a destination.
>
> 「まで」は、"to"、「どうやって」は、"how" の意味です。「どうやって行けばいいですか」という表現を使うことで、目的地までの行き方を尋ねることができます。

Ex.

ジョン　：新宿までどうやって行けばいいですか。
　　　　　しんじゅく　　　　　　　　　　い

駅員　　：総武線で一本ですよ。
えきいん　そうぶせん　いっぽん

Jon　　　: <u>Shinjuku</u> **made dōyatte ikeba ii desu ka**.
Eki-in　 : Sōbu-sen de ippon desu yo.

John	: How do I get to Shinjuku?
Station staff	: You can go straight there with the Sobu-Line.

Practice A

_____ までどうやって行けばいいですか。

🔊 Track 104

Use the following words with the phrase "_____ **made dōyatte ikeba ii desu ka.**"

下記の言葉を使って「_____ までどうやって行けばいいですか」のフレーズを練習してください。

新宿 しんじゅく Shinjuku *Shinjuku*
渋谷 しぶや Shibuya *Shibuya*
東京 とうきょう Tōkyō *Tokyo*
秋葉原 あきはばら Akihabara *Akihabara*

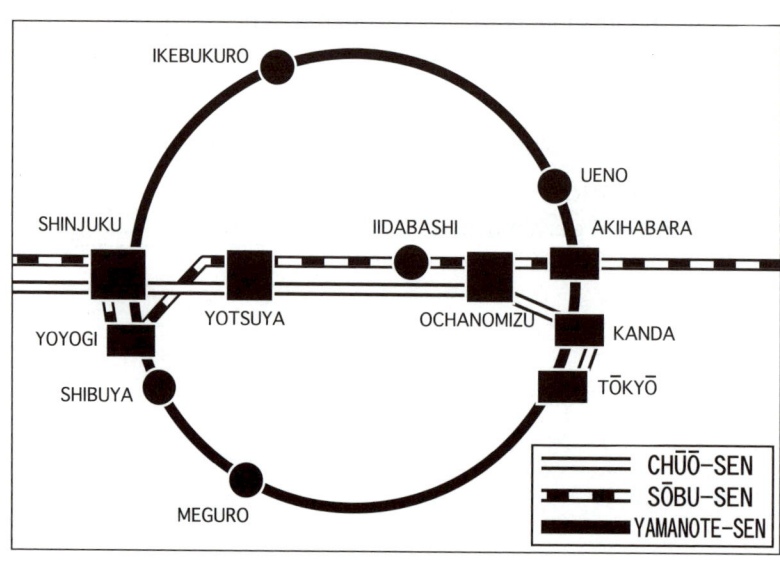

Practice B Ask how to get to the places listed in Practice A using the map on page 94 and following the pattern in (1) or (2) below. 🔊 Track 105

p.94の路線図を使ってPracticeA に挙げた駅への行き方を尋ねてください。答えは(1)あるいは(2)のパターンを使いましょう。

- Currently at Yoyogi - 今、代々木にいます

ジョン ：すみません。^{A-1}〈東京〉まで、どうやって行けばいいですか。

駅員 ：(1)〈山手線〉で一本ですよ。

(2)〈総武線〉に乗って、〈四谷〉で〈中央線〉に乗りかえですよ。

ジョン ：ありがとうございます。

Jon	: Sumimasen. ^{A-1}< Tōkyō > made dōyatte ikeba ii desu ka.
Eki-in	: (1) < Yamanote-sen > de ippon desu yo. (2) < Sōbu-sen > ni notte, < Yotsuya > de < Chūō-sen > ni norikae desu yo.
Jon	: Arigatō gozaimasu.

John	: Excuse me. How do I get to Tokyo?
Station staff	: (1) You can go straight there with the Yamanote-Line. (2) You can take the Sobu-Line and transfer to the Chuo-Line at Yotsuya.
John	: Thank you.

UNIT 7

MEMO

(〜線で)一本／(...sen de) ippon／*directly on the ... line*

(〜線)に乗って／(...sen) ni notte／*get on the ... line*
[the te-form is used in conjunction with other verbs 「て形」は、複数の動詞を接続するのに使います。]

(Aで)B線に乗りかえです。／(A de) B-sen ni norikae desu.／*Transfer to B-line (at A).*

Phrase 3

Ask how much time it takes to get somewhere.

🔊 Track 106

東京から京都までどのぐらいかかりますか。
とうきょう きょうと

Tōkyō kara Kyōto made donogurai kakarimasu ka.

How long does it take from Tokyo to Kyoto?

NOTE "A kara B made" means "from A to B," the word "donogurai" means "how long?" and "kakarimasu" means "take" when referring to time. The phrase "Donogurai kakarimasu ka." is used when asking how much time it takes to get somewhere.

「AからBまで」は、"from A to B" の意味です。また「どのぐらい」は "how long?" で、「かかります」は時間について言及する場合は "take" の意味を持ちます。「どのぐらいかかりますか」は、ある場所までの所要時間を尋ねる表現です。

Ex.

ジョン ：東京から京都までどのぐらいかかりますか。
　　　　とうきょう　きょうと

田中　 ：新幹線で2時間半ぐらいですよ。
たなか　　しんかんせん　　じかんはん

Jon 　　： Tōkyō kara Kyōto made donogurai kakarimasu ka.
Tanaka ： Shinkansen de 2-jikan-han gurai desu yo.

> John 　： How long does it take from Tokyo to Kyoto?
> Tanaka ： It's about two and a half hours by Shinkansen.

_____ までどのぐらいかかりますか。

Use the following words with the phrase "_____ made donogurai kakarimasu ka."

下記の言葉を使って「_____ までどのぐらいかかりますか」のフレーズを練習してください。

🔊 Track 107

① 浅草 あさくさ Asakusa *Asakusa*	② 東京スカイツリー とうきょう Tōkyō sukaitsurī *TOKYO SKYTREE*
③ 箱根 はこね Hakone *Hakone*	④ 日光 にっこう Nikkō *Nikko*

Practice B Look up how to say lengths of time (p. 103) and answer the questions in Practice A using the information below. 🔊 Track 108

p.103で時間の長さの言い方を調べ、下記の情報を使用してPractice A の質問に答えてください。

① 地下鉄 (ちかてつ) → 15分 (ふん)	② 歩いて* (ある) → 20分 (ぷん)
chikatetsu → 15-fun	aruite* → 20-pun
subway / 15 minutes	on foot / 20 minutes
③ 電車 (でんしゃ) → 1時間半 (じかんはん)	④ 車 (くるま) → 2時間半 (じかんはん)
densha → 1-jikan han	kuruma → 2-jikan han
train / 1.5 hours	car / 2.5 hours

＊ When describing how long it takes to walk somewhere, the verb **"aruite"** is used without particles (compare **"densha de"** with **"aruite."**)

＊「徒歩」での所要時間を尋ねる場合、手段の表現は「歩いて」となり、「(乗り物)で」のような助詞の「で」は、使いません。

ジョン：ここから〈浅草(あさくさ)〉までどのぐらいかかりますか。
田中(たなか)：〈地下鉄(ちかてつ)〉で、たぶん〈15分(ふん)〉ぐらいです。
ジョン：そうですか。

Jon : Koko kara < Asakusa > made donogurai kakarimasu ka.
Tanaka : < Chikatetsu > de tabun < 15-fun > gurai desu.
Jon : Sō desu ka.

John : How long does it take to get from here to Asakusa?
Tanaka : On the subway, probably about 15 minutes.
John : Okay.

MEMO
〜ぐらいです。／ ... gurai desu. ／ It's about ... .
たぶん／ tabun ／ probably/I think

UNIT 7

Dialogue

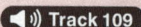 Track 109

Look at the table on the right page and practice the conversation pattern below.
右ページ下の表を見ながら下記の会話例を使って練習しましょう。

ジョン	：鈴木さん、東京から(1)京都までどうやって行けばいいですか。	Jon ：Suzuki-san, Tōkyō kara (1) <u>Kyōto</u> made dōyatte ikeba ii desu ka.
鈴木	：うーん、(2)バスか(3)新幹線ですね。	Suzuki ：Ūn, (2) <u>basu</u> ka (3) <u>shinkansen</u> desu ne.
ジョン	：(2)バスでどのぐらいかかりますか。	Jon ：(2) <u>Basu</u> de donogurai kakarimasu ka.
鈴木	：たぶん(4)6時間ぐらいです。	Suzuki ：Tabun (4) <u>6-jikan</u> gurai desu.
ジョン	：いくらぐらいかかりますか。	Jon ：Ikura gurai kakarimasu ka.
鈴木	：そうですね……。(5)7,000円ぐらいだと思いますよ。	Suzuki ：Sō desu ne....... (5) <u>7,000-en</u> gurai da to omoimasu yo.
ジョン	：そうですか。ありがとうございます。	Jon ：Sō desu ka. Arigatō gozaimasu.

---

①
- (1) 富士山　　　　Fuji-san
- (2) バス　　　　　basu
- (3) 車　　　　　　kuruma
- (4) 2時間半　　　2-jikan-han
- (5) 1,500円　　　1,500-en

②
- (1) 沖縄　　　　　Okinawa
- (2) 船　　　　　　fune
- (3) 飛行機　　　　hikōki
- (4) 3日間　　　　mikka-kan
- (5) 20,000円　　20,000-en

MEMO

バスか新幹線／basu ka shinkansen／bus or sinkansen

いくらぐらいかかりますか。／Ikura gurai kakarimasu ka.／About how much does it cost?

そうですね。／Sō desune.／Let me see.

〜(だ)と思います。／...(da) to omoimasu.／I think that ....

船／fune／ship／boat　　　飛行機／hikōki／airplane

Material

Use the picture below to practice having a conversation.
下記の絵を使って会話練習をしましょう。

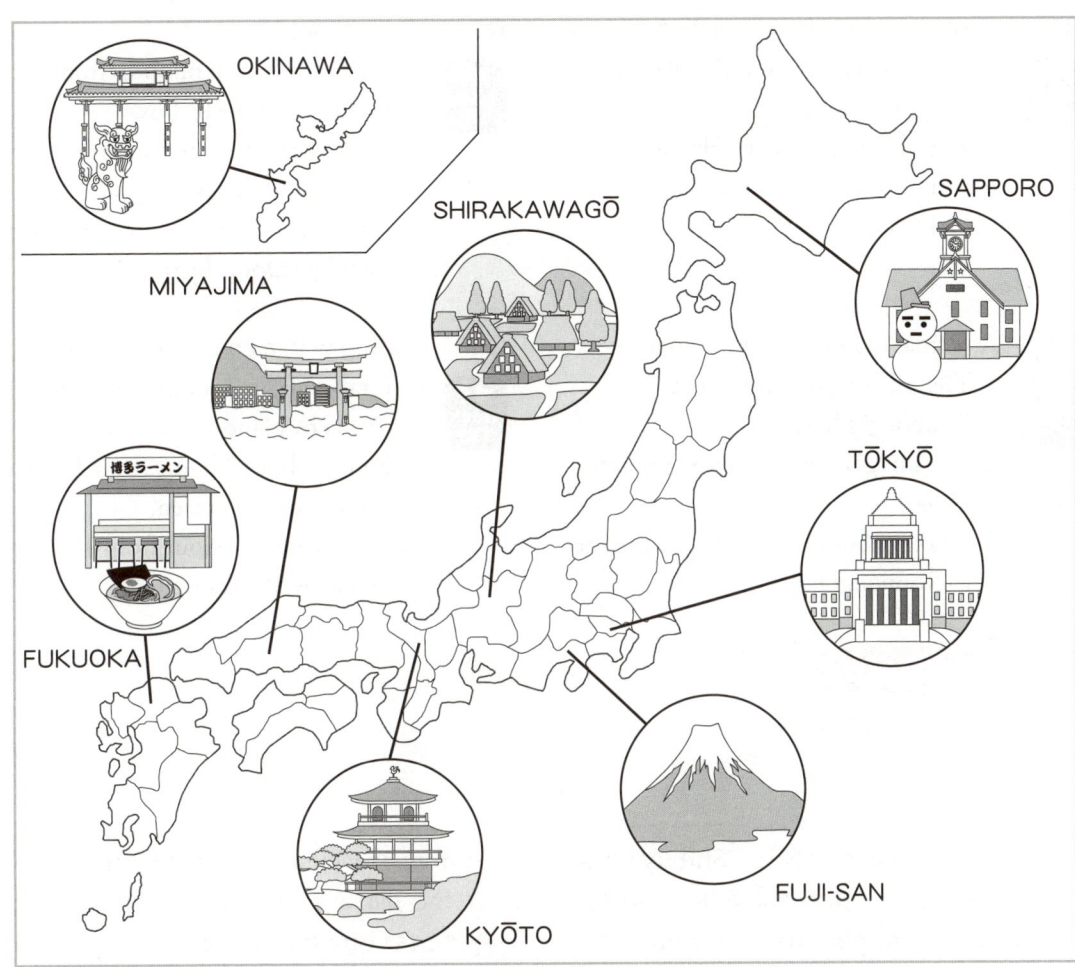

【Time and Cost from Tokyo】

京都 Kyōto		富士山 Fuji-san		沖縄 Okinawa		福岡 Fukuoka	
Bus	Shinkansen	Bus	Car	Airplane	Ship	Airplane	Shinkansen
6 hours	2.5 hours	2.5 hours	2 hours	2.5 hours	3 days	2 hours	5 hours
7,000 yen	20,000 yen	1,500 yen	3,000 yen	30,000 yen	20,000 yen	20,000 yen	25,000 yen

Listening

Listen to the conversation between the man and woman and choose the correct answer.
男の人と女の人の会話を聞いて正しい答えを選んでください。

Q1 On a station platform, pointing at a train

1. The train currently at the platform goes to Hakone.
2. The next train goes to Hakone.
3. A train at a different platform goes to Hakone.

Q3 On a street

1. It takes about 10 minutes from here to Tokyo Dome by bus.
2. It takes about 10 minutes from here to Tokyo Dome by bicycle.
3. It takes about 10 minutes from here to Tokyo Dome by train.

Q2 At a train station ticket counter

1. The subway goes straight to Roppongi Hills.
2. The bus goes straight to Roppongi Hills.
3. It takes a bus and a subway ride to get to Roppongi Hills.

Q4 Talking with a co-worker at work

1. It takes about 3 hours from Tokyo to Osaka by plane.
2. It takes about 3 hours from Tokyo to Osaka by Shinkansen.
3. It takes about 1 hour from Tokyo to Osaka by Shinkansen.

Role playing

Role play using the cards below.
下記のカードを使ってロールプレイしてください。

1.

A: You are currently in Shibuya but want to go to Iidabashi. Ask a person nearby how to get there and how long it takes.

B: You are currently in Shibuya. Look at the picture on page 94 and answer A-san's questions. When there is something you don't know, simply say you don't know.

2.

A: You want to go to B-san's hometown. Ask B-san how to get there, how long it takes, and how much it costs.

B: A-san wants to go to your hometown. Answer his or her questions.

Do you remember?

Use the phrases you have studied in this unit in situations ①–③ below.
このユニットで学習したフレーズを下記の①〜③の状況に合わせて使ってください。

Phrases for This Unit

Unit Phrases

- これ、横浜に行きますか。 — Kore, Yokohama ni ikimasu ka. — *Does this [train] go to Yokohama?*
- 新宿までどうやって行けばいいですか。 — Shinjuku made dōyatte ikeba ii desu ka. — *How do you get to Shinjuku?*
- 東京から京都までどのぐらいかかりますか。 — Tōkyō kara Kyōto made donogurai kakarimasu ka. — *How long does it take from Tokyo to Kyoto?*

Useful expressions

- ～ぐらいです。 — … gurai desu. — *It's about … .*
- たぶん — tabun — *probably/I think*
- いくらぐらいかかりますか。 — Ikura gurai kakarimasu ka. — *About how much does it cost?*
- ～（だ）と思います。 — … (da) to omoimasu. — *I think that … .*

Check!

✓ Now I can...

- ☐ Confirm how to get to a place with public transportation
  公共交通機関で行く方法が確認できる
- ☐ Ask for the best route somewhere with public transportation
  公共交通機関を使った一番いい行き方が尋ねられる
- ☐ Ask about the time and cost required to reach a destination
  目的地までの時間や料金が尋ねられる

Remember and Use!

● TIME and HOURS

TIME 一時（－じ －ji）
-AM / -PM 午前（ごぜん gozen）／午後（ごご gogo）
じゅういちじ jūichi-ji／じゅうにじ jūni-ji／いちじ ichi-ji／にじ ni-ji／さんじ san-ji／よじ yo-ji／ごじ go-ji／ろくじ roku-ji／しちじ shichi-ji／はちじ hachi-ji／くじ ku-ji／じゅうじ jū-ji
what time = 何時（なんじ nan-ji）

MINUTES －分（－ふん -fun / －ぷん -pun)			
5	ごふん go-**fun**	10	じゅっぷん ju**ppun**
15	じゅうごふん jūgo-**fun**	20	にじゅっぷん niju**ppun**
25	にじゅうごふん nijūgo-**fun**	30	さんじゅっぷん／はん sanju**ppun** / han
35	さんじゅうごふん sanjūgo-**fun**	40	よんじゅっぷん yonju**ppun**
45	よんじゅうごふん yonjūgo-**fun**	50	ごじゅっぷん goju**ppun**
55	ごじゅうごふん gojūgo-**fun**	?	なんぷん nam**pun**

→ *See p.177, Grammar*

1. Fill out the Q&A like the example below.
下記の例にならって、質疑応答をしてください。

(1) Q: 今、何時ですか。 Ima nan-ji desu ka.
A: <u>(ごぜん) ごじじゅっぷん</u>です。 <u>(Gozen) go-ji juppun</u> desu.

Ex. 5:10 a.m.　1. 7:40 a.m.　2. 9:15 p.m.　3. 8:50 a.m.　4. 4:05 p.m.　5. 1:30 p.m.

(2) Q: <u>仕事</u>は何時からですか。 <u>Shigoto</u> wa nan-ji kara desu ka.
A: <u>(ごぜん) はちじはん</u>からです。 <u>(Gozen) hachi-ji han</u> kara desu.

Ex. 仕事 shigoto 8:30 a.m.　1. 授業 jugyō 9:50 a.m.　2. 店 mise 10:00 a.m.

HOURS 時間（じかん －jikan）	MINUTES 分（ふん －fun / ぷん -pun）
Ex. 2 hours → にじかん　ni-jikan 4.5 hours → よじかんはん　yo-jikan han	Same as the readings for minutes in a timetable. Note: 3 hours and 20 minutes → さんじかんにじゅっぷん　san-jikan nijuppun

2. Fill out the Q&A like the example below.
下記の例にならって、質疑応答をしてください。

(1) Q: どのぐらいかかりますか。 Donogurai kakarimasu ka.
A: <u>にじかん</u>ぐらいです。 <u>Ni-jikan</u> gurai desu.

Ex. 2 hours　1. 1 hour　2. 2 hours 15 minutes　3. 4 hours 45 minutes　4. 9.5 hours

UNIT 7

● CALENDAR

DAYS −曜日 (−ようび −yōbi)　　　　　　　　　　+ __に / __ni [particle]

Sunday	Monday	Tuesday	Wednesday	Thursday	Friday	Saturday
にちようび	げつようび	かようび	すいようび	もくようび	きんようび	どようび
Nichiyōbi	Getsuyōbi	Kayōbi	Suiyōbi	Mokuyōbi	Kin'yōbi	Doyōbi

DATES −日 (−にち −nichi / −か −ka)　　　　　　　　+ __に / __ni [particle]

1	2	3	4	5	6	7
ついたち	ふつか	みっか	よっか	いつか	むいか	なのか
tsuitachi	**futsuka**	**mikka**	**yokka**	**itsuka**	**muika**	**nanoka**
8	**9**	**10**	11	12	13	**14**
ようか	ここのか	とおか	じゅういちにち	じゅうににち	じゅうさんにち	じゅうよっか
yōka	**kokonoka**	**tōka**	jūichi-nichi	jūni-nichi	jūsan-nichi	**jūyokka**
15	16	17	18	19	**20**	21
じゅうごにち	じゅうろくにち	じゅうしちにち	じゅうはちにち	じゅうくにち	はつか	にじゅういちにち
jūgo-nichi	jūroku-nichi	jūshichi-nichi	jūhachi-nichi	jūku-nichi	**hatsuka**	nijūichi-nichi
22	23	**24**	25	26	27	28
にじゅうににち	にじゅうさんにち	にじゅうよっか	にじゅうごにち	にじゅうろくにち	にじゅうしちにち	にじゅうはちにち
nijūni-nichi	nijūsan-nichi	**nijūyokka**	nijūgo-nichi	nijūroku-nichi	nijūshichi-nichi	nijūhachi-nichi
29	30	31				
にじゅうくにち	さんじゅうにち	さんじゅういちにち				
nijūku-nichi	sanjū-nichi	sanjūichi-nichi				

* Exceptional readings are in **bold pink**
* 例外的な読み方については赤の太字で示してあります

MONTH −月 (−がつ −gatsu)　　　　　　　　　　+ __に / __ni [particle]

1 January	2 February	3 March	4 April	5 May	6 June
いちがつ	にがつ	さんがつ	しがつ	ごがつ	ろくがつ
ichi-gatsu	ni-gatsu	san-gatsu	shi-gatsu	go-gatsu	roku-gatsu
7 July	8 August	9 September	10 October	11 November	12 December
しちがつ	はちがつ	くがつ	じゅうがつ	じゅういちがつ	じゅうにがつ
shichi-gatsu	hachi-gatsu	ku-gatsu	jū-gatsu	jūichi-gatsu	jūni-gatsu

VOCABULARY + ~~に~~ / ~~ni~~　　　　DURATION OF THE TIME

	Last	This	Next		1	2
Year	きょねん kyonen	ことし kotoshi	らいねん rainen	Year	+ねん(かん) +nen(kan)	いちねん(かん) ichi-nen(kan)	にねん(かん) ni-nen(kan)
Month	せんげつ sengetsu	こんげつ kongetsu	らいげつ raigetsu	Month	+かげつ(かん) +kagetsu(kan)	いっかげつ ikkagetsu(kan)	にかげつ ni-kagetsu(kan)
Week	せんしゅう senshū	こんしゅう konshū	らいしゅう raishū	Week	+しゅうかん +shūkan	いっしゅうかん isshūkan	にしゅうかん ni-shūkan
Day	きのう kinō	きょう kyō	あした ashita	Day	[Date](+かん) [Date](+kan)	いちにち* ichi-nichi	ふつか(かん) futsuka(kan)

* Note the difference between "ichi-nichi" (one day) and "tsuitachi" (the 1st day of the month)
* 「いちにち（期間）」と「ついたち（日付）」の意味の違いに注意しましょう

I'm going to an art museum.

美術館に行きます。
Bijutsukan ni ikimasu.

Talking about plans and activities
予定や行動について話す

GOALS FOR UNIT 8

- Talk about plans and what you are about to do
  予定について話す

- Ask about things that have happened and places people have been to
  行った場所やそこでしたことについて話す

- Talk about interests and wants
  興味のあることやしたいことについて話す

Phrase 1 — Talk about what you are about to do.

🔊 Track 114

美術館に行きます。
びじゅつかん　い

Bijutsukan ni ikimasu.

I'm going to an art museum.

> **NOTE** "[Place] ni ikimasu" means "[I am] going to go to [place]." The phrase "___ ni ikimasu" can be combined with verb stems to indicate a purpose for going, as in "tabe ni ikimasu" (= "I am going to eat.")
>
> 「[場所]に行きます」は、"[I am] going to go to [place]" の意味です。また、「_____に行きます」は、[ます形]の語幹を伴い (ex. 食べに行きます＝I am going to eat.)、その場所に行く目的を表します。

Ex.

田中　：どこに行きますか。
たなか　　　　　　い

ジョン：美術館に行きます。
　　　　びじゅつかん　　い

Tanaka : Doko ni ikimasu ka.
Jon   : Bijutsukan ni ikimasu.

> Tanaka : Where are you going?
> John   : I'm going to an art museum.

Practice A

_____ に行きます。
　　　い

Use the following words with the phrase "_____ ni ikimasu."
下記の言葉を使って「_____に行きます」のフレーズを練習してください。

🔊 Track 115

美術館 (びじゅつかん) bijutsukan — *art museum*	新宿 (しんじゅく) Shinjuku — *Shinjuku*	友だちのうち (とも) tomodachi no uchi — *a friend's house*
本屋 (ほんや) hon-ya — *bookstore* → See Appendix, Shops	買い物 (か もの) kaimono — *shopping*	公園 (こうえん) kōen — *park*
飲み (の) nomi — *... to drink*	ごはんを食べ (た) gohan o tabe — *... to have food*	うちに帰ります* (かえ) uchi ni kaerimasu* — *go home*

* "**Kaerimasu**" is used instead of "**ikimasu**" when one is going to one's own house.
* 自分のうちに向かう場合、「行きます」ではなく「帰ります」を使います。

Practice B Put the words from Practice A in < > and practice having a conversation.
Practice Aの言葉を〈　〉に入れて会話練習をしてください。　🔊 Track 116

John-san runs into his co-worker Tanaka-san on the way home from work.
ジョンさんは仕事帰りに同僚の田中さんにばったり会いました。

ジョン：おつかれさまです。

田中：おつかれさまです。ジョンさん、これからどこに行きますか。

ジョン：〈新宿〉に行きます。田中さんは？

田中：私はうちに帰ります。

ジョン：じゃ、駅まで一緒に行きましょう。

田中：はい、行きましょう。

Jon　　：Otsukaresama desu.
Tanaka：Otsukaresama desu. Jon-san, korekara doko ni ikimasu ka.
Jon　　：< Shinjuku > ni ikimasu. Tanaka-san wa?
Tanaka：Watashi wa uchi ni kaerimasu.
Jon　　：Ja, eki made issho ni ikimashō.
Tanaka：Hai, ikimashō.

John　：Hello.
Tanaka：Hello. John-san, where are you going right now?
John　：I'm going to Shinjuku. How about you, Tanaka-san?
Tanaka：I'm going home.
John　：Well, then let's go to the station together.
Tanaka：Okay, let's do that.

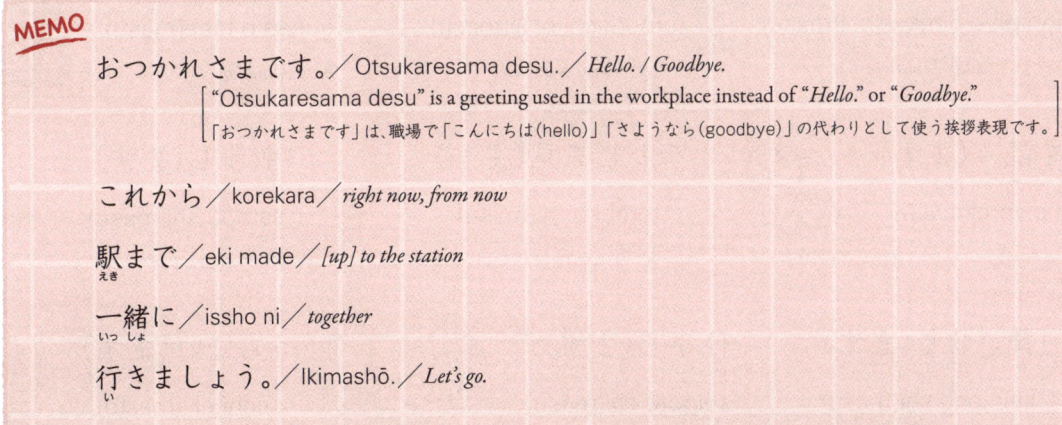

MEMO

おつかれさまです。／Otsukaresama desu.／Hello. / Goodbye.
　"Otsukaresama desu" is a greeting used in the workplace instead of "Hello." or "Goodbye."
　「おつかれさまです」は、職場で「こんにちは(hello)」「さようなら(goodbye)」の代わりとして使う挨拶表現です。

これから／korekara／right now, from now

駅まで／eki made／[up] to the station

一緒に／issho ni／together

行きましょう。／Ikimashō.／Let's go.

Phrase 2 — Talk about prior actions.

🔊 Track 117

昨日はうちで日本語を勉強し**ました**。
きのう　　　　　にほんご　べんきょう

Kinō wa uchi de Nihon-go o benkyō shi**mashita**.

*I **studied** Japanese at home yesterday.*

NOTE: In the past tense, masu verbs end in **"-mashita."** The particle **"de"** is used to indicate the place where an action occurred. **"Nani o shimashita ka"** means **"What did you do?"**

過去時制では、[ます形]は「＿＿＿ました」となり、助詞の「で」は、その動作が起こる場所を示します。「何をしましたか」は、"What did you do?"という意味になります。

Ex.

田中：昨日は何をしましたか。
たなか　きのう　なに

ジョン：(昨日は)うちで日本語を勉強しました。
　　　　きのう　　　　にほんご　べんきょう

Tanaka : Kinō wa nani o shimashita ka.
Jon : (Kinō wa) uchi de Nihon-go o benkyō shi**mashita**.

Tanaka : What did you do yesterday?
John : I studied Japanese at home (yesterday).

Practice A-1

＿＿＿ました。

Change the **"masu"** portion of the following words to **"＿＿＿ mashita."**

下記の言葉の「ます」の部分を「ました」に変えてください。

🔊 Track 118

日本語を勉強し(ます) にほんご　べんきょう Nihon-go o benkyō shi(masu) *study Japanese*	友だちに会い(ます) とも　　あ tomodachi ni ai(masu) *meet a friend*	ごはんを食べ(ます) た gohan o tabe(masu) *have some food*
本を読み(ます) ほん　よ hon o yomi(masu) *read a book*	テレビを見(ます) み terebi o mi(masu) *watch TV*	散歩し(ます) さんぽ sampo shi(masu) *take a walk*
買い物し(ます) か　もの kaimono shi(masu) *go shopping*	仕事し(ます) しごと shigoto shi(masu) *work*	うちにい(ます) uchi ni i(masu) *stay at home*

Practice A-2

_____ は、何 (なに) をしましたか。
Use the following words with the phrase "_____ wa nani o shimashita ka."
下記の言葉を使って「_____は何をしましたか」のフレーズを練習してください。

🔊 Track 119

昨日 (きのう)	週末 (しゅうまつ)	先週 (せんしゅう)
kinō	shūmatsu	senshū
yesterday	weekend	last week → See p.104, Calendar

Practice B

Put the words from Practice A-1 and A-2 in < > below and the name of a place in _____ practice having a conversation.
Practice A-1やA-2の言葉を〈 〉に、場所の名前を_____に入れて会話練習をしてください。

🔊 Track 120

田中 : ジョンさん、^A-2〈昨日(きのう)〉は何(なに)をしましたか。
ジョン : 新宿(しんじゅく)に行(い)きました。／うちにいました。
田中 : 新宿(しんじゅく)／うちで何(なに)をしましたか。
ジョン : ^A-1〈日本語(にほんご)を勉強(べんきょう)し〉ました。それから、^A-1〈ごはんを食(た)べ〉ました。
　　　　田中(たなか)さんは、^A-2〈昨日(きのう)〉何(なに)をしましたか。
田中 : 私(わたし)はうちで^A-1〈本(ほん)を読(よ)み〉ました。

Tanaka : Jon-san, ^A-2< kinō > wa nani o shimashita ka.
Jon : <u>Shinjuku</u> ni ikimashita. / Uchi ni imashita.
Tanaka : <u>Shinjuku / uchi</u> de nani o shimashita ka.
Jon : ^A-1< Nihon-go o benkyō shi > mashita.
　　Sorekara, ^A-1<gohan o tabe> mashita.
　　Tanaka-san wa ^A-2< kinō > nani o shimashita ka.
Tanaka : Watashi wa <u>uchi</u> de ^A-1<hon o yomi> mashita.

Tanaka : John-san, what did you do yesterday?
John : I went to Shinjuku. / I stayed at home.
Tanaka : What did you do at Shinjuku / home?
John : I studied Japanese. Then, I had something to eat. What did you do yesterday, Tanaka-san?
Tanaka : I read a book at home.

UNIT 8

MEMO

それから／sorekara／and, after that

[Place]で[Verb]／[Place] de [Verb]／*[Verb] at [place]*
　　　　　　　　　　*denotes the location of an action　その動作をする場所を示す構文です。

Phrase 3 — Talk about what you want to do.

🔊 Track 121

すもうを見たいです。
Sumō o mitai desu.

I want to watch sumo wrestling.

NOTE The verb-ending "_____ tai desu" attaches to verb stems to mean "I want to/would like to [verb]." For example, "tabemasu" → "tabetai desu" (I want to eat.)

「_____たいです」はます形の語幹を伴い、"I want/would like to [verb]" という意味になります。例えば、「食べます（ます形）」が「食べたいです」になると、"I want to eat" という意味になります。

Ex.

田中　：今度の休み、何をしますか。
ジョン：すもうを見たいです。

Tanaka : Kondo no yasumi, nani o shimasu ka.
Jon　　: Sumō o mitai desu.

Tanaka : What are you going to do next holiday?
John　 : I want to watch sumo wrestling.

Practice A-1

_____たいです。
Change the **"masu"** portion of the following words to **"_____ tai desu."**
下記の言葉の「ます」の部分を「_____たいです」に変えてください。

🔊 Track 122

すもうを見(ます)	服を買い(ます)	日本語を勉強し(ます)
sumō o mi(masu)	fuku o kai(masu)	Nihon-go o benkyō shi(masu)
watch sumo wrestling	*buy clothes*	*study Japanese*
遊びに行き(ます)	旅行に行き(ます)	海／山に行き(ます)
asobi ni iki(masu)	ryokō ni iki(masu)	umi/ yama ni iki(masu)
go hang out (with friends)	*go on a trip*	*go to the beach / mountains*
家族に会い(ます)	ジョギングし(ます)	ゆっくりし(ます)
kazoku ni ai(masu)	jogingu shi(masu)	yukkuri shi(masu)
see (my) family	*jog*	*relax/take it easy*

Practice A-2

_____、何をしますか。
Use the following words with the phrase **" [Time period] , nani o shimasu ka."**
下記の言葉を使って「_____、何をしますか」のフレーズを練習してください。

🔊 Track 123

今度の休み こんど やす kondo no yasumi *the next holiday/day off*	週末 しゅうまつ shūmatsu *weekend*	ゴールデンウィーク gōruden wīku *Golden Week**	夏休み なつ やす natsu-yasumi *summer break*

* "Golden week" is a series of week-long holidays that occurs from late April to early May.
*「ゴールデンウイーク」とは、4月末から5月初めにかけての連休のことを言います。

Practice B

Put the words from Practice A-1 and A-2 in < > and practice having a conversation.
Practice A-1やA-2の言葉を〈 〉に入れて会話練習をしてください。

🔊 Track 124

田中 ：ジョンさん、^A-2〈今度の休み〉、何をしますか。
ジョン：^A-1〈すもうを見〉たいです。田中さんは？
田中 ：私も^A-1〈すもうを見〉たいです。／私は^A-1〈ゆっくりし〉たいです。

Tanaka : Jon-san, ^A-2< kondo no yasumi >, nani o shimasu ka.
Jon : ^A-1< Sumō o mi > tai desu. Tanaka-san wa?
Tanaka : Watashi mo ^A-1< sumō o mi > tai desu.
 / Watashi wa ^A-1<yukkuri shi> tai desu.

> Tanaka : John-san, what are you doing on your next day off?
> John : I want to see some sumo. How about you?
> Tanaka : I want to see sumo wrestling, too. /
> I want to relax.

UNIT 8

Column

The English language uses the phrase "Would you like …?" to make recommendations or invite a person to do something, but the Japanese when making invitations phrase **"…tai desu ka."** is not used in Japanese.

For example, the phrase "Would you like a coffee?" translates into Japanese as **"Kōhī o nomimasu ka."** or **"Kōhī o nomimasen ka."**, or literally **"Will you/Won't you have coffee?"**

Ending these sorts of question with **"masu ka"** asks the listener for his or her intent, while **"masen ka"** is more of an invitation.

Dialogue

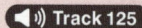

Practice having a conversation by replacing the words in (1)–(4) with the words below.
(1)〜(4)の言葉をピンクの枠内の言葉に置き換えて会話練習をしてください。

田中　：ジョンさん、週末、何をしましたか。
ジョン：(1)新宿でごはんを食べました。
　　　　田中さんは？
田中　：私はうちでゆっくりしました。
　　　　今度の週末は何をしますか。
ジョン：(2)こどもと(3)公園に行きます。
田中　：そうですか。
　　　　(3)公園で何をしますか。
ジョン：(4)写真を撮りたいです。
田中　：いいですね。

Tanaka : Jon-san, shūmatsu nani o shimashita ka.
Jon : (1)Shinjuku de gohan o tabemashita.
Tanaka san wa?
Tanaka : Watashi wa uchi de yukkuri shimashita.
Kondo no shūmatsu wa nani o shimasuka.
Jon : (2)Kodomo to (3)kōen ni ikimasu.
Tanaka : Sō desu ka.
(3)Kōen de nani o shimasuka.
Jon : (4)Shashin o toritai desu.
Tanaka : Ii desu ne.

①
(1) サイクリングしました　saikuringu shimashita
(2) 友だち　tomodachi
(3) 海　umi
(4) 本を読みたい　hon o yomitai

②
(1) 友だちに会いました　tomodachi ni aimashita
(2) 家族　kazoku
(3) ショッピングモール　shoppingu-mōru (= *shopping mall*)
(4) おみやげを買いたい　omiyage o kaitai (*omiyage* = *souvenir*)

MEMO

[Person]と[verb]／[Person] to [verb]／*[verb] with a [person]*

To say "*by myself*" or "*alone*," use the phrase "ひとりで hitori de."
"by myself"や"alone"は「ひとりで」と言います。

Listening

Listen to the conversation between the man and woman and choose the correct answer.
男の人と女の人の会話を聞いて正しい答えを選んでください。

Q1 After work

1. The woman is going to a drug store.
2. The man is going to buy food with a friend.
3. The woman is going to a bookstore.

Q2 Monday morning at work

1. The woman went to a park with her family.
2. The man is going to work on the weekend.
3. The man and woman went to a park.

Q3 Two friends are talking about the summer break

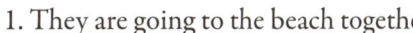

1. They are going to the beach together.
2. The man doesn't want to go to the beach.
3. The woman wants to relax at home.

Q4 Two friends are talking

1. The man wants to study Japanese on the weekend.
2. The man wants to go out somewhere.
3. The man wants to study with the woman.

Role playing

Role play using the cards below.
下記のカードを使ってロールプレイしてください。

1.

A: You are showing B-san around Tokyo. Ask B-san questions like where he/she wants to go or what he/she wants to eat, then decide where the two of you will go and what you will do.

B: A-san will show you around Tokyo. Tell A-san what you want to do and decide what to do together.

2.

A: You are back at work after a weeklong holiday. Talk to B-san about your time off (think about what you did on your own). B-san is also taking some time off next week, so ask about his/her upcoming plans.

B: Ask A-san questions like where he/she went for the holiday and what he/she did. Also talk with A-san about your plans for the time off you are taking next week (think about what you will do on your own).

UNIT 8

Do you remember?

Use the phrases you have studied in this unit in situations ①–③ below.
このユニットで学習したフレーズを下記の①～③の状況に合わせて使ってください。

①

②

③

Phrases For This Unit

Unit Phrases

- 美術館に行きます。 — Bijutsukan ni ikimasu. — *I'm going to an art museum.*
- 昨日はうちで日本語を勉強しました。 — Kinō wa uchi de Nihon-go o benkyō shimashita. — *I studied Japanese at home yesterday.*
- すもうを見たいです。 — Sumō o mitai desu. — *I want to watch Sumo wresting.*

Useful expressions

- おつかれさまです。 — Otsukaresama desu. — *Hello. / Goodbye.* [a greeting used in the workplace instead of "*Hello.*" or "*Goodbye.*"]
- 一緒に行きましょう。 — Issho ni ikimashō. — *Let's go together.*
- これから — korekara — *from now*
- [Place]で[verb] — [Place] de [verb] — *[verb] at [place]*
- [Person]と[verb] — [Person] to [verb] — *[verb] with a [person]*

UNIT 8

Check!

✓ Now I can...

☐ **Talk about plans and what you are about to do**
予定について話せる

☐ **Ask about things that have happened and places people have been to**
行った場所やそこでしたことについて話せる

☐ **Talk about interests and wants**
興味のあることやしたいことについて話せる

Remember and Use!

● Verb Conjugations (masu-form) ●

	Non-past	Past
Affirmative	_____ます / ____masu	_____ました / ____mashita
Negative	_____ません / ____masen	_____ませんでした / ____masendeshita

→ *See p.171, Grammar*

● "____ni ____masu" Verbs ●

[place / person]に_____ます   [place / person] ni ____masu

go
行きます／ikimasu
行く／iku

come
来ます／kimasu
来る／kuru

return / go home
帰ります／kaerimasu
帰る／kaeru

meet
会います／aimasu
会う／au

→ *See Appendix, Verb Conjugation List*

1. Make affirmative and negative sentences in different tenses using a noun with the particle "ni."
   助詞の「に」がつく名詞を使って異なる時制の肯定文・否定文を作ってください。

Ex.　来週、アメリカに帰ります。
　　　Raishū, Amerika **ni** kaerimasu.　　*I'm going back to America next week.*

2. Make yes-or-no questions and then answer them.
   Yes/No疑問文を作り、それに答えてください。

Ex.　Q: 昨日、友だちに会いましたか。
　　　　Kinō, tomodachi **ni** aimashita ka.　　*Did you meet with a friend yesterday?*
　　　A: はい、会いました。／いいえ、会いませんでした。
　　　　Hai, aimashita. / Iie, aimasendeshita.　　*Yes, I did. / No, I didn't.*

3. Make questions using the word "itsu" (= when) and answer them.
   「いつ」という言葉を使って疑問文を作り、それに答えてください。

Ex.　Q: **いつ**日本に来ましたか。
　　　　Itsu Nihon ni kimashita ka.　　*When did you come to Japan?*
　　　A: 去年の８月に来ました。／先月~~に~~来ました。
　　　　Kyonen no 8-gatsu **ni** kimashita. / Sengetsu ~~ni~~ kimashita.　　*Last August. / Last month.*

＊ When answering a "when" question, some time words require the particle **"ni,"** but not all do.
　→ *See p.104, Calendar*
＊「いつ」の質問に答える際、時を表すいくつかの言葉には助詞の「に」が必要ですが全ての言葉に必要なわけではありません。p.104のカレンダー参照。

● "___ o ___masu" Verbs ●

[object]を___ます [object] o ___masu	
eat 食(た)べます／tabemasu 食(た)べる／taberu	**drink** 飲(の)みます／nomimasu 飲(の)む／nomu
look, see, watch 見(み)ます／mimasu 見(み)る／miru	**read** 読(よ)みます／yomimasu 読(よ)む／yomu
buy 買(か)います／kaimasu 買(か)う／kau	**listen, hear** 聞(き)きます／kikimasu 聞(き)く／kiku
take photos (写真(しゃしん)を)撮(と)ります／(shashin o) torimasu 撮(と)る／toru	**study** 勉強(べんきょう)します／benkyō shimasu 勉強(べんきょう)する／benkyō suru

1. **Make affirmative and negative sentences in different tenses using a noun with the particle "o."**
   助詞の「を」がつく名詞を使って異なる時制の肯定文・否定文を作ってください。

   Ex. 昨日(きのう)、日本のテレビを見(み)ました。
   Kinō, Nihon no terebi **o** mimashita.   *I watched Japanese TV yesterday.*

2. **Make questions using verbs and answer them.**
   動詞を使って疑問文を作り、それに答えてください。

   Ex. Q: 昨日(きのう)、ビールを飲(の)みましたか。
   Kinō, biru **o** nomimashita ka.   *Did you drink beer yesterday?*

   A: はい、飲(の)みました。／いいえ、飲(の)みませんでした。
   Hai, nomimashita. / Iie, nomimasen deshita.   *Yes, I did. / No, I didn't.*

3. **Make questions using the phrase "doko de" (= where at) and answer them.**
   「どこで」という言葉を使って疑問文を作り、それに答えてください。

   Ex. Q: **どこで**そのカメラを買(か)いましたか。
   Doko de sono kamera **o** kaimashita ka.   *Where did you buy that camera?*

   A: 秋葉原(あきはばら)で買(か)いました。
   Akihabara **de** kaimashita   *At Akihabara.*

UNIT 8

Good to Know

① Point card service

Japanese stores often have point cards, and cashiers will ask customers for their point card when they make a purchase. Some shops offer gifts or discounts if a certain amount of points are accrued. Here is a sample conversation.

Clerk:	Do you have point card?	Pointo kādo, omochi desu ka.
Customer:	No, I don't.	Arimasen.
Clerk:	Would you like to make one?	Otsukuri shimasu ka.
Customer:	No thanks. / Yes, please.	Kekkō desu. / Onegai shimasu.

② Customer Service

When buying a present for someone at a Japanese shop, several stores will provide free giftwrapping upon request. However, boxes and special wrapping may come at a fee, so be sure to confirm this beforehand.

Stores will also give multiple bags for multiple items at the customer's request. Department stores, large grocery stores, and stores that sell furniture and electronics typically provide home delivery. The cost of delivery depends on the distance traveled, with nearby places sometimes being free, so be sure to confirm before making any arrangements.

● **Helpful Phrases**

1. Requesting giftwrapping

(1) すみません、ラッピングしてもらえますか。

　　Sumimasen, rappingu shite moraemasu ka.
　　Excuse me, would you giftwrap this for me?

(2) 無料*ですか。有料*ですか。

　　Muryō* desu ka. Yūryō* desu ka.
　　Is wrapping here free or does it cost something?
　　*muryō= free / yūryō= paid

2. Arranging delivery

(1) すみません、これ、配達してもらえませんか。

　　Sumimasen, kore, haitatsu shite moraemasen ka.
　　Excuse me, could I have this delivered?

(2) 〜まで、いくらかかりますか。

　　... made ikura kakarimasu ka.
　　How much does it cost [to have it delivered] to ... ?

What you must provide		
住所	jūsho	address
名前	namae	name
電話番号	denwa bangō	phone number
配達日時	haitatsu-nichiji	delivery date and time

How do you like living in Japan?

日本の生活はどうですか。
に ほん せい かつ
Nihon no seikatsu wa dō desu ka.

Talking about impressions
感想を言う

GOALS FOR UNIT 9

- Talk about your life in Japan
  日本での生活について話す

- Talk about your impression of things that happened in the past
  過去の経験について自分の感想を話す

Phrase 1 — Talk about your impression of something.

🔊 Track 130

日本(にほん)の生活(せいかつ)**は**どうですか。

Nihon no seikatsu wa dō desu ka. *How do you like living in Japan?*

NOTE "____ **wa dō desu ka.**" means "How is ____?" or "How do you like ____?" and can be used to ask someone what they think of something.

「____はどうですか」は "How is ____?" あるいは "How do you like ____?" という意味で、ある話題についての感想を求める表現です。

Ex.

田中(たなか) ：日本(にほん)の生活(せいかつ)はどうですか。
ジョン ：楽(たの)しいです。

Tanaka ： <u>Nihon no seikatsu</u> **wa dō desu ka.**
Jon ： Tanoshii desu.

Tanaka : How do you like living in Japan?
John : It's fun.

Practice A-1

____です。
Make sentences ending in "____ **desu**" using the words below.
下記の言葉の文末に「____です」をつけてください。

🔊 Track 131

楽(たの)しい 😊 tanoshii *fun / enjoyable*	おもしろい 😊 omoshiroi *fun / interesting*	おいしい 😊 oishii *delicious / tasty*
つまらない ☹ tsumaranai *boring / unexciting*	大変(たいへん) taihen *hard / tough*	むずかしい ☹ muzukashii *difficult*
いい 😊 ii *good*	便利(べんり) benri *convenient*	きれい 😊 kirei *clean / beautiful*

Practice A-2

_____ はどうですか。

Make questions using the following words with the phrase **"_____ wa dō desu ka."**

下記の言葉に「_____ はどうですか」をつけて文を作ってください。

🔊 Track 132

日本の生活 にほんせいかつ Nihon no seikatsu *life in Japan*	日本料理 にほんりょうり Nihon ryōri *Japanese food*	日本語 にほんご Nihon-go *the Japanese language*	今住んでいるところ います ima sundeiru tokoro *the place where you/I live now*

Practice B

Put the words from Practice A-1 or A-2 in < > and practice having a conversation.

Practice A-1やA-2の言葉を〈　　〉に入れて会話練習をしてください。

🔊 Track 133

田中（たなか）：ジョンさん、^A-2〈日本（にほん）の生活（せいかつ）〉はどうですか。

ジョン：（すごく）^A-1〈楽（たの）しい〉です。

田中（たなか）：そうですか。^A-2〈今（いま）住（す）んでいるところ〉はどうですか。

ジョン：（とても）^A-1〈便利（べんり）〉ですよ。

Tanaka : Jon-san, ^A-2< Nihon no seikatsu > wa dō desu ka.
Jon : (Sugoku) ^A-1< tanoshii > desu.
Tanaka : Sō desu ka. ^A-2< Ima sundeiru tokoro > wa dō desu ka.
Jon : (Totemo) ^A-1< benri > desu yo.

> Tanaka : John-san, how do you like living in Japan?
> John : It's really fun.
> Tanaka : How's the place where you're living right now?
> John : It's very convenient.

UNIT 9

MEMO

すごく ／sugoku／ *very/extremely* [casual　カジュアルな表現です。]

とても ／totemo／ *very* [polite　丁寧な表現です。]

Phrase 2
Talk about your impression of something that happened in the past.

🔊 Track 134

旅行<ruby>（りょこう）</ruby>はどうでしたか。

Ryokō wa dō deshita ka.   *How was your trip?*

> **NOTE** **"Dō deshita ka"** is the past tense of **"dō desu ka"** and is used to ask a person for their impression of something that has already happened.
> → See the MEMO on p.123 for the past tense of different adjectives.
>
> 「どうでしたか」は「どうですか」の過去時制で、過去にあったことについての感想を求める表現です。形容詞の過去形についてはp.123のMEMOを参照。

Ex.

田中<ruby>（たなか）</ruby>：旅行<ruby>（りょこう）</ruby>はどうでしたか。
ジョン：よかったです。

Tanaka : Ryokō wa dō deshita ka.
Jon   : Yokatta desu.

> *Tanaka : How was your trip?*
> *John   : It was good.*

Practice A-1

_____はどうでしたか。
Use the following words with the phrase "_____ **wa dō deshita ka.**"
下記の言葉を使って「_____はどうでしたか」のフレーズを練習してください。

🔊 Track 135

旅行 ryokō *trip*	パーティー pāthī *party*	飲み会 nomikai *drinking party at izakaya**	週末 shūmatsu *weekend*

* izakaya = Japanese-style pub
※「居酒屋」とは日本式飲み屋です。

Practice A-2

_____です。
Answer the questions in Practice A-1 with a sentence ending in "_____ **desu.**"
下記の言葉の文末に「_____です」をつけてPractice A-1の質問に答えてください。

🔊 Track 136

よかった  yokatta *(it was) good*	楽しかった tanoshikatta *(it was) fun/enjoyable*	おもしろかった omoshirokatta *(it was) fun/interesting*
すばらしかった subarashikatta *(it was) wonderful*	つまらなかった tsumaranakatta *(it was) boring*	いそがしかった isogashikatta *(it was) busy*

Practice A-3 ＿＿＿でした。
Answer the questions in Practice A-1 with sentences ending in **"＿＿＿ deshita."**
下記の言葉の文末に「＿＿＿でした」をつけてPractice A-1の質問に答えてください。

🔊 Track 137

まあまあ	ひま	大変(たいへん)
māmā	hima	taihen
(it was) so-so	(it was) free/not busy	(it was) terrible/hard/tough

Practice B Put words from Practice A-1, A-2, or A-3 in < > and practice having a conversation. Use positive adjectives in ① and negative adjectives in ②.
Practice A-1、A-2、A-3の言葉を〈　　〉に入れて会話練習をしてください。①には肯定的な形容詞、②には否定的な形容詞を使ってください。

🔊 Track 138

①

田中　：ジョンさん、^A-1〈旅行〉はどうでしたか。
ジョン：^A-2〈楽しかった〉です。
田中　：それはよかったですね。

Tanaka : Jon-san, ^A-1< ryokō > wa dō deshita ka.
Jon　　: ^A-2< Tanoshikatta> desu.
Tanaka : Sore wa yokatta desu ne.

> Tanaka : John-san, how was your trip?
> Jon　　: It was fun.
> Tanaka : I'm glad to hear that.

②

田中　：ジョンさん、^A-1〈旅行〉はどうでしたか。
ジョン：^A-2 ^A-3〈つまらなかった〉です／でした。
田中　：そうですか。

Tanaka : Jon-san, ^A-1< ryokō > wa dō deshita ka.
Jon　　: ^A-2 ^A-3< Tsumaranakatta > desu/deshita.
Tanaka : Sō desu ka.

> Tanaka : Jon-san, how was your trip?
> John　 : It was boring.
> Tanaka : Was it?

MEMO

それはよかったですね。／Sore wa yokatta desu ne.／*That's good. / I'm glad to hear that.*

* There are two types of adjectives in Japanese, i-adjectives and na-adjectives, both of which conjugate differently. Practice A-2 describes i-adjectives, while na-adjectives are taken up in Practice A-3. ／→ See p.129
* 日本語の形容詞には「い形容詞」「な形容詞」の２つがあり、それぞれ活用の形が異なります。Practice A-2は「い形容詞」、Practice A-3は「な形容詞」の練習です。

UNIT 9

Dialogue

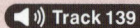 Track 139

Practice having a conversation by replacing the words (1)–(5) with the words below. You can expand part of the conversation using the information on the right page.
(1)–(5)をピンクの枠内の言葉に置き換えて会話練習をしましょう。　の部分には右ページの情報を使ってみてください。

佐藤　：(1)週末はどうでしたか。

カレン：すごく (2)楽しかったです。
　　　　はじめて(3)京都に行きました。
　　　　京都の町はとてもよかったです。

佐藤　：そうですか。
　　　　(4)日本のお寺はどうですか。

カレン：とても (5)きれいです。

Satō　 : (1)Shūmatsu wa dō deshita ka.

Karen : Sugoku (2)tanoshikatta desu.
　　　　Hajimete (3)Kyōto ni ikimashita.
　　　　Kyōto no machi wa totemo yokatta desu.

Satō　 : Sō desu ka.
　　　　(4)Nihon no otera wa dō desu ka.

Karen : Totemo (5)kirei desu.

---

① (1) 昨日のパーティー　　　　kinō no pātī
　 (2) よかった　　　　　　　　yokatta
　 (3) お好み焼きを食べました　okonomiyaki o tabemashita
　 (4) 日本料理　　　　　　　　Nihon ryōri
　 (5) おいしい　　　　　　　　oishii

② (1) 休み　　　　　　　　　　yasumi (= *holiday/day off*)
　 (2) おもしろかった　　　　　omoshirokatta
　 (3) カラオケに行きました　　karaoke ni ikimashita
　 (4) 日本のカラオケ　　　　　Nihon no karaoke
　 (5) すばらしい　　　　　　　subarashii (= *wonderful*)

③ Make your own conversation.
　 自分で会話を作ってみましょう。

MEMO

はじめて / hajimete / *for the first time*

お寺 / otera / *temple*

Material

Look at the picture below and practice the conversation on the left page.
下記の絵を見ながら左ページの会話練習をしてください。

Ex.

カレン／Karen

京都に行きました。Kyōto ni ikimashita.
- 町 machi (*town*) → よかった yokatta
- 食べ物 tabemono (*food*) → おいしかった oishikatta
- 京都の人 Kyōto no hito (*people in Kyoto*) → やさしかった yasashikatta (*kind*)

①

ジョン／Jon

お好み焼きを食べました。okonomiyaki o tabemashita.
- お好み焼き okonomiyaki → おいしかった oishikatta
- 店 mise (*shop*) → 小さかった chiisakatta (*small*)
- 店の人 mise no hito (*shop staff*) → 元気 genki (*energetic*)

②

クマール／Kumāru

カラオケに行きました。karaoke ni ikimashita.
- 料金 ryōkin (*fee, price*) → 高かった takakatta
- 日本の歌 Nihon no uta (*Japanese songs*) → むずかしかった muzukashikatta
- カラオケ karaoke → 楽しかった tanoshikatta

③

You

_____ました。
mashita.

_____は_____です／でした。
wa　　　　　desu/deshita.

→ ***See Appendix p.6, Adjective Conjugation List***
別冊語彙表p.6「形容詞活用リスト」参照

Listening

Listen to the conversation between the man and woman and choose the correct answer.
男の人と女の人の会話を聞いて正しい答えを選んでください。

Q1 Two friends are talking after not seeing each other for a while
1. The woman enjoys her life in Japan.
2. The woman's apartment is very expensive.
3. Tokyo is very beautiful.

Q3 Two friends are talking
1. The hotel was quiet.
2. The man had a good trip.
3. The man was very busy on his trip.

Q2 Two co-workers are talking at work
1. The food was neither good nor bad.
2. The party at the izakaya was neither good nor bad.
3. The party at the izakaya was fun.

Q4 Two friends are talking
1. Japanese temples are beautiful.
2. Japanese temples are expensive.
3. Japanese temples are old.

Role playing

Role play using the cards below.
下記のカードを使ってロールプレイしてください。

1.

A: You went on a trip last week. Tell B-san what you thought of your trip (think of the place you went on your own).

B: Ask A-san questions about his/her trip, such as how was the weather, food, and hotel. Also, if possible, ask what A-san did on the trip.

2.

A: You have recently moved to a town in Japan. Tell B-san what you think of it (talk about where you currently live).
new=atarashii, town=machi, house/your place=uchi

B: A-san has recently moved. Ask about A-san's new town (=atarashii machi), house (=uchi), and what life is like there.

Do you remember?

Use the phrases you have studied in this unit in situations ①–③ below.
このユニットで学習したフレーズを下記の①〜③の状況に合わせて使ってください。

Phrases for This Unit

Unit Phrases

- 日本の生活はどうですか。 | Nihon no seikatsu wa dō desu ka. | *How do you like living in Japan?*
- 旅行はどうでしたか。 | Ryokō wa dō deshita ka. | *How was your trip?*

Useful expressions

- それはよかったですね。 | Sore wa yokatta desune. | *That's good. / I'm glad to hear that.*
- すごく | sugoku | *very* [casual]
- とても | totemo | *very* [polite]
- はじめて | hajimete | *for the first time*

Check! Now I can...

- ☐ Talk about my life in Japan
  日本での生活について話せる

- ☐ Talk about my impression of things that happened in the past
  過去の経験について自分の感想が話せる

Remember and Use!

● I-adjective conjugations ● い形容詞の活用形

	Non-past	Past
Affirmative	_____いです _____i desu	_____かったです _____katta desu
Negative	_____くないです _____kunai desu	_____くなかったです _____kunakatta desu

→ **See p.176, Grammar**
 p.176を参照

NOTE

The i-adjective "いい ii" conjugates irregularly.
「いい」の活用は以下のようになります。

	Non-past	Past
Affirmative	いいです ii desu	よかったです yokatta desu
Negative	よくないです yokunai desu	よくなかったです yokunakatta desu

● 10 Basic i-adjectives ● 基本のい形容詞10

hot あつい atsui		*cold* [weather] 寒い samui	
big 大きい ōkii		*small* 小さい chiisai	
expensive / high 高い takai		*cheap* 安い yasui	
difficult むずかしい muzukashii	*easy / kind* やさしい yasashii	*fun / interesting* おもしろい omoshiroi	*delicious / tasty* おいしい oishii

→ **See Appendix p.6, Adjective Conjugation List**
 形容詞の活用形リストは別冊語彙集のp.6を参照

UNIT 9

● Na-adjective conjugations   な形容詞の活用形

	Non-past	Past
Affirmative	＿＿＿です ＿＿＿desu	＿＿＿でした ＿＿＿deshita
Negative	＿＿＿じゃありません ＿＿＿ja arimasen	＿＿＿じゃありませんでした ＿＿＿ja arimasendeshita

● Basic na-adjectives 4   基本のな形容詞4

convenient	*clean / beautiful*	*quiet*	*energetic / fine*
便利（べんり）　benri	きれい　kirei	静か（しず）　shizuka	元気（げんき）　genki

1. Make affirmative and negative sentences in different tenses.
異なる時制の肯定文・否定文を作ってください。

Ex.　日本語はむずかしくないです。　　　　Nihon-go wa muzukashikunai desu.
　　　京都は静かでした。　　　　　　　　　Kyōto wa shizuka deshita.

2. Make questions using adjectives and answer them.
形容詞を使って質問を作り、それに答えてください。

Ex.　Q: 東京はあついですか。　　　　　　　Tōkyō wa atsui desu ka.
　　　A: はい、あついです。　　　　　　　 Hai, atsui desu.
　　　　 いいえ、あつくないです。　　　　 Iie, atsukunai desu.

　　　Q: ホテルはきれいでしたか。　　　　 Hoteru wa kirei deshita ka.
　　　A: はい、きれいでした。　　　　　　 Hai, kirei deshita.
　　　　 いいえ、きれいじゃありませんでした。 Iie, kirei ja arimasendeshita.

3. Have a free conversation about the topics below. → *See pp.120-123 and Appendix*
下記のトピックについて自由に会話練習をしてください。→ p.120-123 と別冊語彙集を参照

東京（とうきょう） Tōkyō *Tokyo*	会社（かいしゃ） kaisha *your company*	うち uchi *your house*	日本語の先生（にほんごのせんせい） Nihon-go no sensei *Japanese teachers*
昨日の晩ごはん（きのうのばん） kinō no bangohan *what you had for dinner last night*	Languages you have studied	Places you have been on	Places you have lived

What does that taste like?

それ、どんな味ですか。
Sore, donna aji desu ka.

Eating
食事

GOALS FOR UNIT 10

- Understand and use taste words
  味の言葉を理解し、使う

- Say what a food probably tastes like based on its appearance
  食べ物の見た目からどんな味がしそうかを言う

- Politely refuse foods you do not like/do not eat
  好きではない / 食べられないものについて丁寧に断る

Phrase 1 — Ask what something tastes like.

> それ、どんな味(あじ)ですか。
>
> Sore, **donna aji desu ka.**
>
> *What does that taste like?*

🔊 Track 144

NOTE "**Donna**" and "**aji**" mean "**what kind of**" and "**taste**," and are used to ask what something tastes like.

「どんな」は "what kind of"、「味」は "taste" の意味で、あるものの味について尋ねる表現です。

Ex.

ジョン ：それ、**どんな**味(あじ)ですか。

田中(たなか) ：**あまい**です。おいしいですよ。

Jon ： Sore, **donna aji desu ka.**
Tanaka ： <u>Amai</u> **desu.** Oishii desu yo.

> John ： What does that taste like?
> Tanaka ： It's sweet. It tastes good.

Practice A

_____ です。

Answer the question "**Donna aji desu ka.**" using a phrase that ends in "_____ **desu.**"

下記の言葉に「_____ です」をつけて「どんな味ですか」の質問に答えてください。

🔊 Track 145

あまい amai *sweet*	からい karai *spicy / hot*	すっぱい suppai *sour*
しょっぱい shoppai *salty*	にがい nigai *bitter*	油(あぶら)っこい aburakkoi *oily*
あまからい amakarai *sweet and salty*	さっぱりした味(あじ) sapparishita aji *refreshing taste*	おもしろい味(あじ) omoshiroi aji *interesting taste*

おいしい	おいしくない	味（あじ）があまりない
oishii	oishikunai	aji ga amari nai
delicious/good	*not delicious/not good*	*doesn't taste like much*

Practice B

Put the words from Practice A in < > and practice having a conversation.
→ See Pre-text p. i - viii for additional food words.

🔊 Track 146

Practice Aの言葉を〈　　〉に入れて会話練習をしてください。
→他の食べ物の言葉は 巻頭写真を参照。

— At a restaurant — レストランで

クマール：それ、どんな味（あじ）ですか。
田中（たなか）：〈あまい〉ですよ。食（た）べてみますか。
クマール：じゃ、食（た）べてみます。／いいえ、いいです。

Kumāru : Sore, donna aji desu ka
Tanaka : < Amai > desu yo. Tabete mimasu ka.
Kumāru : Ja, tabete mimasu. / Iie, ii desu.

> Kumar: What does that taste like?
> Tanaka: It's sweet. Would you like to try it?
> Kumar: I think I will. / No, that's okay.

MEMO

食（た）べてみますか。／ Tabete mimasu ka. / *Would you like to try it?*
[used for food　食べ物に対して使います。]

食（た）べてみます。／ Tabete mimasu. / *I'll have a taste. / I'll try it.*
[used for food　食べ物に対して使います。]

いいえ、いいです。／ Iie, ii desu. / *No, that's okay.*

Phrase 2

Say what a food probably tastes like based on its appearance.

🔊 Track 147

おいしそうですね。

Oishisō desu ne.   *That looks delicious.*

> **NOTE** "_____ sō desu." means "(That) looks _____." and can be used to describe something based on its physical appearance. The final **"i"** or **"na"** of an adjective is removed before being attached to **"sō desu."**
>
> 「_____そうです」は"(That) looks _____"の意味で、あるものの見かけからその印象を言う表現です。「_____そうです」の前にくる形容詞は[い形容詞]の場合、最後の「い」を除き、[な形容詞]の場合、最後の「な」を除いた形になります。

Ex.

ジョン ：おいしそうですね。

田中(たなか) ：そうですね。

Jon : Oishisō desu ne.
Tanaka : Sō desu ne.

> John : That looks delicious.
> Tanaka : It really does.

Practice A

_____そうです。
Change the **"i"** portion of the follwing words to "_____ sō desu."
下記の言葉の「い」の部分を「_____そうです」に合うよう変えてください。

🔊 Track 148

おいし(い)	あつ(い)	から(い)
oishi(i)	atsu(i)	kara(i)
delicious	*hot*	*spicy/hot*

あま(い)	まず(い)	すっぱ(い)
ama(i)	mazu(i)	suppa(i)
sweet	*gross/bad*	*sour*

やわらか(い)	油っこ(い) あぶら	体によさ* からだ
yawaraka(i)	aburakko(i)	karada ni yosa*
soft	*oily*	*healthy/good for you*

* The adjective **"ii"** (good) conjugates exceptionally to **"yosasō desu."**
* 「いい」の活用形は例外で、「よさそう」になります。

134

Put the words from Practice A in < > and practice having a conversation.
Practice Aの言葉を〈 〉に入れて会話練習をしてください。　🔊 Track 149

- Looking at a menu at a restaurant -　レストランでメニューを見ながら

佐藤（さとう）：何（なん）にしますか。これはどうですか。
ジョン：うーん、ちょっと〈油（あぶら）っこ〉そうですね。
佐藤（さとう）：じゃ、これはどうですか。
ジョン：うん、〈おいし〉そうですね。
佐藤（さとう）：じゃ、これにしましょう。

Satō : Nan ni shimasu ka. Kore wa dō desu ka.	Sato : What should we get? How about this?
Jon : Ūn, chotto < aburakko > sō desu ne.	John : Hm, that looks a little oily.
Satō : Ja, kore wa dō desu ka.	Sato : Then how about this?
Jon : Un, < oishi >sō desu ne.	John : Yeah, that looks good.
Satō : Ja, kore ni shimashō.	Sato : Okay, let's get this, then.

MEMO

何（なん）にしますか。／ Nan ni shimasu ka. ／ *What are we/you going to have?*

これはどうですか。／ Kore wa dō desu ka. ／ *How about this?*

ちょっと〜そうですね。／ Chotto …sō desu ne. ／ *It looks a little ….*

これにしましょう。／ Kore ni shimashō. ／ *Let's have this.*

Phrase 3

Politely refuse foods you do not like.

豚肉(ぶたにく)**はちょっと……**。

Butaniku **wa chotto……** . *I can't really eat pork.*

Track 150

> **NOTE** "____ **wa chotto……** ." can be used to convey negative feelings, with an implication that you don't like or don't want to do something. Follow a "**wa chotto……** ." statement with a reason followed by " ____ **nan desu**" to provide a polite explanation.
>
> 「____はちょっと」は、否定的なニュアンスを持ち、それが好きではない、あるいはしたくないと、暗に伝えることができる表現です。「____はちょっと」のあとには「____なんです」という理由の説明文をつけ加えます。

Ex.

田中(たなか)　：これ、おいしいですよ。

クマール：すみません。豚肉(ぶたにく)はちょっと……。
　　　　　ベジタリアンなんです。

Tanaka　：Kore, oishii desu yo.
Kumāru　：Sumimasen. Butaniku **wa chotto……** .
　　　　　Bejitarian nan desu.

Tanaka : This is really good.
Kumar : I'm sorry, but I can't eat pork.
*　　　　(The thing is) I'm a vegetarian.*

Practice A-1

____はちょっと……。

Use the following words with the phrase "____ **wa chotto……** ."
下記の言葉を使って「____はちょっと」のフレーズを練習してください。

Track 151

| 豚肉(ぶたにく) butaniku — pork | 牛肉(ぎゅうにく) gyūniku — beef | 卵(たまご) tamago — egg | 生もの(なま) namamono — raw food |
| わさび wasabi → See Pre-text p.iv | シーフード shīfūdo — seafood | からいもの karai mono — spicy things | あまいもの amai mono — sweet things |

136

Practice A-2 Explain why you can't eat the foods in Practice A-1 using the following words with the phrase _____ **nandesu.**
Practice A-1 の食べ物が食べられない理由を「＿＿＿なんです」に下記の言葉を入れて説明してください。

🔊 Track 152

ベジタリアン	アレルギー	苦手（にがて）	宗教（しゅうきょう）でだめ
bejitarian	arerugī	nigate	shūkyō de dame
vegitarian	*allergy*	*do not really like / not good at*	*for religious reasons*

Practice B Put the words from Practice A-1 or A-2 in < > and practice having a conversation.
Practice A-1 やA-2の言葉を〈　〉に入れて会話練習をしてください。

🔊 Track 153

田中（たなか）　：これ、どうですか。
クマール　：A-1〈豚肉（ぶたにく）〉ですか。A-1〈豚肉（ぶたにく）〉はちょっと……。
田中（たなか）　：そうなんですか。
クマール　：はい、A-2〈苦手（にがて）〉なんです。

Tanaka　　: Kore, dō desu ka.
Kumāru　 : A-1< Butaniku > desu ka.
　　　　　　　A-1< Butaniku > wa chotto...... .
Tanaka　　: Sō nan desu ka.
Kumāru　 : Hai, A-2< nigate > nan desu.

> *Tanaka : How about this?*
> *Kumar : Is it pork? I can't eat pork.*
> *Tanaka : Oh really?*
> *Kumar : Yes, I don't care for the taste.*

MEMO

そうなんですか。／ Sō nan desu ka. ／ *Oh really? / Is that so?*
[indicates a feeling of surprise　驚きを示します。]

UNIT 10

Dialogue

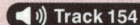 Track 154

Replace the words in (1) – (4) below and practice having a conversation.
(1)〜(4)の言葉をピンクの枠内の言葉に置き換えて会話練習をしてください。

ジョン：(1)<u>肉じゃが</u>って、どんな味ですか。	Jon ：(1) <u>Nikujaga</u> tte donna aji desu ka.
鈴木：(2)<u>あまい</u>ですよ。おいしいです。	Suzuki：(2) <u>Amai</u> desu yo. Oishii desu.
ジョン：そうですか。 *Pointing at another food* これは(3)<u>からそう</u>ですね。	Jon ：Sō desu ka. *Pointing at another food* Kore wa (3) <u>karasō</u> desu ne.
鈴木：ええ、(4)<u>からい</u>ですよ。	Suzuki：Ee, (4) <u>karai</u> desu yo.
ジョン：そうですか。(4)<u>からい</u>ものはちょっと……。苦手なんです。	Jon ：Sō desu ka. (4) <u>Karai</u> mono wa chotto... . Nigate nan desu.
鈴木：じゃ、他のにしましょう。これは？	Suzuki：Ja, hoka no ni shimashō. Kore wa?
ジョン：おいしそうですね。	Jon ：Oishisō desu ne.
鈴木：じゃ、これにしましょう。	Suzuki：Ja, kore ni shimashō.

① (1) こんにゃく　　　　　　　konnyaku (→ See Pre-text p.iv)
　(2) 味があまりない　　　　　aji ga amari nai
　(3) 油っこそう　　　　　　　aburakkosō
　(4) 油っこい　　　　　　　　aburakkoi

② (1) うめぼし　　　　　　　　umeboshi (→ See Pre-text p.iii)
　(2) すっぱい　　　　　　　　suppai
　(3) あまそう　　　　　　　　amasō
　(4) あまい　　　　　　　　　amai

MEMO

〜って／...tte → See p.55 MEMO
もの／mono／*thing(s)*
他のにしましょう。／Hoka no ni shimashō.／*Let's have something else/another one.*
これにしましょう。／Kore ni shimashō.／*Let's have this.*

Listening

Listen to the conversation between the man and woman and choose the correct answer.
男の人と女の人の会話を聞いて正しい答えを選んでください。

Q1 Pointing at the food on the table

1. The food is spicy.
2. The food is refreshing.
3. The food is sour.

Q3 Looking at a menu

1. The salad looks oily.
2. The salad looks light.
3. The salad looks healthy.

Q2 Looking at the food on the next table

1. The man wants to order beef.
2. The man doesn't like beef.
3. The man is going to try the beef.

Q4 Looking at a menu

1. They will order spicy food.
2. They will not order spicy food.
3. They will not order anything.

Role playing

Role play using the cards below
下記のカードを使ってロールプレイしてください。

A: You are at an izakaya with B-san. Ask what dish B-san recommends, then ask what it tastes like, give a reason why you cannot eat it, and refuse the food.

B: You are at an izakaya with A-san. Look at the menu in the pre-text and recommend your favorite food.

UNIT 10

Do you remember?

Use the phrases you have studied in this unit in situations ①–③ below.
このユニットで学習したフレーズを下記の①〜③の状況に合わせて使ってください。

Phrases for This Unit

Unit Phrases

- それ、どんな味ですか。 — Sore, donna aji desu ka. — *What does it taste like?*
- おいしそうですね。 — Oishisō desu ne. — *It looks delicious.*
- 豚肉はちょっと……。 — Butaniku wa chotto....... . — *I can't really eat pork.*

Useful expressions

- 食べてみますか。 — Tabete mimasu ka. — *Would you like to try it?* [used with food]
- 食べてみます。 — Tabete mimasu. — *I'll have a taste.* [used with food]
- いいえ、いいです。 — Iie, ii desu. — *No, that's okay.*
- これにしましょう。 — Kore ni shimashō. — *Let's have this.*
- 苦手なんです。 — Nigate nan desu. — *I'm not good at it.* [a common refusal]
- そうなんですか。 — Sō nan desu ka. — *Oh, really? / Is that so?* [indicates surprise]

Check!

Now I can...

☐ **Understand and use taste words**
味の言葉を理解し、使える

☐ **Say what a food probably tastes like based on its appearance**
食べ物の見た目からどんな味がしそうかが言える

☐ **Politely refuse foods I do not like/do not eat**
好きではない / 食べられないものについて丁寧に断れる

UNIT 10

Good to Know

Common menu "*kanji*"

Ingredients 食材

1. 豚肉
butaniku / *pork*

2. 牛肉
gyūniku / *beef*

3. 鶏肉（鳥肉）
toriniku / *chicken*

4. 卵（玉子）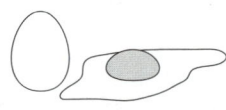
tamago / *egg*

5. 魚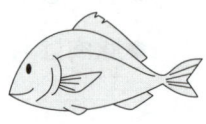
sakana / *fish*

6. 貝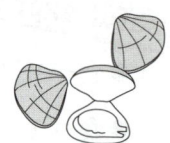
kai / *shellfish*

7. 野菜
yasai / *vegetables*

8. 豆腐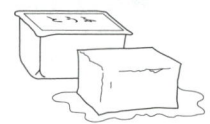
tōfu / *tofu*

Cooking Method 調理法

1. 焼く
ya-ku / *grill*

2. 炒める
ita-meru / *stir-fry*

3. 揚げる
a-geru / *deep fry*

4. 蒸す
mu-su / *steam*

5. 煮る
ni-ru / *boil, simmer*

6. 温かい
atata-kai / *warm*

7. 冷たい
tsume-tai / *cold*

It's nice weather today, isn't it?

今日（きょう）はいい天気（てんき）ですね。
Kyō wa ii tenki desu ne.

Socializing I - Making Small Talk
世間話をする

GOALS FOR UNIT 11

- Start a conversation after saying hello
  挨拶して会話を始める

- Make simple small talk by asking about a person's family and job
  家族や仕事について世間話をする

- Learn other ways to say goodbye than *sayōnara*
  「さようなら」以外の別れの挨拶を学ぶ

Phrase 1 — Have a simple conversation about the weather.

🔊 Track 159

今日はいい天気ですね。
きょう　　　てんき

Kyō wa ii tenki desu ne.

It's nice weather today, isn't it?

> **NOTE** "____desu ne." is frequently used when the speaker feels like the listener will agree with what he or she is saying.
>
> 「____ですね」は話し手が、聞き手も同意するであろう事柄について言及する時に使われます。

Ex.

ジョン　：今日はいい天気ですね。
　　　　　　きょう　　　てんき

田中　　：そうですね。
たなか

Jon　　　: **Kyō wa ii tenki desu ne.**
Tanaka　: Sō desu ne.

> John　　: It's nice weather today, isn't it?
> Tanaka : It sure is.

Practice A

今日は____ですね。
きょう

Use the following words with the phrase "**Kyō wa ____ desu ne.**"

下記の言葉を使って「今日は____ですね」のフレーズを練習してください。

🔊 Track 160

いい天気 (ii tenki) — good weather	嫌な天気 (iyana tenki) — bad weather	雨 (ame) — rain
蒸し暑い (mushiatsui) — humid / muggy	風が強い (kaze ga tsuyoi) — windy 	暑い (atsui) — hot 
寒い (samui) — cold	暖かい* (atatakai*) — warm	涼しい (suzushii) — cool 

* "**Atatakai**" is frequently abbreviated to "**attakai**" in casual conversation.
* くだけた会話文の中では、「あたたかい」は「あったかい」と発音されることが多いです。

Practice B

Put the words from Practice A in < > and practice having a conversation.
Practice Aの言葉を〈　〉に入れて会話練習をしてください。

🔊 Track 161

-John-san runs into the janitor of his apartment building on his way out-
ジョンさんはアパートを出た時に、管理人に会いました

ジョン　　：おはようございます。

管理人　　：おはようございます。

ジョン　　：今日**は**〈いい天気〉ですね。／今日**も**〈いい天気〉ですね。

管理人　　：そうですね。最近／毎日、〈暑い〉ですね。

ジョン　　：本当ですね。じゃ、いってきます。

管理人　　：いってらっしゃい。

Jon	: Ohayō gozaimasu.
Kanri-nin	: Ohayō gozaimasu.
Jon	: Kyō wa < ii tenki > desu ne. / Kyō mo <ii tenki> desu ne.
Kanri-nin	: Sō desu ne. Saikin / Mainichi < atsui > desu ne.
Jon	: Hontō desu ne. Ja, ittekimasu.
Kanri-nin	: Itterasshai.

John	: Good morning.
Janitor	: Good morning.
John	: It's nice weather today, isn't it? / The weather is nice again today, isn't it?
Janitor	: It sure is. It's been hot lately/everyday.
John	: It sure has. See you later.
Janitor	: Have a nice day.

MEMO

毎日／mainichi／*everyday*

最近／saikin／*lately / most recent*

本当ですね。／Hontō desu ne.／*It really is. / I'll say.*

いってらっしゃい。／Itterasshai.／*Have a nice day.*
　　　　　　[said to someone who is leaving　その場を去る人に対して言うことばです。]

いってきます。／Ittekimasu.／*See you later.*
　　　　　　[said by a person about to leave　その場を去る人が言うことばです。]

UNIT 11

Phrase 2

Talk about how you have been recently.

🔊 Track 162

最近、仕事はどうですか。
さいきん　しごと

Saikin, shigoto wa dō desu ka.   *How has your job been lately?*

NOTE "Saikin ____ wa dō desu ka" means "How has [topic] been lately?" The phrase "Saikin, dō desu ka." is also often used to ask a person how they have been.

「最近、____はどうですか」は "How has [topic] been lately?" という意味です。「最近、どうですか」とだけ言えば、今までどうしていたか（元気だったかどうか）を尋ねる文になります。

Ex.

佐藤　：最近、仕事はどうですか。
さとう　　さいきん　しごと

ジョン：順調です。
　　　じゅんちょう

Satō : **Saikin, shigoto wa dō desu ka.**
Jon : Junchō desu.

Sato : How has your work been lately?
John : It's been going well.

Practice A-1

最近、____はどうですか。
さいきん

Use the following words with the phrase " **Saikin, ____ wa dō desu ka.** "

下記の言葉を使って「最近、____はどうですか」のフレーズを練習しましょう。

🔊 Track 163

| 仕事
しごと
shigoto
job / work | 調子
ちょうし
chōshi
condition | ご家族
かぞく
go-kazoku
(your) family | 学校／勉強
がっこう／べんきょう
gakkō / benkyō
school / study |

Practice A-2

____です。

Answer the questions above with the following words followed by " ____ desu."

下記の言葉に「____です」をつけて上記の質問に答えてください。

🔊 Track 164

順調 じゅんちょう junchō *going well*	元気 げんき genki *fine*	楽しい たの tanoshii *fun / enjoyable*
忙しい いそが isogashii *busy* 	まあまあ māmā *so-so*	大変 たいへん taihen *hard / tough*

Practice B — Put the words from Practice A-1 and A-2 in < > and practice having a conversation.
Practice A-1とA-2の言葉を〈 〉に入れて会話練習をしてください。 🔊 Track 165

-John-san runs into his former teacher- ジョンさんは昔の先生に偶然会いました

ジョン ：先生、お久しぶりです。
先生　 ：あ、ジョンさん。お久しぶりです。お元気ですか。
ジョン ：はい、おかげさまで。
先生　 ：最近、A-1〈仕事〉はどうですか。
ジョン ：おかげさまでA-2〈順調〉です。
　　　　 先生はいかがですか。
先生　 ：私もA-2〈順調〉ですよ。／A-2〈忙しい〉ですよ。

Jon   : Sensei, ohisashiburi desu.
Sensei : A, Jon-san, ohisashiburi desu.
          O-genki desu ka.
Jon   : Hai, okagesama de.
Sensei : Saikin, A-1< shigoto > wa dō desuka.
Jon   : Okagesama de A-2< junchō > desu.
          Sensei wa ikaga desu ka.
Sensei : Watashi mo A-2< junchō > desu yo.
          / A-2< Isogashii > desu yo.

John   : Sensei, I haven't seen you for quite a while.
Former teacher: Oh, John-san, it has been a long time.
                How are you doing?
John   : I'm doing well, thank you.
Former teacher: How has your work been?
John   : It's been going well, fortunately.
                How about you?
Former teacher: I've been well. / I've been busy.

MEMO

お久しぶりです。／Ohisashiburi desu. ／*Long time no see. / It's been a while.*

おかげさまで。／Okagesama de. ／*Thanks to you.*
[an expression of gratitude indebting a person for your success, health, and wellbeing; often used as a term of greeting to strengthen human relations even when no favors have been exchanged
自分自身の成功や健康、幸福において恩義を感じている人へ感謝の意を表します。実際にお世話になっていなくても人間関係を築くための挨拶表現として使うこともあります。]

いかがですか。／Ikaga desu ka. ／*How about you?*
[a polite way of saying "dō desu ka."「どうですか」の丁寧な表現です。]

UNIT 11

Phrase 3 — Use natural-sounding Japanese when saying goodbye.

🔊 Track 166

じゃ、また。

Ja, mata.

See you later.

NOTE **"Ja,"** a contraction of **"dewa,"** is used to mean **"well"** or **"then"** to end a topic of conversation. **"Ja"** is also used in modern Japanese as a way to say goodbye, akin to **"see you"** in English.

「じゃ」は「では」の縮約形です。「では」は、"well" や "then" を意味し、会話を終わらせる機能を持つ表現です。「じゃ」は、英語の "See you" のように、立ち去る時の挨拶表現としても使われます。

Ex.

ジョン ：**じゃ、<u>また</u>**。

佐藤(さとう)：じゃ、また来週(らいしゅう)。

Jon : **Ja,** <u>mata</u>.
Satō : Ja, mata raishū.

John : See you later.
Sato : See you next week.

Practice A

じゃ、_____。

Use the following words with the phrase **"Ja, _____."**

下記の言葉を使って「じゃ、_____」のフレーズを練習してください。

🔊 Track 167

また mata *See you (later).* 	また来週(らいしゅう) mata raishū *See you next week.*	また今度(こんど) mata kondo *See you next time.*
また後(あと)で*¹ mata atode*¹ *See you later.*	お大事(だいじ)に o-daiji ni *Get well soon.*	気(き)をつけて ki o tsukete *Take care.*
(お先(さき)に*²)失礼(しつれい)します (o-saki ni*²) shitsurei shimasu *Goodbye.*	また連絡(れんらく)します mata renraku shimasu *I'll be in touch (soon).*	お元気(げんき)で o-genki de *Be well. / Take care of yourself.*

＊1 The phrase **"mata ato de"** is used when you expect to see a person later that day or within a similar time interval.
＊1 「またあとで」は、その日のうち、あるいは一定期間内に再度会うことが期待される場合に使います。
＊2 The phrase **"o-saki ni"** means **"before you."** **"Shitsurei shimasu"** is often used as a way to say goodbye when leaving work before other people or when exiting a meeting, and is frequently shortened to **"o-saki ni"** in casual conversation.
＊2 「お先に」は「あなたより先に～します」という意味です。「失礼します」は、他の人より先に退社する時や、会議から退出する際に「さようなら」の意味で使われる表現です。くだけた会話の中では「お先に」という短縮形で使うことも多いです。

Practice B

Use words from practice A in < > to practice having a conversation.
* Choose words suitable for the situation.
Practice Aの言葉を〈　〉に入れて会話練習をしてください。
＊状況に合わせた言葉を選んでください。

🔊 Track 168

① Leaving work before co-worker Tanaka-san
同僚の田中さんより先に帰る時

ジョン　：じゃ、〈　　　　　〉。
田中（たなか）：おつかれさまでした。

Jon　　　: Ja, <　　>.
Tanaka　: Otsukaresama deshita.

John　　: See you <　>.
Tanaka : Goodbye.

② To a friend who is ill
病気の友達に

ジョン　：じゃ、〈　　　　　〉。
佐藤（さとう）：ありがとう。

Jon　　: Ja, <　　>.
Satō　　: Arigatō.

John　　: <　>.
Sato　　: Thank you.

③ To a friend you will not see for a long time
この後しばらく会う予定のない友達に

ジョン　：じゃ、〈　　　　　〉。
友達（ともだち）：〈　　　　　〉。

Jon　　　　: Ja, <　　>.
Tomodachi : <　　>.

John　: <　>.
Friend : <　>.

UNIT 11

MEMO

おつかれさまでした。／Otsukaresama deshita. ／ *Good work today. / Goodbye.*

["Otsukaresama deshita" is a greeting used in the workplace instead of *"Goodbye."*
「おつかれさまでした」は職場で「さようなら(goodbye)」の代わりに使う挨拶表現です。]

149

Dialogue

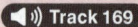

Have a practice conversation replacing the words in (1) - (5).
(1)〜(5)の言葉をピンクの枠内の言葉に置き換えて会話練習をしてください。

- At a party - パーティーで

田中 ：こんにちは。今日は(1)寒いですね。
クマール：本当ですね。
　　　　最近、(2)お仕事はどうですか。
田中 ：(3)順調です。クマールさんは？
クマール：(4)忙しいです。

- Later - 数時間後

クマール：すみません、
　　　　今日はそろそろ帰ります。
田中 ：そうですか。じゃ、気をつけて。
クマール：じゃ、(5)また。

- At a party -

Tanaka ： Konnichiwa. Kyō wa (1)samui desu ne.
Kumāru ： Hontō desu ne.
　　　　Saikin, (2)o-shigoto wa dō desu ka.
Tanaka ： (3)Junchō desu. Kumāru-san wa?
Kumāru ： (4)Isogashii desu.

- Later -

Kumāru ： Sumimasen,
　　　　kyō wa sorosoro kaerimasu.
Tanaka ： Sō desu ka. Ja, ki o tsukete.
Kumāru ： Ja, (5)mata.

①
(1) 暑い — atsui
(2) 調子 — chōshi
(3) まあまあ — māmā
(4) 私もまあまあ — watashi mo māmā
(5) また来週 — mata rai-shū

②
(1) いやな天気 — iyana tenki
(2) ご家族 — go-kazoku
(3) 元気 — genki
(4) うちもみんな元気 — uchi mo minna genki
(5) お先に失礼します — o-saki ni shitsurei shimasu

MEMO
そろそろ帰ります。／Sorosoro kaerimasu.／*I have to leave now.*
うちもみんな元気です。／Uchi mo minna genki desu.／*Everyone at home is doing well.*

Listening

Listen to the conversation between the man and woman and choose the correct answer.
男の人と女の人の会話を聞いて正しい答えを選んでください。

Q1 Two neighbors are talking in the morning

1. It's hot everyday.
2. It's cool everyday.
3. It's warm everyday.

Q2 Two colleagues from different departments are talking

1. The woman is busy.
2. The woman is not doing well.
3. The man is busy.

Q3 At work

1. The woman is leaving now.
2. The man is leaving now.
3. The man and woman are meeting tomorrow.

Q4 Two friends are talking after not seeing each other for a while

1. The man isn't doing too well.
2. The man is doing well.
3. The man is coming down with a cold.

Role playing

Role play using the cards below.
下記のカードを使ってロールプレイしてください

1.

A: You run into B-san, your former co-worker, whom you haven't seen for a long time. Ask B-san how his/her job and family have been.

B: You run into A-san, former co-worker, whom you haven't seen for a long time. Ask how A-san is doing.

2.

A: You run into your neighbor B-san on the street. Talk about how the weather has been recently and say goodbye.

B: You run into your neighbor A-san on the street. Say hello.

UNIT 11

Do you remember?

Use the phrases you have studied in this unit in situations ①–③ below.
このユニットで学習したフレーズを下記の①〜③の状況に合わせて使ってください。

①

②

③

Phrases for This Unit

Unit Phrases

- 今日はいい天気ですね。　　Kyō wa ii tenki desu ne.　　*It's nice weather today, isn't it?*
- 最近、仕事はどうですか。　Saikin, shigoto wa dō desu ka.　*How has your job been lately?*
- じゃ、また。　　　　　　　Ja, mata.　　　　　　　　　　*See you later.*

Useful expressions

- 本当ですね。　　　　　　　Hontō desu ne.　　　　　　　*It really is. / I'll say.*
- おつかれさまでした。　　　Otsukaresama deshita.　　　*Good work today. / Goodbye.*
- お久しぶりです。　　　　　Ohisashiburi desu.　　　　　*Long time no see. / It's been a while.*
- そろそろ帰ります。　　　　Sorosoro kaerimasu.　　　　*I have to leave now.*

Check!

✓ Now I can...

- ☐ **Start a conversation after saying hello**
  挨拶して会話を始められる

- ☐ **Make simple small talk by asking about a person's family and job**
  家族や仕事について世間話ができる

- ☐ **Learn other ways to say goodbye than *sayōnara***
  「さようなら」以外の別れの挨拶が言える

UNIT 11

One More Step

● Talking about the weather 天気について話す

Month	Season	Temperature/Feel	Weather
3-gatsu *Mar.*		あたたかい atatakai *warm*	晴れ はれ hare *sunny*
4-gatsu *Apr.*	春 はる haru *spring*	さわやかな天気ですね。 Sawayaka na tenki desu ne. *It's nice (balmy) outside today.*	
5-gatsu *May*			くもり kumori *cloudy*
6-gatsu *Jun.*	梅雨 つゆ tsuyu *rainy season*	蒸し暑い む あつ mushiatsui *humid*	
7-gatsu *Jul.*			雨 あめ ame *rain*
8-gatsu *Aug.*	夏 なつ natsu *summer*	暑い あつ atsui *hot*	雷 かみなり kaminari *thunder*
9-gatsu *Sep.*		涼しい すず suzushii *cool*	
10-gatsu *Oct.*	秋 あき aki *autumn*	気持ちいい天気ですね。 き も Kimochi ii tenki desu ne. *It feels so nice.*	台風 たいふう taifū *typhoon*
11-gatsu *Nov.*			
12-gatsu *Dec.*			風 かぜ kaze *wind*
1-gatsu *Jan.*	冬 ふゆ fuyu *winter*	寒い さむ samui *cold*	雪 ゆき yuki *snow*
2-gatsu *Feb.*			

→ See p.104, Calendar

Would you like to have a cup of tea?

お茶を飲みませんか。
Ocha o nomimasen ka.

Socializing II - Invitations -
誘う

GOALS FOR UNIT 12

- Talk about your own experiences and ask about those of others
  自分の経験について話したり、他の人の経験について尋ねたりする

- Invite a person to do or have something
  人を誘ったり、何かを勧めたりする

- Accept and refuse invitations
  誘いを受けたり、断わったりする

Phrase 1 — Invite a friend or co-worker to do something.

🔊 Track 174

お茶を飲み**ませんか**。
ちゃ の

Ocha o nomi**masen ka**. *Would you like to have a cup of tea?*

> **NOTE** The negative question form of a masu verb, **"[verb-stem]masen ka,"** means "Would you like to [verb]?" or "Why don't you [verb]?" and is used when inviting someone to do something with you.
>
> 否定疑問文の「[ます形語幹]ませんか」は "Would you like to [verb]?" あるいは "Why don't you [verb]?" を意味し、何かを一緒にしようと誘う表現です。

Ex.

カレン：鈴木さん、これからお茶を飲みませんか。
　　　　すずき　　　　　　　　　ちゃ　の
鈴木　：いいですね。そうしましょう。
すずき

Karen : Suzuki-san, korekara ocha o nomi**masen ka**.
Suzuki : Ii desu ne. Sō shimashō.

> Karen : Suzuki-san, would you like to have a cup of tea right now?
> Suzuki : Sounds good. Let's do it.

Practice A-1

_____ ませんか。

Change the **"masu"** portion of the following words to **"_____ masen ka."**

下記の言葉の「ます」の部分を「_____ ませんか」に変えてください。

🔊 Track 175

お茶を飲み（ます）	サイクリングをし（ます）	映画を見（ます）
ocha o nomi(masu)	saikuringu o shi(masu)	eiga o mi(masu)
have a cup of tea [lit. drink tea]	*go cycling*	*see a movie*
ごはんを食べに行き（ます）	飲みに行き（ます）	遊びに行き（ます）
gohan o tabe ni iki(masu)	nomi ni iki(masu)	asobi ni iki(masu)
go out to eat	*go out for a drink*	*go out to have fun*

Practice A-2

Add the following words to the phrases above to make invitations using **"_____ masen ka."**

上のフレーズに下記の言葉をつけて「_____ ませんか」を使って誘ってください。

🔊 Track 176

これから	今晩	週末	明日
korekara	komban	shūmatsu	ashita
right now	*tonight*	*weekend*	*tomorrow* → See p.104, Calendar

Practice B Put the words from Practice A-1 or A-2 in < > and practice having a conversation. Fill in [ ] with the name of a place. 🔊 Track 177

Practice A-1とA-2の言葉を〈　〉に入れて会話練習をしてください。
[　]には場所の名前を入れてください。

①

鈴木　：ジョンさん、^A-2〈これから〉一緒に^A-1〈お茶を飲み〉ませんか。
ジョン：いいですね。どこに行きましょうか。
鈴木　：[　　]はどうですか。
ジョン：いいですね。そうしましょう。

Suzuki : Jon-san, ^A-2< korekara > issho ni ^A-1< ocha o nomi > masen ka.
Jon : Ii desu ne. Doko ni ikimashō ka.
Suzuki : [　] wa dō desu ka.
Jon : Ii desu ne. Sō shimashō.

Suzuki : Jon-san, would you like to get tea with me right now?
John : That sounds nice. Where should we go?
Suzuki : How does [　] sound?
John : That sounds great. Let's go there.

②

鈴木　：ジョンさん、^A-2〈明日〉一緒に^A-1〈映画を見〉ませんか。
ジョン：すみません、^A-2〈明日〉はちょっと……。
鈴木　：そうですか。じゃ、また今度。
ジョン：すみません。また誘ってください。

Suzuki : Jon-san, ^A-2< ashita > issho ni ^A-1< eiga o mi >masen ka.
Jon : Sumimasen, ^A-2< ashita > wa chotto…….
Suzuki : Sō desu ka. Ja, mata kondo.
Jon : Sumimasen. Mata sasotte kudasai.

Suzuki : Jon-san, would you like to go see a movie tomorrow?
John : I'm sorry, tomorrow's not good for me.
Suzuki : Okay. Well, next time, then.
John : Thanks. Please invite me again.

MEMO

どこに行きましょうか。／Doko ni ikimashō ka. ／ *Where should we go?*

〜はどうですか。／… wa dō desu ka. ／ *How about …? / How does … sound?*

そうしましょう。／Sō shimashō. ／ *Let's do that/it.*

〜はちょっと……。／… wa chotto…. ／ *… is no good for me.*

じゃ、また今度。／Ja, mata kondo. ／ *Well, next time, then.*

また誘ってください。／Mata sasotte kudasai. ／ *Please invite / ask me again.*
[Often said after refusing an invitation　誘いを断ったあとに使うことが多い表現です。]

UNIT 12

Phrase 2 — Talk about things you have done.

🔊 Track 178

温泉に行った**ことがありますか。**
おんせん い

Onsen ni itta koto ga arimasu ka.

Have you ever been to an onsen (hot spring)?

NOTE "**[Verb-ta] + koto ga arimasu**" means "(I) have [done...]" and is used to talk about one's experience. →*See p.173, Grammar: Ta-form*

「[た形]ことがあります」は"(I) have [done]"という意味で、経験について話す時に使われます。p.173文法ページ参照。

Ex.

田中　：温泉に行ったことがありますか。
たなか　　おんせん　い

ジョン：はい、あります。よかったですよ。

Tanaka : <u>Onsen ni itta</u> **koto ga arimasu ka.**
Jon　　: Hai, arimasu. Yokatta desu yo.

Tanaka : Have you ever been to an onsen?
John　　: Yes, I have. It was nice.

 Practice A **[verb-ta]ことがありますか。**
Use the following words with the phrase "**[verb-ta] koto ga arimasu ka.**"
下記の言葉を「[た形]ことがありますか」を使って練習してください。

🔊 Track 179

温泉に行った おんせん い onsen ni itta *went to an onsen (hot spring)*	カラオケに行った い karaoke ni itta *went to karaoke*	スノーボードをした sunō-bōdo o shita *went snowboarding*
花見をした はな み hanami o shita *went flower-viewing*	日本の花火を見た に ほん はな び み Nihon no hanabi o mita *saw Japanese fireworks*	歌舞伎を見た か ぶ き み kabuki o mita *saw kabuki* → **See Appendix**
お好み焼きを食べた この や た okonomiyaki o tabeta *ate okonomiyaki*	焼酎を飲んだ しょうちゅう の shōchū o nonda *drank shochu*	着物を着た き もの き kimono o kita *wore a kimono*

Practice B

Put the words from Practice A in < > and practice having a conversation.
Fill in [ ] with an adjective. → See Unit 9.
🔊 Track 180

Practice Aの言葉を〈　〉に入れて会話練習をしてください。
[　]には形容詞を入れてください。→ ユニット9参照。

①

佐藤：ジョンさん、〈温泉に行った〉ことがありますか。

ジョン：はい、あります。

佐藤：そうですか。どうでしたか。

ジョン：とても[よかったです]。

→ See Appendix, Adjective Conjugation List

Satō	: Jon-san, < onsen ni itta > koto ga arimasu ka.
Jon	: Hai, arimasu.
Satō	: Sō desuka. Dō deshita ka.
Jon	: Totemo [yokatta desu].

Sato	: John-san, have you ever been to an onsen hot spring?
John	: Yes, I have.
Sato	: I see. How did you like it?
John	: It was really nice.

②

佐藤：ジョンさん、〈カラオケに行った〉ことがありますか。

ジョン：いいえ、ありません。

佐藤：じゃ、今度、一緒に行きませんか。

ジョン：いいですね。そうしましょう。

Satō	: Jon-san, < karaoke ni itta > koto ga arimasu ka.
Jon	: Iie, arimasen.
Satō	: Ja, kondo, issho ni ikimasen ka.
Jon	: Ii desu ne. Sō shimashō.

Sato	: John-san, have you ever been to karaoke?
John	: No, I haven't.
Sato	: Oh, then would you like to go with me sometime?
John	: That sounds great. Let's do it.

UNIT 12

Dialogue

🔊 Track 181

Replace the words (1) - (3) and put your own answers in < > to practice having a conversation. You can also use words and grammatical devices from Unit 8 to expand ▨ part of the conversation.
(1)〜(3)の言葉をピンクの枠内の言葉に置き換え、〈　〉内に自分自身の答えを入れて会話練習をしてください。ユニット8で学んだ言葉や文型を使って、▨の部分の会話をさらに展開させることもできます。
→ See p.104, Calendar

Expand your conversation　　　　　　　　　会話を展開してみましょう

田中　：クマールさん、いつ日本に来ましたか。
クマール：〈去年の9月〉に来ました。

Tanaka　：Kumāru-san, itsu Nihon ni kimashita ka.
Kumāru　：< Kyonen no 9-gatsu > ni kimashita.

・・・

田中　：(1)花見をしたことがありますか。
クマール：いいえ、ありません。
田中　：よかったら、日曜日に(2)一緒に(3)行きませんか。
クマール：いいですね。(3)行きましょう。
田中　：じゃ、後で連絡しますね。
クマール：わかりました。楽しみにしています。

Tanaka　：(1)Hanami o shita koto ga arimasu ka.
Kumāru　：Iie, arimasen.
Tanaka　：Yokattara, nichi-yōbi ni (2)issho ni (3)ikimasen ka.
Kumāru　：Ii desu ne. (3)Ikimashō.
Tanaka　：Ja, atode renraku shimasu ne.
Kumāru　：Wakarimashita. Tanoshimi ni shite imasu.

① (1) スノーボードをした　　　　　　　　　sunō-bōdo o shita
　 (2) みんなで　　　　　　　　　　　　　　minna de
　 (3) 行き　　　　　　　　　　　　　　　　iki

② (1) 焼酎を飲んだ　　　　　　　　　　　　shōchū o nonda
　 (2) 一緒に　　　　　　　　　　　　　　　issho ni
　 (3) 飲み　　　　　　　　　　　　　　　　nomi

MEMO

よかったら／yokattara／*if you would like to, if it's alright with you*

後で連絡します。／Atode renraku shimasu.／*I will contact you/be in touch later.*

楽しみにしています。／Tanoshimi ni shite imasu.／*I'm looking forward to it.*

みんなで／minna de／*with everyone*

Listening

Listen to the conversation between the man and woman and choose the correct answer.
男の人と女の人の会話を聞いて正しい答えを選んでください。

Q1 After work

1. They are going to have dinner.
2. They are going out for a drink.
3. They are going home.

Q2 Two co-workers are talking at the office one morning

1. The man asked her out tonight.
2. The man is eating with the woman tonight.
3. The man is eating with the woman tomorrow.

Q3 Two friends are talking

1. The man and woman and no one else are going to see fireworks.
2. The man is going to the fireworks with her.
3. The man is going to see Japanese fireworks by himself.

Q4 Two friends are talking

1. The man is going to see kabuki tonight.
2. The woman has seen kabuki before.
3. They are going to see kabuki on the weekend.

Role playing

Role play using the cards below
下記のカードを使ってロールプレイしてください。

A: You want to go see a kabuki performance next month. Ask if B-san has ever seen kabuki, then invite him/her to join you when you go.

B: You have never seen a kabuki before. Accept A-san's invitation.

UNIT 12

Do you remember?

Use the phrases you have studied in this unit in situations ①–③ below.
このユニットで学習したフレーズを下記の①〜③の状況に合わせて使ってください。

① Would you like to …?

② Have you ever …?

③ Would you like to … right now?

Phrases for This Unit

Unit Phrases

- お茶を飲みませんか。 — Ocha o nomimasen ka. — *Would you like to have a cup of tea?*
- 温泉に行ったことがありますか。 — Onsen ni itta koto ga arimasu ka. — *Have you ever been to an onsen (hot spring)?*

Useful expressions

- どこに行きましょうか。 — Doko ni ikimashō ka. — *Where shall we go?*
- そうしましょう。 — Sō shimashō. — *Let's do that/it.*
- 〜はどうですか。 — ... wa dō desu ka. — *How about ...? / How does ... sound?*
- 〜はちょっと……。 — ... wa chotto .... — *... is no good for me.*
- また誘ってください。 — Mata sasotte kudasai. — *Please invite/ ask me again.*
- 楽しみにしています。 — Tanoshimi ni shite imasu. — *I'm looking forward to it.*

Check!

Now I can...

- ☐ **Talk about my own experiences and ask about those of others**
  自分の経験について話したり、他の人の経験について尋ねたりできる
- ☐ **Invite a person to do or have something**
  人を誘ったり、何かを勧めたりできる
- ☐ **Accept and refuse invitations**
  誘いを受けたり、断わったりできる

UNIT 12

One More Step

Look at the pictures and talk about events throughout the year.
下のイラストを見ながら、年中行事について話しましょう。

● **Seasonal Event**

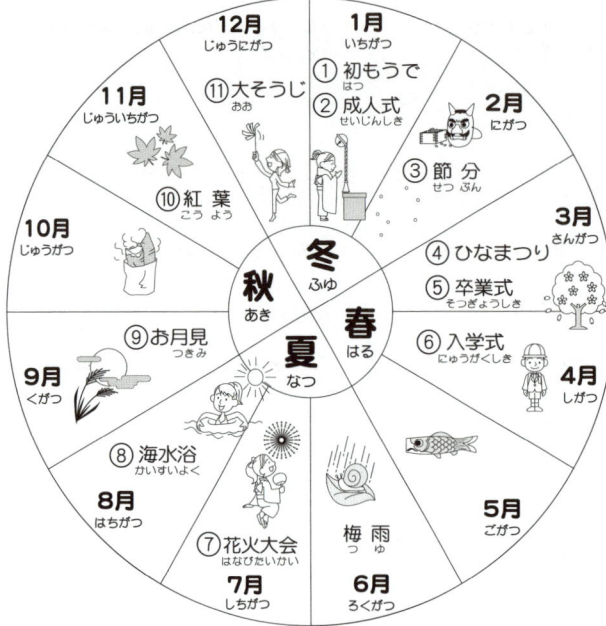

① Hatsumōde / *The first visit to a shrine of the new year*
② Seijin-shiki / *Coming-of-Age, Ceremony for people turning 20*
③ Setsubun (Mame-maki) / *Ceremony for the end of winter (bean throwing)*
④ Hina-matsuri / *Girls' Day, the Doll Festival*
⑤ Sotsugyō-shiki / *School graduations*
⑥ Nyūgaku-shiki / *Entrance ceremonies*
⑦ Hanabi-taikai / *Fireworks festivals*
⑧ Kaisuiyoku / *Sea-bathing*
⑨ O-tsukimi / *Moon-viewing*
⑩ Kōyō / *Changing of the leaves*
⑪ Ōsōji / *Year-end cleaning*

do / have done	**go / have been**	**see / have seen**
(__を) します　(__o) shimasu	(__に) 行きます　(__ni) ikimasu	(__を) 見ます　(__o) mimasu
→ (__を) した　(__o) shita	→ (__に) 行った　(__ni) itta	→ (__を) 見た　(__o) mita

Talk about the seasonal event like the example below using the verbs above.
上記の動詞を使って、下の例のような季節の行事について話してみてください。

(1)　日本では、<u>4月</u> に <u>入学式</u> をします。
　　　Nihon de wa, <u>4-gatsu</u> ni <u>nyūgaku-shiki</u> o shimasu.
　　　We have entrance ceremonies in April.
→ Explain a tradition in your country*.　　　*my country = watashi no kuni
　　あなたの国の伝統を説明してください。

(2)　<u>初もうで</u> をしたことがありますか。
　　　<u>Hatsumōde</u> o shita koto ga arimasu ka.
　　　Have you ever done hatsumode? [the first visit to a shrine of the new year]
→ You can expand the scope of the conversation using the phrases below.
　　以下のフレーズを使って、会話の幅を広げることができます。

"Doko ni ikimashita ka." (Unit 8), "Dō deshita ka." (Unit 9), or "Kondo issho ni ikimasen ka." (Unit 12)

Grammar | 文法

I Sentence Structure

1. Basic Sentence Patterns
In broad terms, Japanese sentences can be divided into the following three patterns.

Watashi wa Nihon-jin desu.	*I am a Japanese person.*	**[Noun Phrase]**
Meari-san wa isogashii desu.	*Mary-san is busy.*	**[Adjective Phrase]**
Tanaka-san wa rāmen o tabemasu.	*Tanaka-san eats ramen.*	**[Verb Phrase]**

"Desu" has a similar function to **"to be"** in English, and comes at the end of Noun and Adjective Phrases. Verb Phrases end with **[-masu]**.

"Wa" is a particle that denotes topics and subjects. (The particles **"ga"** and **"mo"** can also indicate a subject. → See p.166 for more information on particles)

2. Negative Sentences
Negative Sentences are made by modifying the end of a predicate, which is typically the last part of a sentence. This grammatical structure is the reason that one must listen to the very end of a Japanese sentence to know whether it is negative or affirmative.

Watashi wa Nihon-jin <u>ja arimasen</u>.	*I <u>am not</u> a Japanese person.*	**[Negative Noun Phrase]**
Meari-san wa isogashi<u>ku nai</u> desu.	*Mary-san <u>is not</u> busy.*	**[Negative Adjective Phrase]**
Tanaka-san wa rāmen o tabe<u>masen</u>.	*Tanaka-san <u>does not</u> eat ramen.*	**[Negative Verb Phrase]**

Please refer to individual chapters for more detailed information on how to make negative sentences using all parts of speech.

3. Interrogative Sentences (Questions)
Attach **"ka"** to the end of a Declarative Sentence to create an Interrogative Sentence.

Meari-san wa isogashii desu <u>ka</u>.	*Is Mary-san busy?*
Tanaka-san wa rāmen o tabemasu <u>ka</u>.	*Does Tanaka-san eat ramen?*

→ See p.179 for more information on interrogative words and sentences with wh-words (who, what, when, where, why, and how).

II Particles

Creating longer sentences in Japanese typically involves inserting different kinds of information in between the subject and predicate. Grammatical units known as **"particles"** help simplify this process.

Japanese particles are similar to English prepositions, words like **"in"** and **"at."** As shown below, while English uses prepositions, which precede the noun, clause, or phrase they modify, Japanese uses postpositions, which come after the clause or phrase.

Kare no heya de bangohan o tabemashita.	*We had dinner in his room.*
Maiasa roku-ji ni okimasu.	*I wake up at six o'clock every morning.*

Although particles themselves do not carry any meaning, they provide an important role in sentence formation.

For example, English does not use particles and thus relies on word order within a sentence. Changing the order of words in an English sentence can result in a completely different meaning.

I gave her my dog. ≠ *I gave my dog her.

However, what is crucial in a Japanese sentence is not word order, but the units of information made up of a particle and the noun, clause, or phrase it modifies.

Watashi wa kanojo ni inu o ageta. = Watashi wa inu o kanojo ni ageta.   (*I gave her my dog.*)

Even if the words of a sentence appear in a different order, as long as the particles remain the same, the meaning of the sentence does not change.

There are different types of particles. Take a look at the different particles and their functions below.

1. **wa**

【Subject】
    Watashi **wa** Tai-jin desu.   *I am a Thai person.*
    Kore **wa** gohyaku-en desu.   *This costs 500 yen.*

【Topic】
    Kinō **wa** izakaya ni ikimashita.   *Yesterday I went to an izakaya.*
    Natsu-yasumi **wa** nani o shimashita ka.   *What did you do over the summer break?*

【Comparisons】
    Sushi **wa** suki desu ga, sashimi **wa** kirai desu.   *I like sushi, but I don't like sashimi.*

2. o
【Object】

Shimbun **o** yomimasu.	*I read newspapers.*
Kōhī **o** nomimasu.	*I drink coffee.*

3. ni
【Object】

Tomodachi **ni** aimasu.	*I'm going to see my friend.*
Chichi **ni** nekutai o agemasu.	*I'm going to give my dad a necktie.*
Basu **ni** norimasu.	*I'm going to get on the bus.*

【Destination】

Chūgoku **ni** ikimasu.	*I'm going to China.*
Nihon **ni** kimasu.	*I'm coming to Japan.*
Uchi **ni** kaerimasu.	*I'm going back home.*

*The particle **"e"** is used to indicate a general direction as well as a destination, and is interchangeable with **"ni."**

【Time】

Shichi-ji **ni** okimasu.	*I get up at seven o'clock.*
Jūichi-ji **ni** nemasu.	*I go to bed at eleven o'clock.*
San-ji **ni** modorimasu.	*I'll come back at three o'clock.*

【Location】

Otōto no heya **ni** terebi ga arimasu.	*There's a TV in my little brother's room.*
Uchi **ni** neko ga imasu.	*There's a cat in the house.*

4. de
【Place of action】

Resutoran **de** bangohan o tabemasu.	*I eat dinner at restaurants.*

【Means】

Basu **de** ikimasu.	*I'll go by bus.*
Hashi **de** tabemasu.	*I eat with chopsticks.*

【Selection】

- Waiter: Would you like bread or rice? -	
Pan **de** onegaishimasu.	*Bread, please.*

5. no
【Possession】

watashi **no** kuruma	*my car*
tomodachi **no** hon	*my friend's book*

【Affiliation】
　A-sha **no** shain　　　　　　　　　*an employee of Company A*
　A-daigaku **no** gakusei　　　　　　*a student at University A*
【Attribute (Type/Nature)】
　Nihon-go **no** sensei　　　　　　　*a teacher of the Japanese language*
　ichigo **no** shābetto　　　　　　　 *strawberry sherbet*
【Apposition】
　tomodachi **no** Yōko-san　　　　　*my friend, Yoko-san*
　otto **no** Tomu　　　　　　　　　　*my husband, Tom*
【Pronoun】
　akai **no**　　　　　　　　　　　　 *the red one*
　atsui **no**　　　　　　　　　　　　*the hot one*

6. to
【A partner in action】
　Tomodachi **to** eiga o mimashita.　　*I saw a movie with my friend.*
　Eri-san **to** kekkon shimashita.　　　*I married Eri-san.*
　Shachō **to** hanashimasu.　　　　　　*I'll talk with the CEO.*
【Parallel phrases】
　pan **to** tamago　　　　　　　　　　*bread and eggs*

7. mo
【Sameness/Agreement】
　Kore **mo** onegaishimasu.　　　　　*I'll have this, too, please.*
　Watashi **mo** eiga ga suki desu.　　*I also like movies.*
【Emphasis】
　Wain o go-hon **mo** nomimashita.　 *I drank five bottles of wine!*

8. kara
【Origin of duration or motion】
　Uchi **kara** gakkō made samjuppun　*It takes thirty minutes from our house to the*
　kakarimasu.　　　　　　　　　　　　*school.*

9. made
【End of duration or motion】
　Ku-ji kara jūichi-ji **made** benkyō shimasu.　*I study from nine until eleven o'clock.*

10. ga

Although the particle **"ga"** essentially follows the subject of a sentence, it sometimes provides a function similar to other particles. Because this can make **"ga"** confusing to use, try to remember the five patterns below.

【The subject of an interrogative sentence that uses an interrogative word】

Dare **ga** kimasu ka.	*Who's coming?*
Itsu **ga** ii desu ka.	*When would be a good time?*

【The subject of a sentence denoting possession or location】

Uchi ni jitensha **ga** arimasu.	*We have a bicycle at our house.*
Toire ni neko **ga** imasu.	*There's a cat in the restroom.*

【The subject of an embedded clause modifying a noun phrase】

Kore wa Bētōben **ga** tsukutta kyoku desu.	*This is a piece of music that is composed by Beethoven.*

【Objects】 → See p.18

(1) suki, kirai, jōzu, heta　(*like, dislike, be good at, be bad at*)
　　Sakkā **ga** suki desu.　　　　　　　　*I like soccer.*
(2) wakaru, dekiru, mieru, kikoeru　(*understand, can do, can see, can hear*)
　　Koko kara Fuji-san o miru koto **ga** dekimasu.　*It is possible to see Mount Fuji from here.*
(3) hoshii, shitai　(*want, want to do*)
　　Atarashii terebi **ga** hoshii desu.　　　*I want a new TV.*
　　Nihon-go **ga** benkyō shitai desu.　　 *I want to study Japanese.*

【An aspect of part of the subject】

Imōto wa kami **ga** nagai.	*My younger sister has long hair.*
Nihon wa hanzai **ga** sukunai.	*Japan has little crime.*

III Demonstratives

There are four types of Japanese demonstratives, which begin with **"ko-," "so-," "a-,"** and **"do-"** respectively.　　→ See p.28, p.40

The table below shows how they are used.

【Table 1】

Demonstrative	**"ko-"** Close to the speaker	**"so-"** Farther than "ko-" or closer to the listener	**"a-"** Farther than "so-" or far from both the speaker and listener	**"do-"** Which, what, where
Thing	kore	sore	are	dore
	kono [+noun]	sono [+noun]	ano [+noun]	dono [+noun]
Place	koko	soko	asoko	doko
Direction	kocchi	socchi	acchi	docchi
(Polite)	(kochira)	(sochira)	(achira)	(dochira)
Area	kono hen	sono hen	ano hen	dono hen

S=Speaker
L=Listener

IV Existential and Possessive Sentences

An Existential Sentence is a sentence with a phrase describing a location or time in which a noun exists. When the subject of an Existential Sentence is animate (capable of moving), the verb **"imasu/iru"** is used, while **"arimasu/aru"** is used for inanimate objects.　　→ See p.24, p.26, p.38

Kōen ni kodomo ga **imasu**.　　*A little kid is in the park.*
Ekimae ni takushī ga **imasu**.　　*Taxis are in front of the station.*
Uchi no mae ni kombini ga **arimasu**.　　*There's a convenience store in front of our house.*
Niwa ni ki ga **arimasu**.　　*There's a tree in the garden.*

Although a taxi is not alive, because the driver inside is capable of moving, it is consider animate. Likewise, although a tree is a living thing, because it cannot move on its own it is considered inanimate.

"imasu" and **"arimasu"** can also denote possession and scheduling, which are usages derived from their original meaning of existence.

-At a store- Kasa, **arimasu** ka.	*Do you have umbrellas?*
Ashita kaigi ga **arimasu**.	*I have a meeting tomorrow.*
Watashi wa imōto ga futari **imasu**.	*I have two younger sisters.*
Kodomo no koro, uchi ni inu ga **imashita**.	*We had a dog at our house when I was a kid.*

Although the subject of an Existential Sentence is primarily marked by **"ga,"** there are cases when it is denoted by the topic marker **"wa."** → See p.166

V Verbs

Verbs provide a great deal of information in Japanese, including affirmation/negation, tense, and politeness. In broad terms, Japanese verbs can be divided into **polite** and **plain forms**, while Japanese tense is either **past** or **non-past** (used for present and future actions). → See Unit 8

Although some verbs have irregular conjugations, for the most part they follow the same basic rules.

1. Basic Verb Conjugations and Functions

Polite verbs end in [-masu]. This conjugation is known as either the **masu-form** or the **polite form**.

【Table 2】

Masu-form		Affirmative	Negative
ikimasu	Non-past	ikimasu	ikimasen
Go	Past	ikimashita	Ikimasendeshita

To find a verb in the dictionary, you need to search for the **dictionary form** which is non past affirmative of the plain form.

【Table 3】

Dictionary Form		Affirmative	Negative
taberu Eat	Non-past	taberu (dictionary form)	tabenai (nai-form)
	Past	tabeta (ta-form)	tabenakatta

In certain contexts, the **masu-form** and **dictionary form** of a verb are used not to express tense or politeness, but to connect grammatical expressions.

Take a look at what sort of sentences can be made using the **masu-form** and **dictionary form** of the verb "nomu" (*drink*).

1. Masu-form

nomimasu

+ tai desu (**Desire**)

   Nani ka **nomi**tai desu.   *I want something to drink.*

+ ni ikimasu (**Destination of motion**)

   Nomi ni ikimasu.   *I'm going drinking.*

2. Dictionary form

nomu

+ no ga suki desu (**Verb nominalization**)

   Bīru o **nomu** no ga suki desu.   *I like drinking beer.*

+ koto ga dekimasu (**Verb nominalization**)

   Sokode nihon-shu o **nomu** koto ga dekimasu.   *I can drink Japanese sake there.*

Additional conjugations include the **nai-form**, **ta-form**, and **te-form**.
Let's take a look at what sort of sentences can be made using different forms of the verb "kaku" (*write*).

3. Nai-form

kakanai

+ nai de kudasai (**Negative request**)

   Koko ni **kaka**nai de kudasai.   *Please don't write here/on this.*

+ nai to ikemasen (**Obligation**)

   Jūsho mo **kaka**nai to ikemasen.   *You must also write down your address.*

4. Ta-form   → *See Unit 12*
   boxed: **kaita**
   + koto ga arimasu (**Experience**)
      Fan-retā o **kaita** koto ga arimasu.   *I've written a fan letter before.*
   + hō ga ii desu (**Advice**)
      Nihon-go de **kaita** hō ga ii desu.   *It'd be better to write it in Japanese.*

The **te-form** is considered to be the most essential and crucial of all verb conjugations.

5. Te-form   → *See Unit 5, Unit 6*
   boxed: **kaite**
   Te-form (**A request to someone familiar**)
      Koko ni namae o **kaite**.   *Write your name here.*
   Te-form (**Verb connector**)
      Tegami o **kaite**, neta.   *I wrote a letter and went to bed.*
   + kudasai (**Request**)
      Koko ni namae o **kaite** kudasai.   *Please write your name here.*
   + imasu (**Progressive action**)
      Ima tegami o kaite imasu.   *I'm writing a letter right now.*
   + mo ii desu ka (**Request for permission**)
      Bōrupen de **kaite** mo ii desu ka.   *May I write with a ballpoint pen?*

2. How to Conjugate Verbs

We will now take a look at each verb conjugation. As mentioned before, although some exceptions do exist, most verbs apart from the two irregular verbs **"suru"** (*do*) and **"kuru"** (*come*) conjugate according to the same rules.

Verbs can be divided into three categories according to their conjugations. In order to memorize how verbs conjugate, it is important to first understand these three categories.

1. Ru-verbs

Verbs that end in [-ru] whose final vowel before [-ru] is [i] or [e].
   Ex. taberu (*eat*), miru (*look*), miseru (*show*), akeru (*open*)
   *Exceptions: kaeru (*go home / return*), hairu (*enter*), hashiru (*run*), shiru (*know*) → **u-verb**

2. U-verbs

Verbs that end in sounds beside [ru], such as [u] or [tsu].
Verbs that end in [ru] whose final vowel before [ru] is [a], [u], or [o].
   Ex. iku (*go*), motsu (*hold*), tobu (*fly*), sawaru (*touch*), uru (*sell*), noru (*get on*)

173

3. Irregular verbs
Two verbs, **"suru"** (*do*) and **"kuru"** (*come*).

Given the above rules, as long as you are aware of a few exceptions, you can categorize all verbs into one of three groups.
Although **ru-verbs** have the simplest rules for conjugations, the majority of verbs are **u-verbs**.

How to make the dictionary form

1. Ru-verbs
Starting from the **masu-form**, replace [masu] with [ru].
  -masu → -ru
  tabemasu → taberu   mimasu → miru

2. U-verbs
Starting from the **masu-form**, remove **[masu]** and replace the final [i] with [u].
  kakimasu → kaku   nomimasu → nomu

Note that sound changes occur when using *kana* from the **sa** and **ta rows**.
  hanashimasu → hanasu   mochimasu → motsu

3. Irregular verbs
  shimasu → suru   kimasu → kuru

How to make the nai-form

1. Ru-verbs
Starting from the **masu-form**, replace [masu] with [nai]
  -masu → -nai
  tabemasu → tabenai   mimasu → minai

2. U-verbs
Starting from the **masu-form**, remove [masu] and replace the final [i] with [anai].
  -imasu → -anai
  kakimasu → kakanai   nomimasu → nomanai

However, if the character before **"masu"** is the vowel **"i,"** it conjugates to **"wa,"** instead of **"a."**
  kaimasu → kawanai   iimasu → iwanai

3. Irregular verbs
shimasu → shinai   kimasu → konai

How to make the te-form

1. Ru-verbs
Starting from the **masu-form**, replace [masu] with [te]
-masu → -te
tabe**masu** → tabe**te**   mi**masu** → mi**te**

2. U-verbs
Although creating the **te-forms** of **u-verbs** is slightly complicated, they all obey certain rules, which are determined based on the final speech sound that remains after removing [masu] from the **masu-form** of each verb.

(1) **-i, -chi, -ri → -tte**
ka**i**masu → ka**tte**   mo**chi**masu → mo**tte**   kae**ri**masu → kae**tte**

(2) **-mi, -bi, -ni → -nde**
no**mi**masu → no**nde**   aso**bi**masu → aso**nde**   shi**ni**masu → shi**nde**

(3) **-ki, -gi → -ite, -ide**
ka**ki**masu → ka**ite**   oyo**gi**masu → oyo**ide**
*Exception: ikimasu → itte

(4) **-shi → -shite**
hana**shi**masu → hana**shite**

3. Irregular verbs
shimasu → shite   kimasu → kite

*The **ta-form** is identical to the **te-form** conjugation.

VI Adjectives

Like Japanese verbs, Japanese adjectives convey crucial information at the end, such as negation and tense. Two types of Japanese adjectives exist, **i-adjectives** and **na-adjectives**, and they each have their own conjugation pattern.

When attaching an adjective to the front of a noun to create a noun phrase, adjectives that end in [i] are known as **i-adjectives**, and adjectives that end in [na] are called **na-adjectives**.

→ See Unit 9, Unit 10, Unit 11

【Table 4】

I-adjectives	Na-adjectives
hiro**i** heya (*a spacious room*)	shizuka **na** heya (*a quiet room*)
furu**i** heya (*an old room*)	kirei **na** heya (*a clean room*)

Adjectives function in two ways depending on if they are used in the predicate of a sentence or as part of a noun phrase.

Kono kaban wa **chiisai desu**.   This bag is **small**.
Kore wa **chiisai** kaban desu.   This is a **small** bag.
Kono mondai wa **kantan desu**.   This problem is **simple**.
Kore wa **kantan na** mondai desu.   This is a **simple** problem.

【Table 5】

	I-adjective*1 hiroi (*wide*)		Na-adjective*2 shizuka (*quiet*)	
	Affirmative	Negative	Affirmative	Negative
Non-past	hiro**i** desu	hiro**kunai** desu	shizuka desu	shizuka **dewa/ja arimasen**
Past	hiro**katta** desu	hiro**kunakatta** desu	shizuka **deshita**	shizuka **dewa/ja arimasendeshita**

*1 I-adjective "**ii** (*good*)" conjugates irregularly.

	Affirmative	Negative
Non-past	ii desu	yokunai desu
Past	yokatta desu	yokunakatta desu

*2 Na-adjectives also include the following conjugation.

	Affirmative	Negative
Non-past	shizuka desu	shizuka janai desu
Past	shizuka datta desu	shizuka janakatta desu

Note that the word [desu] is frequently omitted in casual conversation.

VII Numbers

Japanese has different words for numbers depending on if numbers are said by themselves, or if they are used in conjunction with a counter word.

1. Stand-alone Numbers

Japanese numbers are based around 10, with numbers higher than 10 formed by stating the unit of 10 and then saying the words for 1 through 9.

0 (zero/rei), 1 (ichi), 2 (ni), 3 (san), 4 (yon/shi), 5 (go), 6 (roku), 7 (nana/shichi), 8 (hachi), 9 (kyū/ku), 10 (jū), 11 (jūichi), 12 (jūni), ..., 20 (nijū), ..., 30 (sanjū)

Additionally, individual words exist for units of 10 with additional decimals, ranging from 10 (jū) and 100 (hyaku) to 1,000 (sen) and 10,000 (man). However, numbers higher than these units are composed by combining these four words. There are units of 10,000 x 10,000 is billion (oku) and 1 billion x 10,000 is trillion (chō).

100,000 jūman	1,000,000 hyakuman	10,000,000 (is)senman
100,000,000 (ichi)oku	1,000,000,000,000 (ic)chō	→ See p.47

Stating a phone number: 03-5225-9733 would be [zero san (no) go ni ni go (no) kyū nana san san].

2. Counting time

___ jikan ___ hours

1 ichi-jikan	2 ni-jikan	3 san-jikan	4 <u>yo</u>-jikan	5 go-jikan
6 roku-jikan	7 shichi-jikan	8 hachi-jikan	9 <u>ku</u>-jikan	10 jū-jikan
11 jūichi-jikan	12 jūni-jikan	......	20 nijū-jikan	30 sanjū-jikan

___ ji ___ o'clock

1 ichi-ji	2 ni-ji	3 san-ji	4 <u>yo</u>-ji	5 go-ji
6 roku-ji	7 shichi-ji	8 hachi-ji	9 <u>ku</u>-ji	10 jū-ji
11 jūichi-ji	12 jūni-ji			

___ fun/pun ___ minutes

1 ippun	2 ni-fun	3 sam-pun	4 yon-pun	5 go-fun
6 roppun	7 nana-fun	8 happun	9 kyū-fun	10 juppun
11 jūippun	12 jūni-fun	......	20 nijuppun	30 sanjuppun

Ex. 3:50 = san-ji gojuppun   8:30 = hachi-ji sanjuppun / hachi-ji han (han = *half*) → See p.103

3. Counters

Japanese uses different counter words depending on what is being counted. → See p.29, p.43, p.53

Uchi niwa chīsai sara ga jū-mai arimasu. *I have 10 plates at home.*
Kuruma ga mō ichi-dai hoshii. *I want one more car.*
Hambāgā o futatsu kudasai. *Two hamburgers, please.*

Counters are determined by the quality of the object(s) being counted. Numbers have different readings depending on the counter they are used with.
Note that the numbers 1 (ichi), 3 (san), 6 (roku), 8 (hachi), and 10 (jū) are especially prone to change.

【Table 6】

	-mai	-dai	-ko / -tsu	-kai	-hon	-nin
	Flat objects (paper, plates, shirts)	Large inanimate objects (TVs, PCs, cars, bicycles)	Small inanimate objects (eggs, hamburgers, tomatos)	Floors and number of times something is done	Long, tubular objects (pens, umbrellas, bottles)	People
1	ichi-mai	ichi-dai	**ikko/hitotsu**	**ikkai**	**ippon**	**hitori**
2	ni-mai	ni-dai	ni-ko/**futatsu**	ni-kai	ni-hon	**futari**
3	san-mai	san-dai	san-ko/**mittsu**	san-kai*	**sam-bon**	san-nin
4	yon-mai	yon-dai	yon-ko/**yottsu**	yon-kai	yon-hon	**yo-nin**
5	go-mai	go-dai	go-ko/**itsutsu**	go-kai	go-hon	go-nin
6	roku-mai	roku-dai	**rokko/muttsu**	**rokkai**	**roppon**	roku-nin
7	nana-mai	nana-dai	nana-ko/**nanatsu**	nana-kai	nana-hon	shichi-nin
8	hachi-mai	hachi-dai	hachi-ko/**yattsu**	hachi-kai/**hakkai**	hachi-hon/**happon**	hachi-nin
9	kyū-mai	kyū-dai	kyū-ko/**kokonotsu**	kyū-kai	kyū-hon	kyū-nin
10	jū-mai	jū-dai	**jukko/tō**	**jukkai**	**juppon**	jū-nin
?	nam-mai	nan-dai	nan-ko/**ikutsu**	nan-kai*	nam-bon	nan-nin

*When talking about floors of a building, [san-gai] and [nan-gai] are also permissible.

VIII Interrogatives

This section looks at interrogative sentences that use interrogative words like "what" and "who," and provides a lineup of Japanese interrogatives.

Interrogative sentences are usually formed by using an interrogative word for the information you are asking for and adding **"ka"** to the end of the sentence.

1. what = nani / nan
   Nani ga suki desu ka.   *What do you like?*
   Kore wa nan desu ka.   *What is this?*   → See Unit 4

2. what time = nan-ji
   Nan-ji ni okimasu ka.   *What time do you wake up?*
   Shigoto wa nan-ji made desu ka.   *What time do you finish work?*

3. where = doko   → See Unit 2, Unit 8
   Doko ni ikimasu ka.   *Where will you go?*
   Doko de benkyō shimasu ka.   *Where do you study?*

4. who = dare
   Dare to ikimasu ka.   *Who are you going with?*
   Dare ga kimashita ka.   *Who came?*

When used as the subject of a sentence, interrogative words are always followed by "ga."

5. what + [noun] = nan no + [noun]
   Nan no hon o yomimashita ka.   *What book did you read?*

6. what kind of = donna   → See Unit 10
   Donna hito desu ka.   *What kind of person is he/she?*
   Donna tokoro desu ka.   *What kind of place is it?*

7. how many = nan + [counter] / ikutsu
   Nan-jikan benkyō shimashita ka.   *How many hours did you study?*
   Nan-nin imasu ka.   *How many people are there?*
   Ikutsu arimasu ka.   *How many are there?*

8. how = nan + [counter] / donogurai

Nan-sai desu ka.	*How old are you?*
Donogurai ikimasu ka.	*How often do you go?*
Donogurai tōi desuka.	*How far is it?*
Donogurai kakarimasu ka.	*How long will it take?* → See Unit 7

9. how much = ikura

Ikura desu ka.	*How much is it?* → See Unit 4

10. which = docchi / dochira / dore

with two options	: **Docchi/dochira** ga suki desu ka.	*Which do you prefer?*
with more than two options	: **Dore** ga (ichiban) suki desu ka.	*Which do you like [the most]?*

IX Adverbs

In Japanese, adverbs come before verbs and adjectives and describe their state or degree.

【State adverbs】

Yukkuri hanashite kudasai.	*Please talk slowly.*
Kono machi wa **sukkari** kawatta.	*This town has completely changed.*
Kichinto setsumei shite kudasai.	*Please explain this precisely.*

【Degree adverbs】

Totemo oishii desu.	*It's very delicious.*
Nihon-go to Eigo wa **kanari** chigau.	*Japanese and English are pretty different.*
Itsumo wa biru desu ga, **tamani** shōchū o nomimasu.	*I always drink beer, but sometimes I'll have shochu.*
Eiga wa **amari** suki ja arimasen.	*I don't really like movies.*
Watashi wa kanojo o **zenzen** shiranai.	*I don't know her at all.*

Affirmative adverbs include **"totemo"** and **"kanari"** that describe degree and others like **"itsumo"** and **"tamani"** that describe frequency. For negative statements, there are adverbs such as **"amari"** and **"zenzen,"** which are used with the negative form of verbs and adjectives.

Some adjectives like the ones listed below can be conjugated to function as adverbs.

haya**i**	→	haya**ku**	**Hayaku** tsukimashita.	*I arrived **early**.*
oso**i**	→	oso**ku**	**Osoku** okimashita.	*I woke up **late**.*
sugo**i**	→	sugo**ku**	Fuji-san wa **sugoku** kirei da.	*Mt. Fuji is **amazingly** beautiful.*
shizuka **na**	→	shizuka **ni**	**Shizuka ni** aruite kudasai.	*Please walk **quietly**.*
pojithibu **na**	→	pojithibu **ni**	Motto **pojithibu ni** kangaeyou.	*Let's think more **positively**.*

X Omitting words

Particularly in spoken conversation, certain parts of a Japanese sentence can be omitted. Consider the examples below.

1. Subject omission

(Watashi wa) Jon desu.	*(I am) John.*
(Watashi wa) kaishain desu.	*(I am) a company employee.*
(Watashi wa) Amerika kara kimashita.	*(I am) from the United States.* → See Unit 1

Subjects that can be quickly understood from context in both interrogative and declarative sentences, particularly in ones in which the listener is the subject, are frequently omitted.

It is important to note that the word **"anata,"** which corresponds to the word **"you"** in English, is hardly ever used in Japanese conversation. Instead, a person's name or job title is used when it is necessary to explicitly refer to them in conversation.

(Anata wa) kaishain desu ka.	*(Are you) a company employee?*
(Tanaka-san,) ima, isogashii desu ka.	*(Tanaka-san, are you) busy right now?*
(Sensei wa) rāmen o tabe masu ka.	*(Sensei, do you) eat ramen?*

2. Interrogative omission

When asking a question using an interrogative word in conversation, there are also times when the question word itself is omitted and only the subject is uttered.

O-shigoto wa (nan desu ka)?	*What do you do?*
O-namae wa (nan desu ka)?	*What is your name?* → See Unit 1

Like **"anata"**(*you*), the phrase **"anata no"**(*your*) is also not used when it can be easily inferred from context.

XI Respectful Language

All languages have a method of conveying politeness depending on who someone is speaking to. Japanese is no exception to this, and Japanese **keigo**, or respectful language, is divided into two categories depending on who is speaking to whom. **Sonkei-go**, or honorific language, is used to promote the stature of a respectable person (listener or third party), while **kenjō-go**, or humble language, is used to lower the speaker's own status. The **desu/masu-form** is sometimes referred to as **teinei-go**, or polite language, which can be considered a form of **keigo**, but unlike **sonkei-go** and **kenjō-go**, both listener and speaker can use the **desu/masu-form** to show respect.

For example, the verb **"taberu"** (*eat*) has completely different forms depending on whether it is in teinei-go (*polite*), sonkei-go (*honorific*), or kenjō-go (*humble*).

Ex. 1 **Taberu** (*eat*)
  Teinei-go   tabemasu
  Sonkei-go   meshiagarimasu
  Kenjō-go   itadakimasu

While some verbs like **"taberu"** are replaced with completely different words when using polite language, most verbs follow a simple rule to promote the listener (**o**+**[masu-form stem]**+**ni narimasu**) or to demote the speaker (**o**+**[masu-form stem]**+**shimasu**). Additionally, attaching **[-rareru]** or **[-areru]** to the stem of a **ru-verb** or **u-verb**, respectively, can also be used to promote the listener.

Ex. 2 **Kariru** (*borrow*)
  Teinei-go   karimasu
  Sonkei-go   okari ni narimasu / kariraremasu
  Kenjō-go   okarishimasu

Ex. 3
  - A-san is a librarian at a museum reference room. B-san is a student. -
  A: Kono shiryō, okari ni narimasu ka / kariraremasu ka.
  B: Ee, okari shitai desu.
  A: Would you like to borrow these materials?
  B: Yes, I would [like to borrow them].

Keigo is not only limited to verbs. Nouns can be modified with bika-go, or beautified language, to show respect.
In bika-go, the prefix **"o"** or **"go"** is attached to a noun.

> Ex. o-mizu (*water*), o-sara (*plate*), o-hashi (*chopsticks*)
> go-shusshin (*hometown*), go-kazoku (*family*), go-shumi (*hobby*)

"o" is attached to wago, or native Japanese words, while **"go"** is attached to kango, or words that were borrowed from Chinese.

Keigo is often found in phrases frequently used at places that serve customers, such as shops, facilities, and areas of public transport. Sonkei-go phrases that elevate the status of the customer include "Omachi kudasai." (*Please wait.*), "Yukkuri goran ni natte kudasai." (*Please take your time and have a look.*), and "Irasshaimase." (*Welcome.*)
Kenjō-go phrases that workers use to demote their own status include "Omatase shimashita." (*Thank you for waiting.*), "Sugu omochi shimasu." (*I'll bring that right out.*), and "Densha ga mairimasu." (*A train is coming.*), which can be heard all across Japan.

While the above was a brief introduction to Japanese polite language, keigo is not limited to verbs. Politeness in the Japanese language is an expansive system that extends all the way to nouns and adjectives, and reflects the dynamic between the people who use it and the people to whom it is used. Because of this complexity, keigo is not an aspect of the Japanese language that Japanese people naturally acquire and use without thinking, but a system that must be consciously studied.
Although it may take time for students of Japanese to comfortably use keigo, opportunities to listen to polite language abound at restaurants, buses, trains, and a variety of public places, so please begin your studies by listening to the keigo around you.

Column | コラム

1. Expressions whose meaning changes with context

There are many words in the Japanese language where a single word or phrase has various meanings and usages. Below are some of the typical examples.

(1) Chotto

"Chotto" has the following two major meanings.

1. Quantity or Degree:

"Chotto" primarily means the same as **"a little,"** and is used to describe **"a small amount"** or **"a low degree."**

Chotto matte kudasai.	*Please wait a little.*
Mō chotto yasui no arimasen ka.	*Do you have a little cheaper one?*

2. Euphemistic negation:

In actual use, this **"chotto"** is sometimes used as a euphemistic denial or refusal expression.

Sā, chotto wakarimasen.	*Sorry I don't know.*
Gomennasai, kinyōbi wa chotto…	*Sorry I won't be available Friday…*

"Chotto" used in this context is an expression that makes the refusal softer and more acceptable to the other party.

(2) Sumimasen

"Sumimasen" is one of the most useful expressions in Japanese.
It has the following three typical uses.

1. Calling:

It can be used to call a staff member in a store, etc. and also to call someone to stop suddenly.

2. Apologizing:

It is used as a slightly polite apology. **"Gomen"** and **"gomennasai"** are used as casual expressions, while **"mōshiwake gozaimasen"** is a polite expression.

3. Thanking:

People tend to use **"sumimasen"** more toward people who are distant or superior to them.

Try using the above expressions little by little in your daily life.

(3) Ki o tsukete

It is necessary to note that **"ki o tsukete"** has the following two meanings, which differ in usage from **"take care"** in English.

1. Greetings when seeing someone off:

Since it has a meaning of **"to pray for your safe journey,"** this expression can be used only by the person who is seeing the other person off when parting. If both parties are returning to different places, use an expression such as **"ja mata (ashita, raishū, kondo, etc.)."**

2. Heads-up:

It is said by shop staff to customers because it means **"please be careful."** For example, it is used for hot drinks or food, or to alert the customer to the danger of using a certain product in the wrong way.

(4) Sō desu

The **"sō"** in **"sō desu"** means **"so"** in English and is used in response to what has just been said in order to avoid repeating the same phrase. The addition of the interrogative final particle **"ka,"** the agreeing final particle **"ne"** or the instructive final particle **"yo"** adds a different nuance. Intonation also changes the meaning.

Let's look at the differences in B's reaction to A's statements in i) through iv).

A: Tōkyō no natsu wa mushi atsui desu. / *Tokyo's summer is hot and humid.*
B: i) Sō desu **ka** (↑ (with rising intonation)). / *I don't think so.*
    When used with an ascending intonation, it means that you do not agree with the other person's statement.
    ii) Sō desu **ka** (↓ (with falling intonation)). / *I'm just listening.*
    When used with a descending intonation, it becomes an affable expression of **"I'm listening."**
    iii) Sō desu **ne**. / *I think so, too.*
    This means to agree with the other person's opinion.
    iv) Sō desu **yo**. / *Didn't you know?*
    This conveys the meaning of **"I knew that (you didn't know that)"** in response to the other person's opinion.

(5) Kekkō desu / Daijōbu desu / Ii desu

In Unit 4, you learned about expressions to refuse things you do not need.
In addition to these, there are other expressions to politely decline a proposal, such as, **"kekkō desu," "daijōbu desu," "ii desu."** However, the literal meaning of these expressions is positive, such as **"kekkō desu = that's fine," "daijōbu desu = it's OK," "ii desu = that's good."** It is necessary to note that it is used as a polite expression of refusal only under the following context.

1. **Politely decline proposals:**

    <At restaurants and on visits>
    Q: Ocha **wa** ikaga desu ka. / *Would you like some tea?*
    A: Iie, kekkō desu / daijōbu desu / ii desu. = *No, thank you.*

    When refusing, it is clearer to begin with **"Iie."**
    If you will accept the suggestion, say **"Hai, arigatō gozaimasu / Onegaishimasu."**

    <At stores>
    Q: Fukuro **wa**? / *Would you like a bag?*
    A: Kekkō desu / daijōbu desu / ii desu. = *I am fine. / No, thank you.*

    If you need one, say **"Onegaishimasu."**

2. **Confirmed and granted:**

    In response to the following questions, it can literally convey a positive meaning. Be sure to start with **"hai"** in the sense of consenting that there is no problem.

    Q: Ocha **de** ii desu ka. / *Is tea OK?*
    A: Hai, (ocha de) kekkō desu / daijōbu desu / ii desu. = *Tea is fine.*

2. Expression of taste
This is a supplemental explanation of the flavor expressions covered in Unit 10.

● Nigai
What is perceived as bitter seems to vary from country to country, as well as individual senses. In Japan, vegetables, such as celery and green peppers, drinks, such as beer and tonic water, and even chocolate with low or no sugar or milk content would be described as **"nigai"** (*bitter*).

● Aji ga amari nai
Some may think that **"aji ga amari nai"** (*not much flavor*) is a euphemism for **"mazui"** (*tastes bad*), but in Japan, foods, such as konnyaku and tofu, which are seasoned with dashi, soy sauce, salt, or other seasonings, are often described as having no flavor.

● Omoshiroi aji
This is best used when referring to a flavor you have never personally tasted before. It may also be useful when it is difficult to directly say **"mazui,"** or when you are not sure how to express the taste, such as **"mazuku wa nai ga oishikunai"** (*not bad but not tasty either*).

● Amakarai
Typified by teriyaki sauce, the saltiness of soy sauce and the sweetness of sugar are often combined in seasonings in Japan. The word **"karai"** here does not mean **'spicy'** or **'hot,'** but rather it means **'salty.'** In some regions, **"karai"** is used to mean **'salty.'**

Translation of Dialogue

p.20 UNIT 1

John : How do you do. I'm John. It's nice to meet you.
Tanaka : How do you do. I'm Tanaka. The pleasure is all mine. John-san, what country are you from?
John : The United States.
Tanaka : I see. And where do you live?
John : In Chiba. How about you?
Tanaka : I live in Nakano. Do you like Japanese food?
John : Yes, I like tempura. / No, not really.
Tanaka : Oh, OK.

p.32 UNIT 2

Kumar : Excuse me.
Woman : Yes?
Kumar : I'm trying to get to Sakura Park.
Woman : It's straight down this way.
Kumar : Okay. Oh, also, is there an ATM near here?
Woman : Let me think.... There's a convenience store.
Kumar : Where is the convenience store?
Woman : In front of Sakura Park.
Kumar : Thank you.

p.46 UNIT 3

John : Excuse me, do you have T-shirts?
Clerk : Yes, we do. They're right here.
John : How much does that cost?
Clerk : It's 3,900 yen.
John : Do you have anything a little cheaper?
Clerk : This one is 1,980 yen.
John : OK, then I'll take three of those.
Clerk : Thank you.

p.60 UNIT 4

Waitress : Are you ready to order?
John : What do you recommend?
Waitress : Today's lunch.
John : Then, I'll have one of those, please.
Waitress : What would you like to drink?
John : Cola, please.
Waitress : Would you like dessert with that?
John : No, thank you.
- During the meal -
John : Excuse me, could I have some water?

p.72 UNIT 5

John : Excuse me, I'd like to become a member.
Clerk : Do you have any ID on you today?
John : Would you accept the residence card?
Clerk : Yes, that's alright. Also do you have a picture?
John : Um, can I bring one next time?
Clerk : No problem. Please fill this out, then.
John : Can I borrow this pen?
Clerk : Yes, please.

p.86 UNIT 6

John : Oh, Tanaka-san. Please have a seat.
Tanaka : Thank you.
John : Have something to drink.
Tanaka : Ah, thanks.
John : Should I get you some chopsticks?
Tanaka : I have some so it's okay.
- Later -
John : Excuse me, Tanaka-san, could you pass me the salt?
Tanaka : Here you go.

p.98 UNIT 7

John : How do I get from Tokyo to Kyoto?
Suzuki : By bus or Shinkasen.
John : How long does it take by bus?
Suzuki : About six hours.
John : How much does it cost?
Suzuki : I think it's about 7,000 yen.
John : I see. Thank you.

p.112 UNIT 8

Tanaka : John-san, what did you do on the weekend?
John : I went out to eat in Shinjuku. What about you, Tanaka-san?
Tanaka : I had a relaxing time at home. What are you going to do on your next day off?
John : I'm going to the park with my children.
Tanaka : What will you do there?
John : I want to take pictures.
Tanaka : That sounds nice.

p.124 UNIT 9

Sato : How was last weekend?
Karen : It was very fun! It was my first visit to Kyoto. Kyoto is a very nice town.
Sato : I see. How do you like Japanese temples?
Karen : They're very beautiful.

p.138 UNIT 10

John : What does nikujaga taste like?
Suzuki : It's sweet. It's really good.
John : Okay.
       This looks spicy, doesn't it?
Suzuki : Yes, it does.
John : I see. I'm not too good with spicy food. I can't eat it.
Suzuki : Well, let's get something else. How about this?
John : That looks good.
Suzuki : Then let's have this.

p.150 UNIT 11

Tanaka : Hello. It sure is cold today.
Kumar : It really is. How has your job been lately?
Tanaka : It's been well. How about your job, Kumar-san?
Kumar : I've been busy.
- Later -
Kumar : If you'll excuse me, I need to be going home.
Tanaka : Alright. Take care.
Kumar : See you later.

p.160 UNIT 12

Tanaka : Kumar-san, when did you come to Japan?
Kumar : Last September.
Tanaka : Have you ever gone flower-viewing?
Kumar : No, I haven't.
Tanaka : If you're interested, would you like to go flower-viewing together on Sunday?
Kumar : That sounds great. I'd like to.
Tanaka : Okay. I'll be in touch later.
Kumar : Alright. I'm looking forward to it.

Listening Answers and Script

p.21 **[UNIT 1] Q1** 1 **Q2** 3 **Q3** 1 **Q4** 3

Q1
M: Hajimemashite. Watashi wa Tomu desu. Igirisu-jin desu. Dōzo yoroshiku.
F: Emirī desu. Ōsutoraria kara kimashita. Kochira koso, dōzo yoroshiku.

M: *How do you do. I'm Tom. I'm English. It's nice to meet you.*
F: *I'm Emily. I'm from Australia. The pleasure is mine.*

Q2
F: Nīru-san, go-shusshin wa?
M: Indo desu.
F: O-shigoto wa nan desu ka.
M: Kaishain desu.

F: *Neal-san, where are you from?*
M: *India.*
F: *What do you do?*
M: *I work for a company.*

Q3
M: Ueda-san, karaoke wa suki desu ka.
F: Ūn, watashi wa amari…. Demo, ongaku wa suki desu yo.

M: *Ueda-san, do you like karaoke?*
F: *Well…, not so much. But I do like music.*

Q4
F: Tomu-san, o-sake wa suki desu ka.
M: Hai, suki desu. Bīru ga suki desu. Yamada-san mo o-sake, suki desu ka.
F: Ee, watashi mo suki desu yo.

F: *Tom-san, do you like drinking?*
M: *Yes, I do. I like beer. Do you drink, too?*
F: *Yes, I sure do.*

p.34 **[UNIT 2] Q1** 1 **Q2** 2 **Q3** 1 **Q4** 2

Q1
M: Sumimasen. Kono hen ni denkiya, arimasu ka.
F: Ee, asoko ni arimasu yo.
M: Arigatō gozaimasu.
F: Dō itashimashite.

M: *Excuse me. Is there a electronics store around here?*
F: *Yes, it's over there.*
M: *Thank you.*
F: *You're welcome.*

Q2
F: Sumimasen, reji, doko desu ka.
M: Achira ni narimasu.
F: A, arigatō gozaimasu.

F: *Excuse me, where is the cash register?*
M: *It's over there.*
F: *Ah, thank you.*

Q3
M: Ano…, hon-ya wa nan-kai desu ka.
F: 3-kai ni narimasu.
M: E, mō ichido ii desu ka.
F: 3-kai desu.
M: Arigatō gozaimasu.

M: *Um…, what floor is the bookstore on?*
F: *The third floor.*
M: *Pardon? Could you say that one more time?*
F: *It's on the third floor.*
M: *Thank you.*

Q4
M: Sumimasen,100-en shoppu ni ikitai n desu ga….
F: A, mukō. Ano kombini no ushiro ni arimasu yo.
M: Arigatō gozaimasu.

M: *Excuse me, I'm trying to get to the 100-yen store, but….*
F: *Ah, it's over there. It's behind that convenience store.*
M: *Thank you.*

p.48 **[UNIT 3] Q1** 3 **Q2** 2 **Q3** 2 **Q4** 1

Q1
M: Sumimasen, tabako arimasu ka.
F: Mōshiwake arimasen. Tabako wa nai n desu.
M: A, sō desu ka. Wakarimashita.

M: *Excuse me, do you have cigarettes?*
F: *I'm sorry, but we don't.*
M: *Oh, I see.*

189

Q2

M: Sumimasen, kore, ikura desu ka.
F: Kasa wa…, 600-en desu.
M: Kono pen wa ikura desu ka.
F: Sore wa 800-en desu.
M: A, wakarimashita.

M: *Excuse me, how much is this?*
F: *Umbrellas are… 600 yen.*
M: *How much is this pen?*
F: *That's 800 yen.*
M: *Oh, okay.*

Q3

M: Sumimasen, o-bentō arimasu ka.
F: Hai, kochira desu.
M: Jā, sore futatsu kudasai.
F: Kashikomarimashita.

M: *Excuse me, do you have bento boxes?*
F: *Yes, they're right here.*
M: *Okay, then I'll have two, please.*
F: *Right away.*

Q4

M: Irasshaimase.
F: Sumimasen, kore, mōchotto ōkii no, arimasen ka.
M: Mōshiwake arimasen. Kore dake nandesu.
F: A, wakarimashita.

M: *Welcome*
F: *Excuse me, do you have a bigger one of these?*
M: *I'm sorry, but that's all we have.*
F: *Oh, I see.*

p.62 **[UNIT 4] Q1** 3 **Q2** 1 **Q3** 1 **Q4** 2

Q1

M: Go-chūmon okimari desu ka.
F: Osusume wa nan desu ka.
M: Ikura desu.
F: Ikura tte nan desu ka.
M: Kochira desu. Sāmon-eggu desu yo.
F: Ā, jā, sore hitotsu kudasai.

M: *Are you ready to order?*
F: *What do you recommend?*
M: *Ikura.*
F: *What is ikura?*
M: *This. It's salmon eggs.*
F: *Ooooh. OK, then I'll have one of those, please.*

Q2

F: Irasshaimase. Kochira de omeshiagari desu ka.
M: Hai, koko de.
F: Go-chūmon o dōzo.
M: Chīzu-bāgā to aisu-kōhī onegaishimasu.
F: Kashikomarimashita. Gamu-shiroppu to miruku wa go-riyō desu ka.
M: A, gamu-shiroppu wa, iranai desu.

F: *Welcome. Will you be eating here?*
M: *Yes.*
F: *Please order when you are ready.*
M: *I'll have a cheeseburger and an iced coffee, please.*
F: *Okay. Would you like cream and liquid sugar?*
M: *Ah, no liquid sugar, thank you.*

Q3

M: O-nomimono wa ikaga desu ka.
F: Jā, kore to onaji no o onegaishimasu.
M: Hai, nama-bīru o o-hitotsu desu ne.
F: Hai.

M: *Would you like something (else) to drink?*
F: *I'll have another one of this.*
M: *Okay, so one more draft beer, then.*
F: *Thank you.*

Q4

F: Arigatō gozaimashita. O-kaikei wa go-issho de yoroshii desu ka.
M: A, betsubetsu de.
F: Reshīto wa?
M: Iranai desu.

F: *Thank you. Will you be paying together?*
M: *Um, separate please.*
F: *Do you need a receipt?*
M: *No, thank you.*

p.74 **[UNIT 5] Q1** 1 **Q2** 3 **Q3** 2 **Q4** 2

Q1

M: Sumimasen, koko, tabako o sutte mo ii desu ka.
F: Mōshiwake gozaimasen. Kochira wa kin'en-seki nandesu.
M: Wakarimashita.

M: *Excuse me, but can I smoke here?*
F: *I'm terribly sorry, but these are non-smoking seats.*
M: *I see.*

Q2

F: Anō, kore, moratte mo ii desu ka.
F: Panfuretto desu ne. Ii desu yo. Sampuru mo dōzo.
M: A, dōmo.

M: Um, could I take one of these?
F: You must mean the pamphlets. That's fine. Here's a free sample for you, too.
M: Ah, thanks.

Q3

F: Kochira ni go-kinyū kudasai.
M: Rōma-ji de ii desu ka.
F: Ee, kekkō desu.

F: Please fill this out.
M: Can I write in Roman letters?
F: Yes, that's fine.

Q4

M: 710-en ni narimasu.
F: Sumimasen, ichiman-en satsu de ii desu ka.
M: Ēto, a, daijōbu desu yo.
F: Jā, kore de.
M: Hai, arigatō gozaimashita.

M: That comes to 710 yen.
F: I'm sorry, but could I pay with a 10,000-yen note?
M: Hmm... ah, yes, that's fine.
F: Alright, then out of this, please.
M: Right away.

p.87 **[UNIT 6] Q1** 1 **Q2** 3 **Q3** 1 **Q4** 2

Q1

F: Sumimasen, kasa o kashite moraemasen ka.
M: Kochira de yoroshii desu ka.
F: Hai, arigatō gozaimasu.

F: Excuse me, but would you lend me an umbrella?
M: Is this one okay?
F: Yes, thank you.

Q2

F: Okimari desu ka.
M: Sumimasen, chotto matte kudasai.
F: Hai, kashikomarimashita.

F: Are you ready to order?
M: I'm sorry, could I have a minute?
F: Yes, sir.

Q3

M: Koko massugu desu ka.
F: A, iie. Shingō o hidari ni magatte kudasai.
M: Hai.

M: It's straight down here?
F: Ah, no. Please turn left at the traffic light.
M: Okay.

Q4

M: Anō, kono wain, nonde mo ii desu ka.
F: Dozo, dōzo.
M: A, sumimasen. Sono gurasu, totte moraemasen ka.

M: Can I drink this wine?
F: Yes, yes, please.
M: Ah, thank you. Could you pass me that glass?

p.100 **[UNIT 7] Q1** 2 **Q2** 2 **Q3** 3 **Q4** 2

Q1

F: Sumimasen, kore, Hakone ni ikimasu ka.
M: Iie, Hakone wa tsugi no densha desu yo.
F: Arigatō gozaimasu.

F: Excuse me, does this (train) go to Hakone?
M: No, for Hakone you need the next train.
F: Thank you.

Q2

F: Sumimasen, Roppongi-hiruzu made dōyatte ikeba ii desu ka.
M: Chikatetsu de norikae ka..., asoko kara basu de ippon desu ne.
F: A, sō desu ka. Dōmo.

F: Excuse me, how do you get to Roppongi Hills?
M: You can transfer in the subway, or... you can go straight there with the bus over there.
F: Oh, I see. Thank you.

Q3

M: Sumimasen, koko kara Tōkyō-dōmu made doyatte ikeba ii desu ka.
F: Basu ka densha desu ne.
M: Densha de donogurai kakarimasu ka.
F: 10-pun gurai desu yo.
M: A, sō desu ka. Arigatō gozaimasu.

M: Excuse me, how do you get to Tokyo Dome from here?
F: You can take a bus or a train.
M: How long would a train take?

F: About 10 minutes.
M: Oh, I see. Thank you.

Q4

M: Nakamura-san, Tōkyō kara Ōsaka made donogurai kakarimasu ka.
F: Hikōki de 1-jikan gurai desu yo.
M: Jā, shinkansen wa?
F: Shinkansen de wa 3-jikan gurai desu yo.

M: *Nakamura-san, how far is it from Tokyo to Osaka?*
F: *It's about an hour by plane.*
M: *What about by Shinkansen?*
F: *That's about three hours.*

p.113 **[UNIT 8] Q1** 3 **Q2** 1 **Q3** 1 **Q4** 2

Q1

M: Otsukaresama desu.
F: Otsukaresama.
M: Korekara doko ni ikimasu ka.
F: Korekara hon-ya ni ikimasu. Ōta-san wa?
M: Boku wa korekara, tomodachi to gohan o tabe ni ikimasu.
F: Hē, ii desu ne.

M: *Hey.*
F: *Hello.*
M: *Where are you going now?*
F: *I'm going to the bookstore. How about you?*
M: *I'm going to get something to eat with a friend.*
F: *Oh, that sounds nice.*

Q2

F: Ohayō gozaimasu.
M: Ohayō gozaimasu.
F: Shūmatsu, nani o shimashita ka.
M: Shūmatsu wa shigoto deshita.
F: Sō desu ka.
M: Yamada-san wa?
F: Watashi wa kōen ni ikimashita yo. Kazoku to.
M: Hē, ii desu ne.

F: *Good morning.*
M: *Good morning!*
F: *What'd you do on the weekend?*
M: *My weekend was work....*
F: *Really....*
M: *What about you, Yamada-san?*
F: *I went to the park, with my family.*
M: *Oh, that sounds nice.*

Q3

M: Natsu-yasumi, nani o shimasu ka.
F: Umi ni ikitai desu. Takahashi-san wa?
M: Watashi wa uchi de yukkuri shitai desu. Demo, umi mo ii desu ne.
F: Jā, issho ni ikimashō.
M: Ii desu ne. Ikimashō.

M: *What are you doing for the summer break?*
F: *I'm going to the beach. What about you, Takahashi-san?*
M: *I just want to relax at home. But the beach sounds nice.*
F: *We should go together!*
M: *That sounds great. Let's do it!*

Q4

F: Tomu-san, shūmatsu, nani o shimashita ka.
M: Nihon-go o benkyō shimashita.
F: Sō desu ka. Uchi de?
M: Iie, gakkō de.
F: Hē, kondo no yasumi mo gakkō desu ka.
M: Iie, dokoka asobi ni ikitai desu.
F: Sō desu ka.

F: *Tom-san, what did you do on the weekend?*
M: *I studied Japanese.*
F: *I see. At home?*
M: *No, at school.*
F: *Really! Are you going back to school on your next day off?*
M: *No, I'm going to go have fun somewhere.*
F: *I see.*

p.126 **[UNIT 9] Q1** 1 **Q2** 2 **Q3** 3 **Q4** 1

Q1

M: An-san, Nihon no seikatsu wa dō desu ka.
F: Sugoku omoshiroi desu.
M: Sore wa yokatta. Ima sundeiru tokoro wa dō desu ka.
F: Un, totemo kirei desu yo. Demo, chotto takai desu.
M: Sō desu ne. Tōkyō wa takai desu yo ne.

M: *Ann-san, how do you like living in Japan?*
F: *It's so much fun here.*
M: *I'm happy to hear that. How is where you're living right now?*
F: *Oh yes, it's very clean. Although a little expensive....*
M: *I'll bet. Tokyo sure is expensive, isn't it?*

Q2

F: Hayashi-san, kinō no nomikai wa dō deshita ka.
F: Māmā deshita. A, demo ryōri wa oishikatta desu yo.
M: A, sō desu ka.

M: *Hayashi-san, how was yesterday's drinking party?*
F: *It was alright. Oh, but the food was delicious.*
M: *Oh really?*

Q3

F: Ueda-san, ryokō wa dō deshita ka.
M: Taihen deshita. Totemo isogashikatta desu.
F: Sō desu ka. Hoteru wa dō deshita ka.
M: Ā, hoteru wa yokatta desu yo.
F: Sore wa yokatta desu ne.

F: *Ueda-san, how was your trip?*
M: *It was terrible. I was so busy.*
F: *Really? How was the hotel?*
M: *Oh, the hotel was nice.*
F: *Well, I'm glad to hear that.*

Q4

F: Maikeru-san, yasumi wa dō deshita ka.
M: Tanoshikatta desu. Tomodachi to Kyōto no o-tera ni ikimashita.
F: Sō desu ka. Ii desu ne. Nihon no o-tera wa dō desu ka.
M: Totemo kirei desu. Subarashii desu.

F: *Michael-san, how was your vacation?*
M: *It was fun. I went with a friend to some temples in Kyoto.*
F: *Did you? That sounds nice. How do you like Japanese temples?*
M: *They're so beautiful. They're wonderful.*

p.139 **[UNIT 10]** **Q1** 3 **Q2** 2 **Q3** 3 **Q4** 2

Q1

F: Kimu-san, kore, tabete mimasu ka.
M: Sore, donna aji desu ka.
F: Chotto suppai desu yo. Demo, oishii desu yo.
M: Jā, tabete mimasu.

F: *Kim-san, why don't you try this?*
M: *What does it taste like?*
F: *It's a little sour. But it's good!*
M: *Okay, I'll give it a try.*

Q2

M: Saitō-san, are, oishisō desu ne. Nan desu ka.
F: Ā, are wa, shabu-shabu desu yo. Gyūniku desu.
M: Ā, gyūniku desu ka.
F: Nigate desu ka.
M: Ee, chotto.... Nigate nandesu.

M: *Saito-san, that sure looks good. What is it?*
F: *Oh, that's shabu-shabu. With beef.*
M: *Oh, beef?*
F: *Do you not like beef?*
M: *Yeah, I don't really eat it.*

Q3

F: Nan ni shimasu ka. Kore wa dō desu ka.
M: Kore, nan desu ka.
F: Tōfu to shīfūdo no sarada desu.
M: Hē, karada ni yosasō desu ne. Jā, kore ni shimashō.

F: *What will you have? How about this?*
M: *What is it?*
F: *It's a tofu and seafood salad.*
M: *Wow, that sounds healthy. I'll have that, then.*

Q4

M: Kimuchi wa dō desu ka.
F: Kimuchi? Kimuchi tte, donna aji desu ka.
M: Karai desu yo. Demo, oishii desu.
F: Ā, karai mono wa chotto....
M: Sō desu ka. Jā, hoka no ni shimashō.

M: *How about kimchi?*
F: *Kimchi? What does kimchi taste like?*
M: *It's spicy, but it tastes really good.*
F: *Oh, I'm not so good with spicy foods.*
M: *Oh yeah? Then let's have something else.*

p.151 **[UNIT 11]** **Q1** 3 **Q2** 1 **Q3** 1 **Q4** 2

Q1

F: A, dōmo. Kyō mo ii tenki desu ne.
M: Sō desu ne. Mainichi atatakai desu ne.
F: Hontō desu ne.
M: Jā, ittekimasu.
F: Itterasshai.

F: *Hello. We have nice weather today, too, don't we?*
M: *Yes, it's been warm everyday, hasn't it?*
F: *It really has.*
M: *Well, I'm off.*
F: *Have a nice day.*

Q2

F: Konnichiwa. Saikin, chōshi wa dō desu ka.
M: Okagesama de, genki desu. Yamada-san wa?
F: Watashi mo genki desu. Demo, shigoto ga isogashikute….
M: Taihen desu ne.

F: Hello. How have you been lately?
M: I've been OK, knock on wood. How about you?
F: I've been good, too. But work sure is busy….
M: It's rough, isn't it?

Q3

F: Sumimasen, sorosoro kaerimasu. O-saki ni shitsurei shimasu.
M: Otsukaresama deshita. Ki o tsukete.
F: Jā, mata raishū.

F: Excuse me, but I'm heading home. I'll see you later.
M: Good work today. Take care.
F: See you next week.

Q4

F: Konnichiwa. O-hisashiburi desu ne.
M: O-hisashiburi desu, Yamada-san.
F: O-genki desu ka.
M: Okagesama de. Kyō wa kaze ga tsuyoi desu ne,
F: Hontō. Samui desu ne.

F: Hello! It certainly has been a while.
M: It really has, Yamada-san.
F: How are you doing?
M: I'm good, fortunately. The wind is really strong today, isn't it?
F: I know! It's so cold.

p.161 **[UNIT 12]** Q1 2 Q2 1 Q3 2 Q4 3

Q1

M: Otsukaresama. Emiri-san, korekara issho ni nomi ni ikimasen ka.
F: Ii desu ne. Doko ni ikimashō ka.
M: Shibuya wa dō desu ka.
F: Un, sō shimashō.

M: Hey there, Emily-san. Would you want to go get a drink together?
F: That sounds great. Where should we go?
M: How does Shibuya sound?
F: Great, let's do it.

Q2

F: Ohayō gozaimasu.
M: Ohayō gozaimasu. A, Yamada-san, komban issho ni gohan o tabe ni ikimasen ka.
F: Sumimasen. Komban wa chotto….
M: Sō desu ka. Jā, mata kondo.
F: Sumimasen, mata sasotte kudasai.

F: Good morning.
M: Good morning. Oh, Yamada-san, would you like to get something to eat tonight?
F: I'm sorry, but tonight's not so good.
M: It's not? Well, next time, then.
F: Sorry about that. Do ask me again, though.

Q3

F: Tomu-san, Nihon no hanabi o mita koto ga arimasu ka.
M: Hanabi? Iie, mada desu.
F: Yokattara, shūmatsu minna de hanabi o mimasen ka.
M: Ii desu ne.
F: Jā, atode renraku shimasu ne.

F: Tom-san, have you ever seen fireworks in Japan?
M: Fireworks? No, not yet.
F: If you can, would you want to come see fireworks with everyone this weekend?
M: I sure would!
F: Okay, I'll get in touch with you later.

Q4

M: Natarī-san, kabuki o mita koto ga arimasu ka.
F: Iie, arimasen.
M: Shūmatsu, issho ni ikimasen ka.
F: Ii desu ne. Ikimashō.

M: Natalie-san, have you ever seen kabuki?
F: No, I haven't.
M: Would you want to go this weekend?
F: That sounds great. Let's do it.

Model Answers for Role playing and "Do you remember?"

·········· Role playing ··········

p.21 UNIT1
A: Hajimemashite. Watashi wa Robāto desu. Dōzo yoroshiku.
B: Hajimemashite. Yamada desu. Kochira koso dōzo yoroshiku onegaishimasu. Robāto-san, go-shussin wa?
A: Ōsutoraria no Shidonī desu.
B: Sō desu ka. O-shigoto wa?
A: Shisutemu enjinia desu.
B: O-sumai wa?
A: Nakano desu.
B: Sō desu ka. Nihon ryōri ga suki desu ka.
A: Hai, suki desu. Demo sakana wa amari suki ja nai desu.
B: Sō desu ka.

p.34 UNIT2
1
A: Sumimasen, kono hen ni kombini arimasu ka.
B: Arimasu yo.
A: Doko desu ka.
B: Koko massugu desu yo.
A: Chikai desu ka.
B: Hai, chikai desu yo.

2
A: Sumimasen, basu-tei wa doko desu ka.
B: Basu-tei wa soko desu yo.
A: Gendai bijutsukan ni ikitai n desu ga.
B: Sumimasen. Chotto wakarimasen.
A: Sō desu ka. Arigatō gozaimasu.

p.48 UNIT3
1
A: Sumimasen. Kono sumaho no mobairu batterī arimasu ka.
B: Hai arimasu yo. Kochira desu.
A: Ikura desu ka.
B: 1,500-en desu.
A: Motto yasui no wa arimasen ka.
B: Kore wa 1,000-en desu.

2
A: Sumimasen, kasa arimasu ka.
B: Hai, arimasu. Kochira desu.
A: Kore wa ikura desu ka.
B: 2,800-en desu.
A: Motto chiisai no wa arimasen ka.
B: Arimasu. Kochira wa 1,500-en desu.
A: Arigatō gozaimasu.

p.62 UNIT4
1
A: Sumimasen, menyū onegaishimasu.
B: Dōzo.
A: Pasuta ranchi hitotsu onegaishimasu.
B: O-nomimono wa?
A: Kōhī onegaishimasu.
B: Kashikomarimashita. Miruku to o-satō go-riyō desu ka.
A: O-satō onegaishimasu.
B: Kashikomarimashita. Shōshō omachikudasai.

2
A: Sumimasen. Hambāgā hitotsu to aisu kōhī onegaishimasu.
B: Arigatō gozaimasu. Hambāgā hitotsu to aisu kōhī hitotsu desu ne.
Kochira de omeshiagari desu ka.
A: Iie, mochikaeri de.
B: Kashikomarimashita. Aisu kōhī ni miruku to gamu shiroppu wa go-riyō desu ka.
A: Iie, iranai desu.
B: Kashikomarimashita. Fukuro wa go-riyō desu ka.
A: Iie, iranai desu.

p.74 UNIT5
1
A: Sumimasen, yoyaku nashi de mo ii desu ka.
B: Mōshiwake arimasen. Yoyaku nashi wa chotto….
A: Sō desu ka. Kono kādo moratte mo ii desu ka.
B: Hai, dōzo!

2
A: Sumimasen, kai-in ni naritai n desu ga.
B: Arigatō gozaimasu. Dewa kochira ni go-kinyū kudasai.
A: Uchi de kaite mo ii desu ka.
B: Hai, ii desu yo.
A: Ato, eigo de kaite mo ii desu ka.
B: Hai, ii desu yo.

p.87 UNIT6

1
A: Konnichiwa! Dōzo haitte kudasai.
B: Konnichiwa! Arigatō gozaimasu.
A: Dōzo suwatte kudasai.
B: Arigatō gozaimasu. Kore o-miyage desu. Chokorēto desu.
A: Arigatō gozaimasu! O-cha o dōzo. Nonde kudasai.
B: Arigatō gozaimasu.

2
A: Sumimasen, basu no jikoku-hyo arimasu ka.
B: Hai, arimasu yo.
A: Arigatō gozaimasu.
  Kochira, kopī o moraemasen ka.
B: Hai, dōzo!

p.100 UNIT7

1
A: Sumimasen. Shibuya kara Iidabashi made, dōyatte ikeba ii desu ka.
B: Sō desu ne. Yamanote-sen ni notte, Yoyogi de Sōbu-sen ni norikae desu yo.
A: Sō desu ka. Donogurai kakarimasu ka.
B: Ūn, 20-pun gurai desu.
A: Wakarimasita. Arigatō gozaimashita.

2
A: B-san, go-shussin wa Nagano desu ne?
B: Hai.
A: Nagano made, dōyatte ikeba ii desu ka.
B: Shinkansen de 2-jikan-han gurai desu.
A: Ikura gurai kakarimasu ka.
B: Sō desu ne. 9,000-en gurai da to omoimasu.
A: Arigatō gozaimashita.

p.113 UNIT8

1
A: B-san, Tōkyō de nani o shi tai desu ka.
B: Ūn. Asakusa ni iki tai desu.
A: Ii desu ne. Asakusa de nani o shimasu ka.
B: Omiyage o kai tai desu. Sorekara tendon o tabe tai desu.
A: Wakarimashita. Ja, oishii tendon o tabemashō.

2
A: B-san, kore, Hawai no o-miyage desu. Dōzo.
B: Hawai de nani o shimasita ka.
A: Bīchi de yukkuri shimashita. Sorekara oishii shīfūdo o tabemashita. B-san wa raishū, doko ni ikimasu ka.
B: Watashi wa raishū Tai ni ikimasu.
A: Ii desu ne. Tai de nani o shimasu ka.
B: Massāji o shimasu. Sorekara oishii Tai ryōri o tabe tai desu.

p.126 UNIT9

1
A: Senshū, Hokkaidō ni ikimashita.
B: Ii desu ne. Tenki wa dō deshita ka.
A: Samukatta desu. Demo, totemo yokatta desu.
B: Nani o shimashita ka.
A: Sukī o shimashita.
B: Dō deshita ka.
A: Tanoshikatta desu. Yuki wa totemo kirei deshita.

2
A: Saikin, Yokohama ni hikkoshimashita.
B: Sō desu ka.
A: Totemo kirei desu. Uchi wa atarashii desu.
B: Ii desu ne. Yokohama wa benri desu ka.
A: Hai. Kodomo no gakkō wa chikai desu. Totemo benri desu.

p.139 UNIT10

A: Oishi sō desu ne. B-san no osusume wa nan desu ka.
B: Shīfūdo sarada desu.
A: Nani ga haitte imasu ka.
B: Ēto, kore wa ebi (shrimp) ga haitte imasu.
A: Sō desu ka. Ebi wa chotto….
B: Kirai desu ka.
A: Arerugī nan desu.

p.151 UNIT11

1
A: B-san, ohisashiburi desu.
B: A-san, ohisashiburi desu. O-genki desu ka.
A: Hai, genki desu yo. B-san, saikin, shigoto wa dō desu ka.
B: Totemo isogashii desu. Demo tanoshii desu yo. A-san no go-kazoku wa genki desu ka.
A: Hai, totemo genki desu. B-san no go-kazoku wa?
B: Okagesama de genki desu.

2

A: B-san, konnichiwa. O-genki desu ka.
B: Hai, genki desu. A-san wa?
A: Watashi mo genki desu. Saikin totemo mushiatsui desu ne.
B: Sō desu ne. Chotto taihen desu ne.
A: Sō desu ne. Ja, mata.
B: Ja, o-ki o tsukete.

p.161 UNIT12

A: B-san, kabuki o mita koto ga arimasu ka.
B: Iie. Demo, omoshirosou desu.
A: Watashi mo mita koto ga arimasen. Raigetsu, issho ni ikimasen ka.
B: Ii desu ne. Ikimashō.
A: Ja, atode renraku shimasu.
B: Hai, tanoshimi ni shite imasu.

••••••• **Do you remember?** •••••••

p.22 UNIT1

① Hajimemashite. Watashi wa Jon desu. Enjinia desu. Amerika-jin desu. Dōzo yoroshiku.

② O-kuni wa? Amerika desu.
Go-shussin wa? Chiba-ken desu.

③ Sakkā wa suki desu ka.
Iie, sakkā wa amari.
Demo, basuketto bōru wa suki desu.
Sō desu ka.

p.35 UNIT 2

① Kono hen ni koin rokkā arimasu ka.
Iriguchi no tonari desu.
Arigatō gozaimasu.

② Sumimasen, yūbinkyoku ni ikitai n desu ga.
Gomennasai, chotto wakarimasen.

③ Sumimasen, toire doko desu ka.
Achira de gozaimasu.

p.49 UNIT 3

① Sore, ikura desu ka.
1,900-en desu.

② Mō chotto ōkii no arimasen ka.
Kore dake nan desu.

③ Kono ichigo no shōto kēki mittsu kudasai.
Kashikomarimashita. Arigatō gozaimasu.

④ Sumimasen, Kyōto tsuā no panfuretto arimasu ka.
Hai, arimasu.

p.63 UNIT 4

① Kochira de omeshiagari desu ka.
Iie, mochikaeri de.

② Fukuro iranai desu.

③ Sumimasen, torizara futatsu onegaishimasu.
Kashikomarimashita.

④ Are nan desu ka.
Tendon desu.

197

p.75 UNIT 5

① Sumimasen, kore kite mo ii desu ka.
　Dōzo.

② Sumimasen, shashin o totte mo ii desu ka.
　Mōshiwake arimasen ga, chotto.

③ Sumimasen, kutsu de ii desu ka.
　Mōshiwake arimasen ga, chotto.

④ Sumimasen, koko suwatte mo ii desu ka.
　Hai, dōzo.

p.88 UNIT 6

① Sumimasen, are o totte moraemasen ka.
　Wakarimashita.

② Shingō o migi ni magatte kudasai.
　Kashikomarimashita.

③ Sumimasen, tetsudatte moraemasen ka.
　Kashikomarimashita.

p.101 UNIT 7

① Tōkyō made donogurai kakarimasu ka.
　Densha de 20-pun gurai desu yo.

② Tōkyō made dōyatte ikeba ii desu ka.
　Chūō-sen de ippon desu yo.

③ Kore Tōkyō ni ikimasu ka.
　Iie, Tōkyō wa hantai desu yo.

p.114 UNIT 8

① Kurisumasu, nani o shimasu ka.
　Kazoku ni aitai desu.

② Doko ni ikimasu ka.
　Gohan o tabe ni ikimasu.

③ Kinō wa nani o shimashita ka.
　Kinō, watashi wa uchi de nihon-go o benkyō shimashita.

p.127 UNIT 9

① Ryokō wa dō deshita ka.
　Tanoshikatta desu.

② Ima sundeiru tokoro wa dō desu ka.
　Kirei desu yo.

③ Nomikai wa dō deshita ka.
　Tsumaranakatta desu.

p.140 UNIT 10

① Sore, donna aji desu ka.
　Suppai desu.

② Sore, karasō desu ne.
　Karai desu.

③ Kore, dō desu ka.
　Shīfūdo desu ka, shīfūdo wa chotto.

p.152 UNIT 11

① Kyō wa kaze ga tsuyoi desu ne.
　Sō desu ne.

② Saikin shigoto wa dō desu ka.
　Isogashii desu.

③ Ja o-daiji ni.

p.162 UNIT 12

① Ashita, eiga o mimasen ka.
　Ii desu ne. Sō shimashō.

② Kimono o kita koto ga arimasu ka.
　Hai, arimasu.

③ Korekara karaoke ni ikimasen ka.
　Sumimasen, karaoke wa chotto.

● 著者紹介 ●　　Coto Japanese Academyホームページ　https://cotoacademy.com

渡部 由紀子　WATANABE Yukiko
タイでの日本語教育、帰国後㈱リクルートでの営業職、ボランティア日本語グループWAIWAIで代表を務める。生活者向けの日本語教育に特化した日本語スクール事業を2000年より開始。2012年に法人化。Coto World㈱代表取締役社長。

角谷 佳奈　SUMITANI Kana
Coto Japanese Academyスタッフ兼講師。学習者ニーズ調査やカウンセリング担当。千葉県出身。大学で日本文学・日本語学専攻。通信会社勤務、速記者、ボランティア日本語教師経験後、現職に。海外一人旅にて様々なコミュニケーション術を学ぶ。

左 弥寿子　HIDARI Yasuko
Coto Academy麻布十番校講師。海産物卸売業を営む両親のもと、長崎に生まれる。スコットランドの大学院にて「産業としてのロック音楽」を研究。文化関連のシンクタンク勤務を経て、現職。

緒方 由希子　OGATA Yukiko
静岡県出身。美大卒業後、DTP、帽子デザインなどの仕事に携わる。日本語教師という職業を知り、異文化交流に興味があったことから日本語教師に転向。

制作ご協力者：Steve Kingさん、大場麻佐代さん、左 江里子さん、左 文江さん、駒場整骨院の先生、Matthew Harveyさん、渡部実亜さん・里沙さん、角谷収さん、白戸直人さん、Anahita Riaziさん、桜井愛子さん他いいだばし日本語学院スタッフ

NIHONGO FUN & EASY　Survival Japanese Conversation for Beginners　2nd Edition

2009年12月11日	初版　第1刷発行
2023年 2月21日	改訂版第1刷発行
2025年 6月 2日	改訂版第4刷発行

著者	渡部由紀子、角谷佳奈、左 弥寿子、緒方由希子
DTP	鮫島幹夫、株式会社あるむ
翻訳	Ben Milam、株式会社アミット
イラスト	平塚徳明
装丁・本文デザイン	吉田清美
ナレーション	Jason Hancock、廣瀬和也、深山信嗣、緒方由希子、角谷佳奈、左 弥寿子、中村太亮、鍋井まき子
発行	株式会社アスク 〒162-8558　東京都新宿区下宮比町2-6　　電話: 03-3267-6864　　FAX: 03-3267-6867
発行人	天谷修身
印刷・製本	株式会社光邦

ISBN978-4-86639-563-0　　ⓒOGATA Yukiko, SUMITANI Kana, HIDARI Yasuko, WATANABE Yukiko　　Printed in Japan
乱丁・落丁の場合はお取り替えいたします。

アンケートにご協力ください

PC 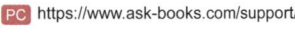 Smartphone

Handy Wordbook
別冊語彙集

Contents | 目次

Verb Conjugation List	動詞活用表	2
Adjective Conjugation List	形容詞活用表	6
Countries and Regions	国・地域	10
List of Useful Words	お役立ち語彙集	11

Jobs	仕事	11	Food	料理	14
Hobbies / Sports	趣味 / スポーツ	11	Cooking Ingredient	食材	16
Shops / Facilities	店 / 施設	12	Drinks	飲み物	17
Clothing / Accessories	衣類 / アクセサリー	13	Tableware	食器類	18
Stationery	文房具	13	Daily Commodities	日用品	18
Furniture / Appliance	家具 / 電化製品	13	Vehicles / Train	乗り物 / 電車	18
Medicine	薬	14	Event	イベント	19
Colors	色	14	Traditional Arts	伝統芸能	19

Verb Conjugation List ｜ 動詞活用表

● U-verb ●

Meaning	Masu-form	Dictionary form	Te-form	Ta-fom	Nai-form
meet	あいます	あう	あって	あった	あわない
keep (a luggage)	あずかります	あずかる	あずかって	あずかった	あずからない
rain	あめがふります	あめがふる	あめがふって	あめがふった	あめがふらない
walk	あるきます	あるく	あるいて	あるいた	あるかない
go	いきます	いく	いって	いった	いかない
hurry	いそぎます	いそぐ	いそいで	いそいだ	いそがない
think/guess/suppose	おもいます	おもう	おもって	おもった	おもわない
buy	かいます	かう	かって	かった	かわない
return (things)	かえします	かえす	かえして	かえした	かえさない
return/go home	かえります	かえる	かえって	かえった	かえらない
it takes (time)/cost	かかります	かかる	かかって	かかった	かからない
write/draw	かきます	かく	かいて	かいた	かかない
lend	かします	かす	かして	かした	かさない
do one's best	がんばります	がんばる	がんばって	がんばった	がんばらない
listen/hear	ききます	きく	きいて	きいた	きかない
sit	すわります	すわる	すわって	すわった	すわらない
smoke (cigarettes)	たばこをすいます	たばこをすう	たばこをすって	たばこをすった	たばこをすわない
use	つかいます	つかう	つかって	つかった	つかわない
make	つくります	つくる	つくって	つくった	つくらない
give one's help	てつだいます	てつだう	てつだって	てつだった	てつだわない
stop/stay(at a hotel)	とまります	とまる	とまって	とまった	とまらない
take (a picture)	とります	とる	とって	とった	とらない
drink	のみます	のむ	のんで	のんだ	のまない
enter	はいります	はいる	はいって	はいった	はいらない
put on (lower body)	はきます	はく	はいて	はいた	はかない
speak	はなします	はなす	はなして	はなした	はなさない
pay	はらいます	はらう	はらって	はらった	はらわない
turn	まがります	まがる	まがって	まがった	まがらない
wait	まちます	まつ	まって	まった	またない
receive/get	もらいます	もらう	もらって	もらった	もらわない
be absent/get rest	やすみます	やすむ	やすんで	やすんだ	やすまない
read	よみます	よむ	よんで	よんだ	よまない
be [inanimate]	あります	ある	あって	あった	ない

• U-verb •

Meaning	Masu-form	Dictionary form	Te-form	Ta-form	Nai-form
meet	aimasu	au	atte	atta	awanai
keep (a luggage)	azukarimasu	azukaru	azukatte	azukatta	azukaranai
rain	ame ga furimasu	ame ga furu	ame ga futte	ame ga futta	ame ga furanai
walk	arukimasu	aruku	aruite	aruita	arukanai
go	ikimasu	iku	itte	itta	ikanai
hurry	isogimasu	isogu	isoide	isoida	isoganai
think/guess/suppose	omoimasu	omou	omotte	omotta	omowanai
buy	kaimasu	kau	katte	katta	kawanai
return (things)	kaeshimasu	kaesu	kaeshite	kaeshita	kaesanai
return/go home	kaerimasu	kaeru	kaette	kaetta	kaeranai
it takes (time)/cost	kakarimasu	kakaru	kakatte	kakatta	kakaranai
write/draw	kakimasu	kaku	kaite	kaita	kakanai
lend	kashimasu	kasu	kashite	kashita	kasanai
do one's best	gambarimasu	gambaru	gambatte	gambatta	gambaranai
listen/hear	kikimasu	kiku	kiite	kiita	kikanai
sit	suwarimasu	suwaru	suwatte	suwatta	suwaranai
smoke (cigarettes)	tabako o suimasu	tabako o suu	tabako o sutte	tabako o sutta	tabako o suwanai
use	tsukaimasu	tsukau	tsukatte	tsukatta	tsukawanai
make	tsukurimasu	tsukuru	tsukutte	tsukutta	tsukuranai
give one's help	tetsudaimasu	tetsudau	tetsudatte	tetsudatta	tetsudawanai
stop/stay(at a hotel)	tomarimasu	tomaru	tomatte	tomatta	tomaranai
take (a picture)	torimasu	toru	totte	totta	toranai
drink	nomimasu	nomu	nonde	nonda	nomanai
enter	hairimasu	hairu	haitte	haitta	hairanai
put on (lower body)	hakimasu	haku	haite	haita	hakanai
speak	hanashimasu	hanasu	hanashite	hanashita	hanasanai
pay	haraimasu	harau	haratte	haratta	harawanai
turn	magarimasu	magaru	magatte	magatta	magaranai
wait	machimasu	matsu	matte	matta	matanai
receive/get	moraimasu	morau	moratte	moratta	morawanai
be absent/get rest	yasumimasu	yasumu	yasunde	yasunda	yasumanai
read	yomimasu	yomu	yonde	yonda	yomanai
be [inanimate]	arimasu	aru	atte	atta	nai

● Ru-verb ●

Meaning	Masu-form	Dictionary form	Te-form	Ta-fom	Nai-form
open	あけます	あける	あけて	あけた	あけない
be [animate]	います	いる	いて	いた	いない
wake up	おきます	おきる	おきて	おきた	おきない
be late	おくれます	おくれる	おくれて	おくれた	おくれない
teach	おしえます	おしえる	おしえて	おしえた	おしえない
change	かえます	かえる	かえて	かえた	かえない
borrow	かります	かりる	かりて	かりた	かりない
put on (upper body)	きます	きる	きて	きた	きない
eat	たべます	たべる	たべて	たべた	たべない
get tired	つかれます	つかれる	つかれて	つかれた	つかれない
go out	でかけます	でかける	でかけて	でかけた	でかけない
sleep	ねます	ねる	ねて	ねた	ねない
show	みせます	みせる	みせて	みせた	みせない
see/look/watch	みます	みる	みて	みた	みない
forget	わすれます	わすれる	わすれて	わすれた	わすれない

● Irregular verb ●

Meaning	Masu-form	Dictionary form	Te-form	Ta-fom	Nai-form
fill in	きにゅうします	きにゅうする	きにゅうして	きにゅうした	きにゅうしない
come	きます	くる	きて	きた	こない
cancel	キャンセルします	キャンセルする	キャンセルして	キャンセルした	キャンセルしない
take a walk	さんぽします	さんぽする	さんぽして	さんぽした	さんぽしない
work	しごとします	しごとする	しごとして	しごとした	しごとしない
try on	しちゃくします	しちゃくする	しちゃくして	しちゃくした	しちゃくしない
do/play	します	する	して	した	しない
jog	ジョギングします	ジョギングする	ジョギングして	ジョギングした	ジョギングしない
order	ちゅうもんします	ちゅうもんする	ちゅうもんして	ちゅうもんした	ちゅうもんしない
phone/call	でんわします	でんわする	でんわして	でんわした	でんわしない
study	べんきょうします	べんきょうする	べんきょうして	べんきょうした	べんきょうしない
bring (things)	もってきます	もってくる	もってきて	もってきた	もってこない
relax	ゆっくりします	ゆっくりする	ゆっくりして	ゆっくりした	ゆっくりしない
reserve	よやくします	よやくする	よやくして	よやくした	よやくしない
contact	れんらくします	れんらくする	れんらくして	れんらくした	れんらくしない

● Ru-verb ●

Meaning	Masu-form	Dictionary form	Te-form	Ta-fom	Nai-form
open	akemasu	akeru	akete	aketa	akenai
be [animate]	imasu	iru	ite	ita	inai
wake up	okimasu	okiru	okite	okita	okinai
be late	okuremasu	okureru	okurete	okureta	okurenai
teach	oshiemasu	oshieru	oshiete	oshieta	oshienai
change	kaemasu	kaeru	kaete	kaeta	kaenai
borrow	karimasu	kariru	karite	karita	karinai
put on (upper body)	kimasu	kiru	kite	kita	kinai
eat	tabemasu	taberu	tabete	tabeta	tabenai
get tired	tsukaremasu	tsukareru	tsukarete	tsukareta	tsukarenai
go out	dekakemasu	dekakeru	dekakete	dekaketa	dekakenai
sleep	nemasu	neru	nete	neta	nenai
show	misemasu	miseru	misete	miseta	misenai
see/look/watch	mimasu	miru	mite	mita	minai
forget	wasuremasu	wasureru	wasurete	wasureta	wasurenai

● Irregular verb ●

Meaning	Masu-form	Dictionary form	Te-form	Ta-fom	Nai-form
fill in	kinyū shimasu	kinyū suru	kinyū shite	kinyū shita	kinyū shinai
come	kimasu	kuru	kite	kita	konai
cancel	kyanseru shimasu	kyanseru suru	kyanseru shite	kyanseru shita	kyanseru shinai
take a walk	sampo shimasu	sampo suru	sampo shite	sampo shita	sampo shinai
work	shigoto shimasu	shigoto suru	shigoto shite	shigoto shita	shigoto shinai
try on	shichaku shimasu	shichaku suru	shichaku shite	shichaku shita	shichaku shinai
do/play	shimasu	suru	shite	shita	shinai
jog	jogingu shimasu	jogingu suru	jogingu shite	jogingu shita	jogingu shinai
order	chūmon shimasu	chūmon suru	chūmon shite	chūmon shita	chūmon shinai
phone/call	denwa shimasu	denwa suru	denwa shite	dennwa shita	denwa shinai
study	benkyō shimasu	benkyō suru	benkyō shite	benkyō shita	benkyō shinai
bring (things)	motte kimasu	motte kuru	motte kite	motte kita	motte konai
relax	yukkuri shimasu	yukkuri suru	yukkuri shite	yukkuri shita	yukkuri shinai
reserve	yoyaku shimasu	yoyaku suru	yoyaku shite	yoyaku shita	yoyaku shinai
contact	renraku shimasu	renraku suru	renraku shite	renraku shita	renraku shinai

Adjective Conjugation List ｜ 形容詞活用表

● I-adjective ●

Meaning	Non-Past		Past	
	Affir.（＋です）	Neg.（＋です）	Affir.（＋です）	Neg.（＋です）
bright	あかるい	あかるくない	あかるかった	あかるくなかった
smart/wise	あたまがいい	あたまがよくない	あたまがよかった	あたまがよくなかった
new	あたらしい	あたらしくない	あたらしかった	あたらしくなかった
hot	あつい	あつくない	あつかった	あつくなかった
dangerous	あぶない	あぶなくない	あぶなかった	あぶなくなかった
good/fine	いい	よくない	よかった	よくなかった
busy	いそがしい	いそがしくない	いそがしかった	いそがしくなかった
noisy	うるさい	うるさくない	うるさかった	うるさくなかった
delicious/tasty	おいしい	おいしくない	おいしかった	おいしくなかった
big	おおきい	おおきくない	おおきかった	おおきくなかった
heavy	おもい	おもくない	おもかった	おもくなかった
interesting/fun	おもしろい	おもしろくない	おもしろかった	おもしろくなかった
good-looking/cool	かっこいい	かっこよくない	かっこよかった	かっこよくなかった
light/lightweight	かるい	かるくない	かるかった	かるくなかった
pretty/cute	かわいい	かわいくない	かわいかった	かわいくなかった
dirty	きたない	きたなくない	きたなかった	きたなくなかった
feel good	きもちいい	きもちよくない	きもちよかった	きもちよくなかった
dark	くらい	くらくない	くらかった	くらくなかった
scary/feel fear	こわい	こわくない	こわかった	こわくなかった
cold [weather]	さむい	さむくない	さむかった	さむくなかった
great	すごい	すごくない	すごかった	すごくなかった
wonderful	すばらしい	すばらしくない	すばらしかった	すばらしくなかった
tall	せがたかい	せがたかくない	せがたかかった	せがたかくなかった
short (in height)	せがひくい	せがひくくない	せがひくかった	せがひくくなかった
narrow	せまい	せまくない	せまかった	せまくなかった
expensive/high	たかい	たかくない	たかかった	たかくなかった
enjoyable/fun	たのしい	たのしくない	たのしかった	たのしくなかった
small	ちいさい	ちいさくない	ちいさかった	ちいさくなかった
close/near	ちかい	ちかくない	ちかかった	ちかくなかった
boring	つまらない	つまらなくない	つまらなかった	つまらなくなかった
cold [thing]	つめたい	つめたくない	つめたかった	つめたくなかった
strong	つよい	つよくない	つよかった	つよくなかった
far	とおい	とおくない	とおかった	とおくなかった
long	ながい	ながくない	ながかった	ながくなかった

• I-adjective •

Meaning	Non-Past		Past	
	Affir.(+desu)	Neg. (+desu)	Affir. (+desu)	Neg. (+desu)
bright	akarui	akarukunai	akarukatta	akarukunakatta
smart/wise	atama ga ii	atama ga yokunai	atama ga yokatta	atama ga yokunakatta
new	atarashii	atarashikunai	atarashikatta	atarashikunakatta
hot	atsui	atsukunai	atsukatta	atsukunakatta
dangerous	abunai	abunakunai	abunakatta	abunakunakatta
good/fine	ii	yokunai	yokatta	yokunakatta
busy	isogashii	isogashikunai	isogashikatta	isogashikunakatta
noisy	urusai	urusakunai	urusakatta	urusakunakatta
delicious/tasty	oishii	oishikunai	oishikatta	oishikunakatta
big	ōkii	ōkikunai	ōkikatta	ōkikunakatta
heavy	omoi	omokunai	omokatta	omokunakatta
interesting/fun	omoshiroi	omoshirokunai	omoshirokatta	omoshirokunakatta
good-looking/cool	kakko ii	kakko yokunai	kakko yokatta	kakko yokunakatta
light/lightweight	karui	karukunai	karukatta	karukunakatta
pretty/cute	kawaii	kawaikunai	kawaikatta	kawaikunakatta
dirty	kitanai	kitanakunai	kitanakatta	kitanakunakatta
feel good	kimochi ii	kimochi yokunai	kimochi yokatta	kimochi yokunakatta
dark	kurai	kurakunai	kurakatta	kurakunakatta
scary/feel fear	kowai	kowakunai	kowakatta	kowakunakatta
cold [weather]	samui	samukunai	samukatta	samukunakatta
great	sugoi	sugokunai	sugokatta	sugokunakatta
wonderful	subarashii	subarashikunai	subarashikatta	subarashikunakatta
tall	se ga takai	se ga takakunai	se ga takakatta	se ga takakunakatta
short (in height)	se ga hikui	se ga hikukunai	se ga hikukatta	se ga hikukunakatta
narrow	semai	semakunai	semakatta	semakunakatta
expensive/high	takai	takakunai	takakatta	takakunakatta
enjoyable/fun	tanoshii	tanoshikunai	tanoshikatta	tanashikunakatta
small	chiisai	chiisakunai	chiisakatta	chiisakunakatta
close/near	chikai	chikakunai	chikakatta	chikakunakatta
boring	tsumaranai	tsumaranakunai	tsumaranakatta	tsumaranakunakatta
cold [thing]	tsumetai	tsumetakunai	tsumetakatta	tsumetakunakatta
strong	tsuyoi	tsuyokunai	tsuyokatta	tsuyokunakatta
far	tōi	tōkunai	tōkatta	tōkunakatta
long	nagai	nagakunai	nagakatta	nagakunakatta

Meaning	Non-Past		Past	
	Affir.（＋です）	Neg.（＋です）	Affir.（＋です）	Neg.（＋です）
wide/large [space]	ひろい	ひろくない	ひろかった	ひろくなかった
old	ふるい	ふるくない	ふるかった	ふるくなかった
taste bad	まずい	まずくない	まずかった	まずくなかった
short	みじかい	みじかくない	みじかかった	みじかくなかった
difficult	むずかしい	むずかしくない	むずかしかった	むずかしくなかった
easy/kind	やさしい	やさしくない	やさしかった	やさしくなかった
cheap	やすい	やすくない	やすかった	やすくなかった
weak	よわい	よわくない	よわかった	よわくなかった
young	わかい	わかくない	わかかった	わかくなかった

● **Na-adjective** ●

Meaning	Non-Past		Past	
	Affirmative	Negative	Affirmative	Negative
safe	あんぜんです	あんぜんじゃありません	あんぜんでした	あんぜんじゃありませんでした
easy	かんたんです	かんたんじゃありません	かんたんでした	かんたんじゃありませんでした
clean/beautiful	きれいです	きれいじゃありません	きれいでした	きれいじゃありませんでした
fine	げんきです	げんきじゃありません	げんきでした	げんきじゃありませんでした
quiet	しずかです	しずかじゃありません	しずかでした	しずかじゃありませんでした
skillful/good	じょうずです	じょうずじゃありません	じょうずでした	じょうずじゃありませんでした
simple	シンプルです	シンプルじゃありません	シンプルでした	シンプルじゃありませんでした
like/favorite	すきです	すきじゃありません	すきでした	すきじゃありませんでした
hard/tough/terrible	たいへんです	たいへんじゃありません	たいへんでした	たいへんじゃありませんでした
lively	にぎやかです	にぎやかじゃありません	にぎやかでした	にぎやかじゃありませんでした
free/not busy	ひまです	ひまじゃありません	ひまでした	ひまじゃありませんでした
complicated	ふくざつです	ふくざつじゃありません	ふくざつでした	ふくざつじゃありませんでした
friendly	フレンドリーです	フレンドリーじゃありません	フレンドリーでした	フレンドリーじゃありませんでした
unskillful/bad	へたです	へたじゃありません	へたでした	へたじゃありませんでした
convenient	べんりです	べんりじゃありません	べんりでした	べんりじゃありませんでした
serious	まじめです	まじめじゃありません	まじめでした	まじめじゃありませんでした
famous	ゆうめいです	ゆうめいじゃありません	ゆうめいでした	ゆうめいじゃありませんでした
selfish	わがままです	わがままじゃありません	わがままでした	わがままじゃありませんでした

Meaning	Non-Past		Past	
	Affir.(+desu)	Neg. (+desu)	Affir. (+desu)	Neg. (+desu)
wide/large [space]	hiroi	hirokunai	hirokatta	hirokunakatta
old	furui	furukunai	furukatta	furukunakatta
taste bad	mazui	mazukunai	mazukatta	mazukunakatta
short	mijikai	mijikakunai	mijikakatta	mijikakunakatta
difficult	muzukashii	muzukashikunai	muzukashikatta	muzukashikunakatta
easy/kind	yasashii	yasashikunai	yasashikatta	yasashikunakatta
cheap	yasui	yasukunai	yasukatta	yasukunakatta
weak	yowai	yowakunai	yowakatta	yowakunakatta
young	wakai	wakakunai	wakakatta	wakakunakatta

• **Na-adjective** •

Meaning	Non-Past		Past	
	Affirmative	Negative	Affirmative	Negative
safe	anzen desu	anzen ja arimasen	anzen deshita	anzen ja arimasen deshita
easy	kantan desu	kantan ja arimasen	kantan deshita	kantan ja arimasen deshita
clean/beautiful	kirei desu	kirei ja arimasen	kirei deshita	kirei ja arimasen deshita
fine	genki desu	genki ja arimasen	genki deshita	genki ja arimasen deshita
quiet	shizuka desu	shizuka ja arimasen	shizuka deshita	shizuka ja arimasen deshita
skillful/good	jōzu desu	jōzu ja arimasen	jōzu deshita	jōzu ja arimasen deshita
simple	shimpuru desu	shimpuru ja arimasen	shimpuru deshita	shimpuru ja arimasen deshita
like/favorite	suki desu	suki ja arimasen	suki deshita	suki ja arimasen deshita
hard/tough/terrible	taihen desu	taihen ja arimasen	taihen deshita	taihen ja arimasen deshita
lively	nigiyaka desu	nigiyaka ja arimasen	nigiyaka deshita	nigiyaka ja arimasen deshita
free/not busy	hima desu	hima ja arimasen	hima deshita	hima ja arimasen deshita
complicated	fukuzatsu desu	fukuzatsu ja arimasen	fukuzatsu deshita	fukuzatsu ja arimasen deshita
friendly	furendorī desu	furendorī ja arimasen	furendorī deshita	furendorī ja arimasen deshita
unskillful/bad	heta desu	heta ja arimasen	heta deshita	heta ja arimasen deshita
convenient	benri desu	benri ja arimasen	benri deshita	benri ja arimasen deshita
serious	majime desu	majime ja arimasen	majime deshita	majime ja arimasen deshita
famous	yūmei desu	yūmei ja arimasen	yūmei deshita	yūmei ja arimasen deshita
selfish	wagamama desu	wagamama ja arimasen	wagamama deshita	wagamama ja arimasen deshita

Countries and Regions | 国・地域

Africa	Afurika	アフリカ
Benin	Benan	ベナン
Cameroon	Kamerūn	カメルーン
Cote d'Ivoire	Kōtojiboāru	コートジボアール
Egypt	Ejiputo	エジプト
Ethiopia	Echiopia	エチオピア
Ghana	Gāna	ガーナ
Guinea	Ginia	ギニア
Kenya	Kenia	ケニア
Madagascar	Madagasukaru	マダガスカル
Morocco	Morokko	モロッコ
Nigeria	Naijeria	ナイジェリア
Senegal	Senegaru	セネガル
South Africa Republic	Minami Afurika kyōwakoku	南アフリカ共和国
Tanzania	Tanzania	タンザニア
Tunisia	Chunijia	チュニジア

Asia/Oceania	Ajia/Oseania	アジア/オセアニア
Afghanistan	Afuganistan	アフガニスタン
Australia	Ōsutoraria	オーストラリア
Bahrain	Bārēn	バーレーン
Bangladesh	Banguradeshu	バングラデシュ
China	Chūgoku	中国
India	Indo	インド
Indonesia	Indoneshia	インドネシア
Iran	Iran	イラン
Iraq	Iraku	イラク
Japan	Nihon	日本
Korea	Kankoku	韓国
Kuwait	Kuwēto	クウェート
Kyrgyzstan	Kirugisu	キルギス
Lebanon	Rebanon	レバノン
Malaysia	Marēshia	マレーシア
Mongolia	Mongoru	モンゴル
Myanmar	Myanmā	ミャンマー
Nepal	Nepāru	ネパール
New Zealand	Nyūjirando	ニュージーランド
Oman	Omān	オマーン
Pakistan	Pakisutan	パキスタン
Philippines	Firipin	フィリピン
Qatar	Katāru	カタール
Saudi Arabia	Sauji Arabia	サウジアラビア
Singapore	Shingapōru	シンガポール
Sri Lanka	Suriranka	スリランカ
Taiwan	Taiwan	台湾
Thailand	Tai	タイ
Turkey	Toruko	トルコ
United Arab Emirates	Arabu shuchōkoku rempō	アラブ首長国連邦
Uzbekistan	Uzubekisutan	ウズベキスタン
Vietnam	Betonamu	ベトナム

Europe	Yoroppa	ヨーロッパ
Austria	Ōsutoria	オーストリア
Belgium	Berugī	ベルギー
Bulgaria	Burugaria	ブルガリア
Croatia	Kuroachia	クロアチア
Czech	Cheko	チェコ
Denmark	Denmāku	デンマーク
Estonia	Esutonia	エストニア
Finland	Finrando	フィンランド
France	Furansu	フランス
Germany	Doitsu	ドイツ
Greece	Girisha	ギリシャ
Hungary	Hangarī	ハンガリー
Iceland	Aisurando	アイスランド
Ireland	Airurando	アイルランド
Israel	Isuraeru	イスラエル
Italy	Itaria	イタリア
Latvia	Ratobia	ラトビア
Lithuania	Ritoania	リトアニア
Luxembourg	Rukusenburuku	ルクセンブルク
Moldova	Morudoba	モルドバ
Netherlands	Oranda	オランダ
Norway	Noruwē	ノルウェー
Poland	Pōrando	ポーランド
Portugal	Porutogaru	ポルトガル
Romania	Rūmania	ルーマニア
Russian Federation	Roshia	ロシア
Spain	Supein	スペイン
Sweden	Suweden	スウェーデン
Switzerland	Suisu	スイス
Ukraine	Ukuraina	ウクライナ
United Kingdom	Igirisu	イギリス

North/Central/South America	Kita/Chuo/Minami Amerika	北・中央・南アメリカ
Argentina	Aruzenchin	アルゼンチン
Brazil	Burajiru	ブラジル
Canada	Kanada	カナダ
Chile	Chiri	チリ
Colombia	Korombia	コロンビア
Costa Rica	Kosutarika	コスタリカ
Cuba	Kyūba	キューバ
Ecuador	Ekuadoru	エクアドル
Guatemala	Guatemara	グアテマラ
Jamaica	Jamaika	ジャマイカ
Mexico	Mekishiko	メキシコ
Paraguay	Paraguai	パラグアイ
Peru	Perū	ペルー
United States of America	Amerika	アメリカ
Uruguay	Uruguai	ウルグアイ
Venezuela	Benezuera	ベネズエラ

List of Useful Words
お役立ち語彙集

The word list for Practice A, Practice B and Dialogue
*ページ番号は、各ユニットでの初出ページです。

Jobs 仕事 しごと **Shigoto**	company worker 会社員 かいしゃいん kaishain p.14	engineer エンジニア えんじにあ enjinia p.14	programmer プログラマー ぷろぐらまー puroguramā	lawyer 弁護士 べんごし bengoshi
accountant 会計士 かいけいし kaikeishi	tax accountant 税理士 ぜいりし zeirishi	banker 銀行員 ぎんこういん ginkōin	consultant コンサルタント こんさるたんと konsarutanto p.14	journalist ジャーナリスト じゃーなりすと jānarisuto
translator 翻訳家 ほんやくか hon'yakuka	interpreter 通訳(者) つうやく(しゃ) tsūyaku(sha)	doctor 医者 いしゃ isha	nurse 看護師 かんごし kangoshi	researcher 研究員 けんきゅういん kenkyūin
teacher 先生／教師 せんせい／きょうし sensei/kyōshi p.14	student 学生 がくせい gakusei p.14	artist アーティスト あーてぃすと āthisuto	architect 建築家 けんちくか kenchikuka	designer デザイナー でざいなー dezainā
musician ミュージシャン みゅーじしゃん myūjishan	cameraman カメラマン かめらまん kameraman	photographer 写真家 しゃしんか shashinka	writer 作家／ライター さっか／らいたー sakka/raitā	chef シェフ／コック しぇふ／こっく shefu/kokku
beautician 美容師 びようし biyōshi	self-employed 自営業 じえいぎょう jieigyō	homemaker 主婦／主夫 しゅふ／しゅふ shufu	not working 仕事をしていません しごとをしていません shigoto o shiteimasen	

Hobbies/Sports 趣味／スポーツ しゅみ／すぽーつ **Shumi/Supōtsu**	movie 映画 えいが eiga p.18, p.156	music 音楽 おんがく ongaku p.18	reading 読書 どくしょ dokusho	leisure walk 散歩 さんぽ sampo p.108
gardening ガーデニング がーでにんぐ gādeningu	paintings 絵 え e	travel/trip 旅行 りょこう ryokō p.18, p.110, p.122	leisure drive ドライブ どらいぶ doraibu	picture/photo 写真 しゃしん shashin p.70, p.84, p.112
shopping 買い物 かいもの kaimono p.106	cooking 料理 りょうり ryōri	volunteer ボランティア ぼらんてぃあ boranchia	bowling ボウリング ぼうりんぐ bōringu	pool/billiard ビリヤード びりやーど biriyādo
karaoke カラオケ からおけ karaoke p.18, p.124, p.158	darts ダーツ だーつ dātsu	video games ゲーム げーむ gēmu	manga/comic まんが まんが manga	the outdoors アウトドア あうとどあ autodoa p.18
the internet インターネット いんたーねっと intānetto	eating tour 食べ歩き たべあるき tabe-aruki	cycling サイクリング さいくりんぐ saikuringu p.112, p.156	jogging ジョギング じょぎんぐ jogingu p.110	soccer/football サッカー さっかー sakkā p.18

baseball 野球 やきゅう yakyū	snowboarding スノーボード すのーぼーど sunōbōdo p.158	skiing スキー すきー sukī	scuba diving スキューバダイビング すきゅーばだいびんぐ sukyūba-daibingu	surfing サーフィン さーふぃん sāfin
yoga ヨガ よが yoga	dancing ダンス だんす dansu	golf ゴルフ ごるふ gorufu	tennis テニス てにす tenisu	ping pong 卓球 たっきゅう takkyū
weight training 筋トレ きんとれ kintore	bouldering ボルダリング ぼるだりんぐ borudaringu	martial arts 格闘技 かくとうぎ kakutōgi	judo 柔道 じゅうどう jūdō p.viii	aikido 合気道 あいきどう aikidō p.viii
karate 空手 からて karate	swimming 水泳 すいえい suiei	mountain climbing 山登り やまのぼり yama-nobori	hiking ハイキング はいきんぐ haikingu	fishing 釣り つり turi

Shops/Facilities 店／施設 みせ／しせつ Mise/Shisetsu	bookstore 本屋 ほんや hon-ya p.28, p.106	flower shop 花屋 はなや hana-ya p.32	restaurant レストラン れすとらん resutoran	café 喫茶店／カフェ きっさてん／かふぇ kissaten/kafe
izakaya/Japanese pub 居酒屋 いざかや izakaya	bakery パン屋 ぱんや pan-ya	ramen house ラーメン屋 らーめんや rāmen-ya	sushi restaurant すし屋 すしや sushi-ya	electronics store 電気屋 でんきや denki-ya p.26
beauty salon 美容院 びよういん biyō-in	barbershop 床屋 とこや tokoya	100-yen store １００円ショップ ひゃくえんしょっぷ hyaku-en shoppu p.26	discount store ディスカウントショップ でぃすかうんとしょっぷ disukaunto shoppu	drugstore ドラッグストア どらっぐすとあ doraggu sutoa p.26
pharmacy 薬局 やっきょく yakkyoku	super market スーパー すーぱー sūpā p.26	convenience store コンビニ こんびに kombini p.26	bank 銀行 ぎんこう ginkō p.30	atm ATM ATM p.26
station 駅 えき eki p.26, p.107	bus stop バス停 ばすてい basu-tei p.26	movie theater 映画館 えいがかん eigakan p.30	museum 美術館 びじゅつかん bijutsukan p.30, 106	zoo 動物園 どうぶつえん dōbutsu-en
police box 交番 こうばん kōban p.26	post office 郵便局 ゆうびんきょく yūbinkyoku p.30	amusement park 遊園地 ゆうえんち yūenchi	park 公園 こうえん kōen p.30, p.106	hotel ホテル ほてる hoteru p.82
guesthouse ゲストハウス げすとはうす gesuto-hausu p.82	gas station ガソリンスタンド がそりんすたんど gasorin sutando	parking lot 駐車場 ちゅうしゃじょう chūshajō p.26	city hall 区役所／市役所 くやくしょ／しやくしょ kuyakusho/shiyakusho	airport 空港 くうこう kūkō
university 大学 だいがく daigaku	school 学校 がっこう gakkō p.146	hospital 病院 びょういん byōin p.30	department store デパート でぱーと depāto	shopping mall ショッピングモール しょっぴんぐもーる shoppingu mōru p.112

English	Japanese	Romaji		
onsen (hot spring) 温泉 おんせん onsen p.158	temple お寺 おてら otera p.124	restroom トイレ といれ toire p.28	cash register レジ れじ reji p.28	elevator エレベーター えれべーたー erebētā
escalator エスカレーター えすかれーたー esukarētā	coin-operated locker コインロッカー こいんろっかー koin rokkā p.28	entrance 入り口 いりぐち iriguchi p.28	exit 出口 でぐち deguchi	

Clothing/Accessories 衣類／アクセサリー いるい／あくせさりー Irui/Akusesarī	T-shirt Tシャツ てぃーしゃつ T-shatsu p.42	dress shirt ワイシャツ わいしゃつ wai-shatsu	shoes 靴 くつ kutsu p.41, p.68	socks 靴下 くつした kutsushita
necktie ネクタイ ねくたい nekutai	shorts 半ズボン／ショートパンツ はんずぼん／しょーとぱんつ han-zubon/shōto-pantsu	pants/trousers ズボン／パンツ ずぼん／ぱんつ zubon/pantsu	jacket ジャケット じゃけっと jaketto	underwear 下着 したぎ shitagi
short/long sleeves 半／長そで はん／ながそで han-/naga-sode	skirt スカート すかーと sukāto	jeans ジーンズ じーんず jinzu	sweater セーター せーたー sētā	jumper ジャンパー じゃんぱー jampā
kimono 着物 きもの kimono p.158	yukata/cotton kimono 浴衣 ゆかた yukata	watch/clock 時計 とけい tokei p.41	scarf マフラー まふらー mafurā p.41	glasses めがね めがね megane
swimsuit 水着 みずぎ mizugi p.72	hat/cap 帽子 ぼうし bōshi p.72	pierced earring ピアス ぴあす piasu	earring イヤリング いやりんぐ iyaringu	necklace ネックレス ねっくれす nekkuresu
glove 手袋 てぶくろ tebukuro	belt ベルト べると beruto	ring ゆびわ ゆびわ yubiwa	handkerchief ハンカチ はんかち hankachi	bag バッグ／かばん ばっぐ／かばん baggu/kaban p.41

Stationery 文房具 ぶんぼうぐ Bumbōgu	notebook ノート のーと nōto	pen ペン ぺん pen p.41, p.70	scissors ハサミ はさみ hasami	file ファイル ふぁいる fairu
eraser 消しゴム けしごむ keshigomu	sticky note 付箋 ふせん fusen	scotch tape セロテープ せろてーぷ serotēpu	packaging tape ガムテープ がむてーぷ gamu-tēpu	staple ホッチキス ほっちきす hocchikisu

Furniture/Appliance 家具／電化製品 かぐ／でんかせいひん Kagu/Denka-seihin	shelf 棚 たな tana	desk 机 つくえ tsukue	chair いす いす isu	table テーブル てーぶる tēburu
bed ベッド べっど beddo	Japanese-style bedding 布団 ふとん futon	refrigerator 冷蔵庫 れいぞうこ reizōko	washing machine 洗濯機 せんたくき sentakuki	dryer 乾燥機 かんそうき kansouki

vacuum cleaner 掃除機 そうじき sōjiki	microwave 電子レンジ でんしれんじ denshi-renji	hairdryer ドライヤー どらいやー doraiyā	air conditioner エアコン えあこん eakon	printer プリンタ ぷりんた purinta
battery charger 充電器 じゅうでんき jūdenki p.38	personal computer パソコン ぱそこん pasokon p.45, p.71	smart phone スマホ(スマートフォン)／携帯 すまほ(すまーとふぉん)／けいたい sumaho (sumātofon)/keitai p.45	wireless earphone ワイヤレスイヤホン わいやれすいやほん waiyaresu iyahon p.45	TV テレビ てれび terebi p.108

Medicine 薬 くすり **Kusuri**	headache medicine 頭痛薬 ずつうやく zutsū-yaku	painkiller 痛み止め いたみどめ itami-dome	cold medicine かぜ薬 かぜぐすり kazegusuri	stomach medicine 胃薬 いぐすり igusuri
gargle うがい薬 うがいぐすり ugaigusuri	eye drops 目薬 めぐすり megusuri	nasal drops 点鼻薬 てんびやく tenbi-yaku	itch medicine かゆみ止め かゆみどめ kayumi-dome	disinfectant 消毒液 しょうどくえき shōdoku-eki
band-aid ばんそうこう ばんそうこう bansōkō	diarrhea medicine 下痢止め げりどめ geri-dome	wet cloth 湿布 しっぷ shippu	insecticide 殺虫剤 さっちゅうざい sacchū-zai	sanitary product 生理用品 せいりようひん seiriyōhin

Colors 色 いろ **Iro**	red 赤(い) あか(い) aka(i) p.i, p.54	blue 青(い) あお(い) ao(i) p.i, p.46	yellow 黄色(い) きいろ(い) kiiro(i) p.i	black 黒(い) くろ(い) kuro(i) p.i, p.46, p.54
white 白(い) しろ(い) shiro(i) p.i, p.54	brown 茶色(い)／ブラウン ちゃいろ(い)／ぶらうん chairo(i)/buraun p.i	green 緑 みどり midori p.i	orange オレンジ おれんじ orenji p.i	pink ピンク ぴんく pinku p.i
yellow-green 黄緑 きみどり kimidori p.i	dark blue 紺 こん kon p.i	light blue 水色 みずいろ mizuiro p.i	purple 紫 むらさき murasaki p.i	gray 灰色／グレー はいいろ／ぐれー haiiro/gurē p.i

Food 料理 りょうり **Ryōri**	Japanese food 日本料理 にほんりょうり Nihon ryōri p.i	sukiyaki すき焼き すきやき sukiyaki p.i	shabu-shabu しゃぶしゃぶ しゃぶしゃぶ shabu shabu p.i	grilled meat 焼肉 やきにく yakiniku p.i
grilled chicken skewers 焼き鳥 やきとり yakitori p.vi	row fish 刺身 さしみ sashimi p.vi	tempura 天ぷら てんぷら tempura p.i, p.20	fried chicken から揚げ からあげ karaage p.vi	pork fried with ginger しょうが焼き しょうがやき shōgayaki p.ii
chicken teriyaki 鶏の照り焼き とりのてりやき tori no teriyaki p.ii	meat and potato stew 肉じゃが にくじゃが nikujaga p.ii	tempura rice bowl 天丼 てんどん tendon p.ii	chicken and egg rice bowl 親子丼 おやこどん oyakodon p.i	beef rice bowl 牛丼 ぎゅうどん gyūdon p.i, p.55
pork cutlet rice bowl かつ丼 かつどん katsudon p.ii	broth with egg, steamed fish cake etc. おでん おでん oden p.i	sushi (お)すし／にぎりずし (お)すし／にぎりずし (o)sushi/nigiri zushi p.i, p.18	sashimi or various toppings on sushi rice ちらしずし ちらしずし chirashi zushi p.i	sushi rice-stuffed fried tofu いなりずし いなりずし inari zushi p.i

English	Japanese (kanji)	Romaji	Page
sushi roll	のり巻き / のりまき	norimaki	p. i
udon with deep-fried tofu	きつねうどん / きつねうどん	kitsune udon	p. ii
udon with tempura batter	たぬきうどん / たぬきうどん	tanuki udon	p. ii
buckwheat noodles with tempura	天ぷらそば / てんぷらそば	tempura soba	p. ii
cold soba with dipping sauce	ざるそば / ざるそば	zaru soba	p. ii
soy sauce based ramen	しょうゆラーメン / しょうゆらーめん	shōyu rāmen	p. ii
salt based ramen	塩ラーメン / しおらーめん	shio rāmen	p. ii
miso based ramen	味噌ラーメン / みそらーめん	miso rāmen	p. ii
pork bone based ramen	とんこつラーメン / とんこつらーめん	tonkotsu rāmen	p. ii
fried noodles	焼きそば / やきそば	yakisoba	p. ii
Japanese pan-fried pizza	お好み焼き / おこのみやき	okonomiyaki	p. ii, p.124, p.158
thin Japanese pan-fried pizza	もんじゃ焼き / もんじゃやき	monjayaki	p. ii
octopus dumpling	たこ焼き / たこやき	takoyaki	p. ii
cold tofu	冷奴 / ひややっこ	hiyayakko	p. vi
deep-fried tofu with broth	揚げ出し豆腐 / あげだしどうふ	agedashi dōfu	p. vi
boiled soybeans	枝豆 / えだまめ	edamame	p. vi
fried rolled egg	卵焼き / たまごやき	tamagoyaki	
rice ball	おにぎり / おにぎり	onigiri	p. ii
rice bowl filled with broth	お茶漬け / おちゃづけ	ochazuke	p. ii
miso soup	味噌汁 / みそしる	misoshiru	p. ii
pork miso soup with vegetables	とん汁 / とんじる	tonjiru	p. ii
bento box	お弁当 / おべんとう	o-bentō	p.41
Japanese Style Western Food	洋食 / ようしょく	Yōshoku	p. ii
croquette	コロッケ / ころっけ	korokke	p. iii
fried shrimp	えびフライ / えびふらい	ebi furai	p. iii
fried oysters	カキフライ / かきふらい	kakifurai	p. iv
pork cutlet	トンカツ / とんかつ	tonkatsu	p. iii
hamburger meat	ハンバーグ / はんばーぐ	hanbāgu	p. iii
curry with rice	カレー（ライス） / かれー（らいす）	karē (raisu)	p. iii, p.52
pork cutlet curry	カツカレー / かつかれー	katsu karē	p. iii
omelette stuffed with rice	オムライス / おむらいす	omuraisu	p. iii
rice with hashed meat	ハヤシライス / はやしらいす	hayashi raisu	p. iii
pizza	ピザ / ぴざ	piza	
spaghetti meat sauce	ミートソース / みーとそーす	mīto sōsu	p. iii
pasta with tomato ketchup	ナポリタン / なぽりたん	naporitan	p. iii
spaghetti with cod roe	タラコスパゲッティ / たらこすぱげってぃ	tarako-supagetthi	
carbonara	カルボナーラ / かるぼなーら	karubonāra	
gratin	グラタン / ぐらたん	guratan	p. iii
rice and cheese casserole	ドリア / どりあ	doria	
hamburger	ハンバーガー / はんばーがー	hambāgā	p.57
cheeseburger	チーズバーガー / ちーずばーがー	chizu bāgā	p.57
teriyakiburger	テリヤキバーガー / てりやきばーがー	teriyaki bāgā	p.57
french fries	（フライド）ポテト / （ふらいど）ぽてと	(furaido)poteto	p.57
salad	サラダ / さらだ	sarada	p.57
potato salad	ポテトサラダ / ぽてとさらだ	poteto sarada	p. iv
Chinese food	中華料理 / ちゅうかりょうり	Chūka ryōri	p. iii
fried rice	チャーハン / ちゃーはん	chāhan	p. iii
pot stickers	餃子 / ぎょうざ	gyōza	p. iii
spring roll	春巻き / はるまき	harumaki	p. iii
steamed meat dumpling	シュウマイ / しゅうまい	shūmai	p. iii
shrimp with chili sauce	エビチリ / えびちり	ebichiri	
meat dumpling	肉まん / にくまん	nikuman	
stir-fried vegetables	野菜炒め / やさいいため	yasai-itame	
chop suey rice bowl	中華丼 / ちゅうかどん	chūkadon	
cold Chinese noodles	冷やし中華 / ひやしちゅうか	hiyashi chūka	
desserts	デザート / でざーと	dezāto	p. iii
strawberry shortcake	ショートケーキ / しょーとけーき	shōto kēki	p. iii
cream puff	シュークリーム / しゅーくりーむ	shukurimu	p. iii
pudding	プリン / ぷりん	purin	
chocolate parfait	チョコレートパフェ / ちょこれーとぱふぇ	chokorēto pafe	p. iii
sweet boiled beans	みつまめ / みつまめ	mitsumame	
mitsumame topped with bean jam	あんみつ / あんみつ	anmitsu	p. iii
dumpling	だんご / だんご	dango	
shaved ice	かき氷 / かきごおり	kakigōri	p. iii
pickled vegetables	漬物 / つけもの	tsukemono	p. iii

pickled plum 梅干 うめぼし umeboshi p.iii, p.138	pickled daikon radish たくあん たくあん takuan p.iii	pickled vegetables in soy sauce ふくじんづけ ふくじんづけ fukujinzuke p.iv	Japanese leek pickles らっきょう らっきょう rakkyō p.iv	Korean style pickles キムチ きむち kimuchi p.iv
Cooking Ingredients 食材 しょくざい **Shokuzai**	seasoning 調味料 ちょうみりょう chōmiryō	salt 塩 しお shio p.38, p.86	pepper こしょう こしょう koshō	sugar 砂糖 さとう satō p.58
soy sauce しょうゆ しょうゆ shōyu p.86	tabasco sauce タバスコ たばすこ tabasuko	mustard マスタード ますたーど masutādo	grated cheese 粉チーズ こなちーず kona-chizu	sauce ソース そーす sōsu
a mixture of red pepper and other spices 七味(とうがらし) しちみ(とうがらし) shichimi (tōgarashi) p.iv	vinegar (お)酢 (お)す o-su	ponzu sauce (made from soy sauce and citrus juice) ポン酢 ぽんず ponzu	mayonnaise マヨネーズ まよねーず mayonēzu	sweet sake (used as a condiment) みりん みりん mirin
ketchup ケチャップ けちゃっぷ kechappu	Chinese chili oil ラー油 らーゆ rā-yu	miso 味噌 みそ miso	condiments 薬味 やくみ yakumi p.iv	nori seaweed のり のり nori p.iv
green nori seaweed 青のり あおのり aonori p.iv	sliced dried bonito かつおぶし かつおぶし katsuobushi p.iv	pickled ginger 紅しょうが べにしょうが beni-shōga p.iv	sesame ごま ごま goma p.iv	green onion ねぎ ねぎ negi p.iv
grated daikon radish 大根おろし だいこんおろし daikon oroshi p.iv	wasabi わさび わさび wasabi p.iv, p.136	mustard からし からし karashi p.iv	fermented soybeans 納豆 なっとう nattō p.iv	tofu 豆腐 とうふ tōfu p.iv
deep-fried tofu 油揚げ あぶらあげ abura-age p.iv	fish paste かまぼこ かまぼこ kamaboko p.iv	konjac potato gel こんにゃく こんにゃく konnyaku p.iv, p.138	wakame seaweed わかめ わかめ wakame p.iv	kombu seaweed こんぶ こんぶ kombu p.iv
salted cod roe たらこ たらこ tarako p.iv	spiced cod roe 明太子 めんたいこ mentaiko p.iv	egg 卵 たまご tamago p.136	seafoods シーフード しーふーど shifūdo p.136	tuna まぐろ まぐろ maguro
shrimp えび えび ebi	squid いか いか ika	scallop ほたて ほたて hotate	octopus たこ たこ tako	abalone あわび あわび awabi
oyster かき かき kaki	sardine いわし いわし iwashi	salmon さけ さけ sake	mackerel さば さば saba	eel うなぎ うなぎ unagi
salmon roe いくら いくら ikura	urchin うに うに uni	crab かに かに kani	blowfish フグ ふぐ fugu	meat 肉 にく niku

pork 豚肉 ぶたにく butaniku p.136	beef 牛肉 ぎゅうにく gyūniku p.136	chicken 鶏肉 とりにく toriniku	minced meat ひき肉 ひきにく hikiniku	vegitables 野菜 やさい yasai
bean sprouts もやし もやし moyashi	lettuce レタス れたす retasu	cucumber きゅうり きゅうり kyūri	eggplant なす なす nasu	bitter melon ゴーヤ ごーや gōya
cabbage キャベツ きゃべつ kyabetsu	carrot にんじん にんじん ninjin	pepper ピーマン ぴーまん piman	onion たまねぎ たまねぎ tamanegi	bamboo shoot たけのこ たけのこ takenoko
spinach ほうれんそう ほうれんそう hōrensō	Japanese pumpkin かぼちゃ かぼちゃ kabocha	potato じゃがいも じゃがいも jagaimo	Japanese sweet potato さつまいも さつまいも satsumaimo	garlic にんにく にんにく ninniku
celery セロリ せろり serori	Chinese cabbage 白菜 はくさい hakusai	daikon radish 大根 だいこん daikon	lotus root レンコン れんこん renkon	burdock ごぼう ごぼう gobō
shiitake mushroom しいたけ しいたけ shiitake	champignon しめじ しめじ shimeji	hackberry えのき えのき enoki	fruits 果物 くだもの kudamono	grape ぶどう ぶどう budō
watermelon すいか すいか suika	apple りんご りんご ringo	tangerine みかん みかん mikan	loquat びわ びわ biwa	peach もも もも momo
strawberry いちご いちご ichigo	pear なし なし nashi	persimmon かき かき kaki	cherry さくらんぼ さくらんぼ sakurambo	

Drinks 飲み物 のみもの **Nomimono** p.v	water 水 みず mizu p.38, p.46, p.60	tea/Japanese tea お茶 おちゃ o-cha	green tea 緑茶 りょくちゃ ryoku-cha p.v	powdered green tea 抹茶 まっちゃ maccha
barley tea 麦茶 むぎちゃ mugi-cha	oolong tea ウーロン茶 うーろんちゃ ūron-cha p.v	black tea 紅茶 こうちゃ kōcha p.v	iced tea アイスティー あいすてぃー aisu-thi p.v, p.57	coffee コーヒー こーひー kōhi p.v
iced coffee アイスコーヒー あいすこーひー aisu-kōhi p.v, p.57	cream (コーヒー)ミルク (こーひー)みるく (kōhi) miruku p.58	liquid sugar ガムシロップ がむしろっぷ gamu shiroppu p.58	café au lait カフェオレ かふぇおれ kafeore	cappucino カプチーノ かぷちーの kapuchino
hot chocolate ココア ここあ kokoa	juice ジュース じゅーす jūsu	cola コーラ こーら kōra p.57	ginger ale ジンジャーエール じんじゃーえーる jinjā ēru	milk 牛乳 ぎゅうにゅう gyūnyū p.38

soy milk 豆乳 とうにゅう tōnyū	alcoholic drink/Japanese sake （お）酒 （お）さけ (o)sake p.20, p.38	(canned/bottled) beer （缶／ビン）ビール （かん／びん）びーる (kan/bin) bīru p.18	draft beer 生ビール なまびーる nama-biru p. v, p.52, p.60	Japanese sake 日本酒 にほんしゅ nihon-shu p. v
hot sake 熱燗 あつかん atsukan p. v	cold sake 冷酒 れいしゅ reishu p. v	red/white wine （赤／白）ワイン （あか／しろ）わいん (aka/shiro) wain p. v	champagne シャンパン しゃんぱん shampan p. v	cocktail カクテル かくてる kakuteru p. v
shochu (Japanese liquor similar to vodka) 焼酎 しょうちゅう shōchū p. v, p.158	with cold water 水割り みずわり mizu-wari p. v	with hot water お湯割り おゆわり oyu-wari	with soda ソーダ割り そーだわり sōda-wari p. v	shochu with lemon and soda レモンサワー れもんさわー remon sawā p. v
whiskey ウイスキー ういすきー uisuki	on the rocks ロック ろっく rokku p. v	straight ストレート すとれーと sutorēto p. v	shochu with tonic water チューハイ ちゅーはい chū-hai	plum wine 梅酒 うめしゅ umeshu p. v
Tableware 食器類 しょっきるい **Shokki-rui**	plate/dish 皿 さら sara p.86	small plate 取り皿 とりざら torizara p.52	cup コップ こっぷ koppu	glass グラス ぐらす gurasu p.52
knife ナイフ ないふ naifu	fork フォーク ふぉーく fōku p.58	Chinese soup spoon れんげ れんげ renge	spoon スプーン すぷーん supūn p.58	chopsticks （お）はし （お）はし (o)hashi p.58, p.86
disposable chopsticks 割りばし わりばし waribashi	straw ストロー すとろー sutorō p.58	rolled wet towel おしぼり おしぼり oshibori p.52	toothpick つまようじ つまようじ tsumayōji	napkin ナプキン なぷきん napukin
Daily Commodities 日用品 にちようひん **Nichiyō-hin**	umbrella かさ かさ kasa p.38	tissue ティッシュ てぃっしゅ thisshu p.38	toothbrush 歯ブラシ はぶらし haburashi	battery/dry cell 電池 でんち denchi
light bulb 電球 でんきゅう denkyū	cigarette たばこ たばこ tabako	ashtray 灰皿 はいざら haizara	towel タオル たおる taoru p.41	soap せっけん せっけん sekken
detergent 洗剤 せんざい senzai	paper bag 紙袋 かみぶくろ kami-bukuro p.41, p.58	bag 袋 ふくろ hukuro p.58	newspaper 新聞 しんぶん shimbun	map 地図 ちず chizu
Vehicles/Train 乗り物／電車 のりもの／でんしゃ **Norimono/Densha**	car/automobile 車／自動車 くるま／じどうしゃ kuruma/jidōsha p.97	motorcycle バイク ばいく baiku	bus バス ばす basu p.98	taxi タクシー たくしー takushi p.30
airplane 飛行機 ひこうき hikōki p.98	bicycle 自転車 じてんしゃ jitensha p.45	boat/ship 船 ふね fune p.98	ferry フェリー ふぇりー feri	train 電車 でんしゃ densha p.93

subway 地下鉄 ちかてつ chikatetsu p.26, p.97	Shinkansen/bullet train 新幹線 しんかんせん shinkansen p.96	platform ホーム ほーむ hōmu p.93	platform no.- 〜番線 〜ばんせん -ban sen p.93	ticket gate 改札 かいさつ kaisatsu
ticket 切符 きっぷ kippu	ticket salespoint 切符売り場 きっぷうりば kippu-uriba	bound for - 〜行き 〜いき -iki	local 普通／各駅停車 ふつう／かくえきていしゃ futsū/kakueki-teisha	rapid 快速 かいそく kaisoku
express 急行 きゅうこう kyūkō	special express 特急 とっきゅう tokkyū	not in service 回送 かいそう kaisō	station employee 駅員 えきいん eki-in	conductor 車掌 しゃしょう shashō
seat 席 せき seki	designated seating 指定席 していせき shitei-seki	free seating 自由席 じゆうせき jiyū-seki	first-class car グリーン車 ぐりーんしゃ gurīn sha	last train 終電 しゅうでん shūden
first train 始発(電車) しはつ(でんしゃ) shihatsu (densha)	priority seating 優先席 ゆうせんせき yūsen-seki	women-only car 女性専用車 じょせいせんようしゃ josei-sen'yō sha	kiosk 売店／キオスク ばいてん／きおすく baiten/kiosuku	station bento 駅弁 えきべん eki-ben

Event イベント いべんと **Ibento**	party パーティー ぱーてぃー pāthī p.122	drinking party at izakaya 飲み会 のみかい nomikai p.122	new year's party 新年会 しんねんかい shinnenkai	year-end party 忘年会 ぼうねんかい bōnenkai
spring break 春休み はるやすみ haru-yasumi	summer break 夏休み なつやすみ natsu-yasumi	winter break 冬休み ふゆやすみ fuyu-yasumi	rice-cake making 餅つき もちつき mochitsuki	concert/gig コンサート／ライブ こんさーと／らいぶ konsāto/raibu
barbecue バーベキュー ばーべきゅー bābekyū	fireworks display 花火大会 はなびたいかい hanabi-taikai p.158	flower(sakura) viewing 花見 はなみ hanami p.158	goodbye party 送別会 そうべつかい sōbetsukai	welcome party 歓迎会 かんげいかい kangeikai
after-party 2次会 にじかい niji-kai	date デート でーと dēto	mixer 合コン ごうこん gō-kon	wedding 結婚式 けっこんしき kekkonshiki	open-air festival 野外フェス やがいふぇす yagai-fesu

Traditional Arts 伝統芸能 でんとうげいのう **Dentō geinō**	kabuki 歌舞伎 かぶき kabuki p.vii, p.158	sumo wrestling すもう すもう sumō p.viii, p.110	noh theatre 能 のう nō p.vii	tea ceremony 茶道 さどう sadō p.vii
flower arrangement 華道 かどう kadō p.vii	calligraphy 書道 しょどう shodō p.vii	haiku poetry 俳句 はいく haiku p.viii	Japanese comedic storytelling 落語 らくご rakugo p.viii	